TOPCIMA

Paper P10

Test of Professional Competence in Management Accounting

CIMA Study Text

KAPLAN
PUBLISHING
FOULKS LYNCH

British Library Cataloguing-in-Publication Data

A catalogue record for this book is available from the British Library.

Kaplan Publishing Foulks Lynch

Unit 2 The Business Centre

Molly Millars Lane,

Wokingham,

Berkshire,

RG41 2QZ

ISBN 1-84390-914-6

978-1-84390-914-9

Printed and bound in Great Britain.

Acknowledgements

We are grateful to the Chartered Institute of Management Accounting for permission to reproduce past examination questions. The answers have been prepared by Kaplan Publishing Foulks Lynch.

We are grateful to the Chartered Institute of Management Accounting for permission to reproduce extracts from their ethical guidelines. The extracts from Student Guide 12 are reproduced here by kind permission of CIMA.

Introduction

The TOPCIMA (Test of Professional Competence in Management Accounting) is a new final assessment. It is based upon a case study and set within a simulated business context. TOPCIMA has no specific syllabus content (material from any part of the syllabus could be potentially relevant). The assessment format of this exam is unique too: pre-seen material is published in advance with the question and new unseen material provided in the exam.

This Study Text has been written to produce an interactive text that will help you to prepare successfully for your final CIMA examination.

Section A introduces the process and principles of the TOPCIMA case.

Section B is a detailed walkthrough, using the March 2006 exam for the Zubinos case, to illustrate the techniques involved.

Sections C and D have additional real exams for further practice.

Where sample solutions are provided, they must be viewed as just one interpretation of the case. Remember that there is no single 'correct' solution. Your own answer might reach different conclusions, and give greater emphasis to some issues and less emphasis to others.

Contents

Learning aims and rationale

Learning aims

The aim of the Test of Professional Competence in Management Accounting (TOPCIMA) is to test the capabilities and competence of students, to ensure that they:

A have a sound technical knowledge of the specific subjects within the curriculum

B can apply technical knowledge in an analytical and practical manner

C can extract, from various subjects, the knowledge required to solve many-sided or complex problems

D can solve a particular problem by distinguishing the relevant information from the irrelevant, in a given body of data

E can, in multi-problem situations, identify the problems and rank them in the order in which they need to be addressed

F appreciate that there can be alternative solutions and understand the role of judgement in dealing with them

G can integrate diverse areas of knowledge and skills

H can communicate effectively with users, by formulating realistic recommendations, in a concise and logical fashion

I can identify, advise on and/or resolve ethical dilemmas.

The Test of Professional Competence in Management Accounting (TOPCIMA) comprises a case study that requires students to primarily apply strategic management accounting techniques to make and support decisions within a simulated business context.

Rationale

The TOPCIMA will provide an integrated test of syllabus content that is mainly included within the three Strategic level papers. However, it will also draw upon content covered within the six Managerial level papers.

The TOPCIMA will require the student to deal with material in less structured situations than those encountered in previous Strategic level papers, and to integrate a variety of tools in arriving at a recommended solution. It is unlikely that there will be a single right answer to a complex business problem and students will be expected to recognise the possible alternatives in dealing with a problem.

The emphasis will be on assessing candidates' capabilities and competence in the practical use of appropriate, relevant knowledge, the ability to demonstrate the application of the higher level skills of synthesis, analysis and evaluation, and skill in effectively presenting and communicating information to users.

A – Preparatory to the TOPCIMA exam

- Analyse and identify the current position of the organisation.
- Analyse and identify the relevant problems facing the organisation

Note: Activities undertaken using published 'pre-seen' case study materials.

B – TOPCIMA exam

- Appraise possible feasible courses of action available.
- Evaluate and then choose specific proposals.
- Identify and evaluate priorities related to the proposals.
- Recommend a course of action.
- Prepare and present information in a format suitable for presentation to senior management.

The examination

Assessment strategy

The Test of Professional Competence provides a final test and can be taken only after all the Strategic level subjects have been successfully completed.

There will be a written TOPCIMA examination paper of three hours (and 20 minutes reading time), with a limited number of questions (requirements). They will normally be answered using the form of a report and/or presentation, with supporting documents, to a variety of users. The questions will be based upon a case study, which will be published on the CIMA website, at least six weeks in advance of the examination. This will provide sufficient time before the examination to allow the student to undertake preparatory analysis based upon the pre-seen material. Further information regarding the case will be added as part of the examination paper.

As a guide to the volume of material within the case, it is likely to be between 8 and 20 sides of A4, published in advance of the exam and up to six sides of A4 contained within the examination paper.

Questions will test the students' capabilities and competence in the application of appropriate knowledge and the processes undertaken in dealing with the problems identified in the examination, together with their ability to present and communicate information.

A 'TOPCIMA Assessment Matrix' will be published on the CIMA website, with the pre-seen case material. The matrix will identify the list of assessment criteria, performance bands and range of marks that will be used to assess the capabilities and competence of candidates.

Maths tables and formulae

Present value of £1 i.e. $(1 + r)^{-n}$ where r = interest rate, n = number of periods until payment or receipt.

Periods (n)	Interest rates (r)									
	1%	2%	3%	4%	5%	6%	7%	8%	9%	10%
1	.990	.980	.971	.962	.962	.943	.935	.926	.917	.909
2	.980	.961	.943	.925	.907	.890	.873	.857	.842	.826
3	.971	.942	.915	.889	.864	.840	.816	.794	.772	.751
4	.961	.924	.888	.855	.823	.792	.763	.735	.708	.683
5	.951	.906	.863	.822	.784	.747	.713	.681	.650	.621
6	.942	.888	.837	.790	.746	.705	.666	.630	.596	.564
7	.933	.871	.813	.760	.711	.665	.623	.583	.547	.513
8	.923	.853	.789	.731	.677	.627	.582	.540	.502	.467
9	.914	.837	.766	.703	.645	.592	.544	.500	.460	.424
10	.905	.820	.744	.676	.614	.558	.508	.463	.422	.386
11	.896	.804	.722	.650	.585	.527	.475	.429	.388	.350
12	.887	.788	.701	.625	.557	.497	.444	.397	.356	.319
13	.879	.773	.681	.601	.530	.469	.415	.368	.326	.290
14	.870	.758	.661	.577	.505	.442	.388	.340	.299	.263
15	.861	.743	.642	.555	.481	.417	.362	.315	.275	.239
16	.853	.728	.623	.534	.458	.394	.339	.292	.252	.218
17	.844	.714	.605	.513	.436	.371	.317	.270	.231	.198
18	.836	.700	.587	.494	.416	.350	.296	.250	.212	.180
19	.828	.686	.570	.475	.396	.331	.277	.232	.194	.164
20	.820	.673	.554	.456	.377	.312	.258	.215	.178	.149

Periods (n)	Interest rates (r)									
	11%	12%	13%	14%	15%	16%	17%	18%	19%	20%
1	.901	.893	.885	.877	.870	.862	.855	.847	.840	.833
2	.812	.797	.783	.769	.756	.743	.731	.718	.706	.694
3	.731	.712	.693	.675	.658	.641	.624	.609	.593	.579
4	.659	.636	.613	.592	.572	.552	.534	.516	.499	.482
5	.593	.567	.543	.519	.497	.476	.456	.437	.419	.402
6	.535	.507	.480	.456	.432	.410	.390	.370	.352	.335
7	.482	.452	.425	.400	.376	.354	.333	.314	.296	.279
8	.434	.404	.376	.351	.327	.305	.285	.266	.249	.233
9	.391	.361	.333	.308	.284	.263	.243	.225	.209	.194
10	.352	.322	.295	.270	.247	.227	.208	.191	.176	.162
11	.317	.287	.261	.237	.215	.195	.178	.162	.148	.135
12	.286	.257	.231	.208	.187	.168	.152	.137	.124	.112
13	.258	.229	.204	.182	.163	.145	.130	.116	.104	.093
14	.232	.205	.181	.160	.141	.125	.111	.099	.088	.078
15	.209	.183	.160	.140	.123	.108	.095	.084	.074	.065
16	.188	.163	.141	.123	.107	.093	.081	.071	.062	.054
17	.170	.146	.125	.108	.093	.080	.069	.060	.052	.045
18	.153	.130	.111	.095	.081	.069	.059	.051	.044	.038
19	.138	.116	.098	.083	.070	.060	.051	.043	.037	.031
20	.124	.104	.087	.073	.061	.051	.043	.037	.031	.026

Cumulative present value of £1

This table shows the Present Value of £1 per annum, Receivable or Payable at the end of each year for n years $\frac{1-(1+r)^{-n}}{r}$

Periods (n)	Interest rates (r)									
	1%	2%	3%	4%	5%	6%	7%	8%	9%	10%
1	0.990	0.980	0.971	0.962	0.952	0.943	0.935	0.926	0.917	0.909
2	1.970	1.942	1.913	1.886	1.859	1.833	1.808	1.783	1.759	1.736
3	2.941	2.884	2.829	2.775	2.723	2.673	2.624	2.577	2.531	2.487
4	3.902	3.808	3.717	3.630	3.546	3.465	3.387	3.312	3.240	3.170
5	4.853	4.713	4.580	4.452	4.329	4.212	4.100	3.993	3.890	3.791
6	5.795	5.601	5.417	5.242	5.076	4.917	4.767	4.623	4.486	4.355
7	6.728	6.472	6.230	6.002	5.786	5.582	5.389	5.206	5.033	4.868
8	7.652	7.325	7.020	6.733	6.463	6.210	5.971	5.747	5.535	5.335
9	8.566	8.162	7.786	7.435	7.108	6.802	6.515	6.247	5.995	5.759
10	9.471	8.983	8.530	8.111	7.722	7.360	7.024	6.710	6.418	6.145
11	10.368	9.787	9.253	8.760	8.306	7.887	7.499	7.139	6.805	8.495
12	11.255	10.575	9.954	9.385	8.863	8.384	7.943	7.536	7.161	6.814
13	12.134	11.348	10.635	9.986	9.394	8.853	8.358	7.904	7.487	7.103
14	13.004	12.106	11.296	10.563	9.899	9.295	8.745	8.244	7.786	7.367
15	13.865	12.849	11.938	11.118	10.380	9.712	9.108	8.559	8.061	7.606
16	14.718	13.578	12.561	11.652	10.838	10.106	9.447	8.851	8.313	7.824
17	15.562	14.292	13.166	12.166	11.274	10.477	9.763	9.122	8.544	8.022
18	16.398	14.992	13.754	12.659	11.690	10.828	10.059	9.372	8.756	8.201
19	17.226	15.679	14.324	13.134	12.085	11.158	10.336	9.604	8.950	8.365
20	18.046	16.351	14.878	13.590	12.462	11.470	10.594	9.818	9.129	8.514

Periods (n)	Interest rates (r)									
	11%	12%	13%	14%	15%	16%	17%	18%	19%	20%
1	0.901	0.893	0.885	0.877	0.870	0.862	0.862	0.847	0.840	0.833
2	1.713	1.690	1.668	1.647	1.626	1.605	1.585	1.566	1.547	1.528
3	2.444	2.402	2.361	2.322	2.283	2.246	2.210	2.174	2.140	2.106
4	3.102	3.037	2.974	2.914	2.855	2.798	2.743	2.690	2.639	2.589
5	3.696	3.605	3.517	3.433	3.352	3.274	3.199	3.127	3.058	2.991
6	4.231	4.111	3.998	3.889	3.784	3.685	3.589	3.498	3.410	3.326
7	4.712	4.564	4.423	4.288	4.160	4.039	3.922	3.812	3.706	3.605
8	5.146	4.968	4.799	4.639	4.487	4.344	4.207	4.078	3.954	3.837
9	5.537	5.328	5.132	4.946	4.772	4.607	4.451	4.303	4.163	4.031
10	5.889	5.650	5.426	5.216	5.019	4.833	4.659	4.494	4.339	4.192
11	6.207	5.938	5.687	5.453	5.234	5.029	4.836	4.656	4.486	4.327
12	6.492	6.194	5.918	5.660	5.421	5.197	4.968	4.793	4.611	4.439
13	6.750	6.424	6.122	5.842	5.583	5.342	5.118	4.910	4.715	4.533
14	6.982	6.628	6.302	6.002	5.724	5.468	5.229	5.008	4.802	4.611
15	7.191	6.811	6.462	6.142	5.847	5.575	5.324	5.092	4.876	4.675
16	7.379	6.974	6.604	6.265	5.954	5.668	5.405	5.162	4.938	4.730
17	7.549	7.120	6.729	6.373	6.047	5.749	5.475	5.222	4.990	4.775
18	7.702	7.250	6.840	6.467	6.128	5.818	5.534	5.273	5.033	4.812
19	7.839	7.366	6.938	6.550	6.198	5.877	5.584	5.316	5.070	4.843
20	7.963	7.469	7.025	6.623	6.259	5.929	5.628	5.353	5.101	4.870

chapter

1

INTRODUCING THE CASE STUDY

Contents

1 Learning aims for TOPCIMA

The syllabus states that the Test of Professional Competence in Management Accounting (TOPCIMA) requires candidates to apply mainly strategic management accounting techniques to make and support decisions within a case study (a simulated business context). CIMA wishes to assess:

- your possession of the higher skills of synthesis, analysis and evaluation, in addition to
- your technical knowledge of management accounting, and
- your skill in presenting and communicating information to users.

The TOPCIMA case study is therefore an attempt to simulate workplace problem solving. This allows examiners to move one step closer to the assessment of competence than is possible with essay-style questions.

Since the examination tests your higher level skills, preparing for this examination needs to be different from studying for a 'traditional' examination paper. The purpose of this study text is to suggest how you might prepare for the examination by developing and practising your skills.

2 How the case study examination works

The TOPCIMA exam is a written examination paper of three hours. Candidates cannot take the examination until they have successfully completed all the 'strategic' level subjects: Risk and Control Strategy, Business Strategy and Financial Strategy.

The exam is based on:

- pre-seen material issued in advance of the exam day, supplemented by
- additional, previously unseen material given to you in the exam room.

There will be a limited number of questions or requirements relating to this material. You will probably be required to answer the questions by presenting a report (but possibly another form of document) to one or more users of the information.

For this purpose, you will be required to present your answer in the role of a professional adviser, such as a management consultant or a newly appointed management accountant.

The pre-seen material is an extended scenario consisting of 15 to 20 pages of information about a business organisation. It is made available at least six weeks before the examination, to give you the opportunity for familiarisation and analysis, and is published on the CIMA website. You therefore have at least six weeks to study the pre-seen material and you should spend as much time as you can doing this, taking notes, analysing the information, doing background reading and research, and revising any technical topics that you think might be relevant.

You cannot take your copy of the pre-seen material, nor any notes or calculations that you have made relating to the material into the examination. Similarly, you will not be allowed to take in any textbook. Normal 'closed book' examination conditions will apply.

In the examination room you will be supplied with a fresh booklet containing the pre-seen material and the unseen material. The unseen material will be up to six pages in length. The pre-seen material might also be altered, for example by including more up-to-date figures in an appendix. When this happens, the examination paper will indicate where the pre-seen material has been changed.

Tables, such as discount tables, will be provided where appropriate.

Typically, the questions in the examination will require you to demonstrate your ability to assess and evaluate the strategic and financial position of the organisation in the case study, and to recommend suitable courses of action to deal with the issues involved. There will not be a 'correct' or 'incorrect' answer, but you will be expected to identify the key issues from the material provided, and to use your judgement in making recommendations, with suitable reasons.

3 The pre-seen material

CIMA releases the pre-seen material at least six weeks before the examination. This is posted on the student area of the CIMA website (www.cimaglobal.com) and it is your responsibility to downloading it and to print off a copy. Candidates without access to download and printing facilities can ask CIMA to post them a copy.

The pre-seen material is an introductory scenario to set the scene for the case study, together with accounting and financial information. Much of the financial information will probably be in the form of appendices to the main text, but the main text of the pre-seen might include some figures too.

The purpose of giving you access to this information in advance of the exam is to enable you to study, analyse and become very familiar with the organisation(s) and industry described.

This should incorporate the following:

- researching the industry involved
- detailed paragraph-by-paragraph analysis
- overall position analysis, incorporating a SWOT
- ratio analysis of financial statements and financial plans
- additional business strategy analysis, including generation of strategic options
- additional financial strategy analysis, including how the business is financed, how future finance could be raised and valuation techniques
- risk and control analysis to identify key risk areas, presence and suitability of management controls and performance measures.

4 The unseen material

In the examination room, you will be provided with:

- a clean copy of the pre-seen material incorporating the further pages of the unseen material
- the questions or requirements
- two blank answer booklets.

You will be required to present your answers in the main answer booklet, and you may use the supplementary booklet for any appendices or workings, if you wish. If you use the supplementary answer booklet for presenting appendices, you should make sure that they are clearly labelled and neatly presented.

The unseen material will be a continuation of the pre-seen and will usually bring the scenario up to date.

In most cases there is a 'twist' in the unseen i.e. a development that most students would not have anticipated from the pre-seen.

A common mistake made by weaker students is that they place too much emphasis on their analysis of the pre-seen material and do not develop the information in the unseen material adequately. Both are important, but the unseen material usually gives the strongest lead on identifying key issues to discuss in your answer.

5 Feedback from the 2006 CIMA lecturers' conference

The main points of note for TOPCIMA that arose from the 2006 CIMA lecturers' conference are as follows:

Prioritisation

- Each of the last five diets has contained a very similar question:
  - prioritise key issues
  - discuss the key issues
  - make appropriate recommendations on the key issues.

  So identifying the top five or six key issues is thus the critical success factor.
- Key issues were described as those that 'could have a substantial effect on the company's future success or even its very survival'.
- It was also stressed that students need to justify their prioritisation more e.g. the cash shortfall in the November 2005 case should be one of the top two issues as Domusco could become bankrupt if it continues to spend as planned.
- All of the key issues should also be in the SWOT.
- Each of the top five or six issues should be 'thoroughly discussed'.

Pre-seen v unseen material

- One of the problems identified was that students rely too much on themes identified in the pre-seen material and do not spend enough time identifying themes in the unseen material. In particular students often seem unprepared/unwilling/unable to cope with the 'twist'.
- Too many students put in pre-prepared analysis whether useful or not e.g. in the May 2005 case a SWOT of Shard would be useful, but SWOTs of ReuseR and NOW were not considered relevant.
- Students need to have the confidence to … be able to adapt (or discard) ideas and pre-prepared material if it is no longer relevant.

Calculations

- There will only be up to 10 marks maximum available for calculations. Some students are spending far too long on lengthy analysis. 'They can pass TOPCIMA with no numbers at all.'

Exam technique

- Students were advised to:
  - list the new topics, and then
  - identify which are the really critical key issues, and then
  - prioritise them,
  - discuss them, and
  - make justified recommendations on them.

  'Then they should pass.'
- Some students seem to forget that TOPCIMA is a strategy exam:

  The company needs a clear, focused report that has identified key, critical issues and makes appropriate well-justified recommendations on its future strategic direction.

chapter

2

ASSESSMENT AND KEY SKILLS

Contents

1 The assessment matrix and marking process

Case study answers will be assessed by the marker using an assessment matrix.

The matrix consists of nine criteria against which your answer will be judged. Marks will be awarded for your performance in relation to each of these criteria, up to a specified maximum limit. The total available for all nine criteria together is 100 marks i.e. the total marks available for the examination.

The format of the assessment matrix is shown on the next page, using the matrix for Zubinos (March and May 2006 case), as an example.

For any specific case study examination, the marks available for each criterion may be a minimum of 5 or a maximum of 20. In this way the distribution of marks can be adjusted to suit the nature of a specific case study (for example one involving more or fewer calculations or a greater or lesser knowledge).

The matrix for Kadgee (September and November 2006 case), for example, had 10 for focus and 20 for judgement rather than 15 for each, as was the situation with Zubinos. This would suggest that there are fewer irrelevant issues in the Kadgee material but that more judgement is required to analyse key issues in depth.

CIMA publishes the assessment matrix in advance on the student area of its website.

After reading through your script, the marker will award marks according to how well you perform against each criterion on the assessment matrix. To guide them, they are required to choose the description that best applies to your script. When all criteria have been assessed, the total mark will be calculated. You must achieve a minimum of 50 marks in order to pass the examination.

Criterion	Marks*	Clear pass	Pass	Marginal pass	Marginal Fail	Fail	Clear fail
Technical	5	Thorough display of relevant technical knowledge. **5**	Good display of relevant knowledge. **4**	Some display of relevant technical knowledge. **3**	Identification of some relevant knowledge, but lacking in depth. **2**	Little knowledge displayed, or some misconceptions. **1**	No evidence of knowledge displayed, or fundamental misconceptions. **0**
Application	10	Knowledge clearly applied in an analytical and practical manner. **9-10**	Knowledge applied to the context of the case. **6-8**	Identification of some relevant knowledge, but not well applied. **5**	Knowledge occasionally displayed without clear application. **3-4**	Little attempt to apply knowledge to the context. **1-2**	No application of knowledge displayed. **0**
Diversity	5	Most knowledge areas identified, covering a wide range of views. **5**	Some knowledge areas identified, covering a range of views. **4**	A few knowledge areas identified, expressing a fairly limited scope. **3**	Several important knowledge aspects omitted. **2**	Many important knowledge aspects omitted. **1**	Very few knowledge aspects considered. **0**
Focus	15	Clearly distinguishes between and irrelevant information. **13-15**	Information used is mostly relevant. **9-12**	Some relevant information ignored, or some less relevant information used. **8**	Information used is sometimes irrelevant. **5-7**	Little ability to distinguish between relevant and irrelevant information. **1-4**	No ability to distinguish between relevant and irrelevant information. **0**
Prioritisation	10	Issues clearly prioritised in a logical order and based on a clear rationale. **9-10**	Issues prioritised with justification. **6-8**	Evidence of issues being listed in order of importance, but rationale unclear. **5**	Issues apparently in priority order, but without a logical justification or rationale. **3-4**	Little attempt at prioritisation or justification or rationale. **1-2**	No attempt at prioritisation or justification. **0**
Judgement	15	Clearly recognises alternative solutions. Judgement exercised professionally. **13-15**	Alternative solutions or options considered. Some judgement exercised. **9-12**	A slightly limited range of solutions considered. Judgement occasionally weak. **8**	A limited range of solutions considered. Judgement sometimes weak. **5-7**	Few alternative solutions considered. Judgement often weak. **1-4**	No alternative solutions considered. Judgement weak or absent. **0**
Integration	10	Diverse areas of knowledge and skills integrated effectively. **9-10**	Diverse areas of knowledge and skills integrated. **6-8**	Knowledge areas and skills occasionally not integrated. **5**	Knowledge areas and skills sometimes not integrated. **3-4**	Knowledge areas and skills often not integrated. **1-2**	Knowledge areas and skills not integrated. **0**
Logic	20	Communication effective, recommendations realistic, concise and logical. **16-20**	Communication mainly clear and logical. Recommendations occasionally weak. **11-15**	Communication occasionally unclear, and/or recommendations occasionally illogical. **10**	Communication sometimes weak. Some recommendations slightly unrealistic. **5-9**	Communication weak. Some unclear or illogical recommendations, or few recommendations. **1-4**	Very poor communication, and/or no recommendations offered. **0**
Ethics	10	Excellent evaluation of ethical aspects. Clear and appropriate advice offered. **9-10**	Good evaluation of ethical aspects. Some appropriate advice offered. **6-8**	Some evaluation of ethical aspects. Advice offered. **5**	Weak evaluation of ethical aspects. Little advice offered. **3-4**	Poor evaluation of ethical aspects. No advice offered. **1-2**	No evaluation of ethical aspects. Unethical, or no, advice offered. **0**
TOTAL	100	*Note The number of available marks allocated to each criterion will normally be as shown.					*© CIMA – January 2006*

2 Technical skills

The aim of this part of the assessment matrix is to test whether you 'have a sound technical knowledge of the specific subjects of the curriculum'.

2.1 CIMA Student Guide 12 *Understanding the assessment matrix*

The CIMA Student Guide 12 *Understanding the assessment matrix* gives the following guidance on technical skills:

> Unlike the previous Case Study exam, the TOPCIMA directly credits the quality of your technical knowledge. The reason for this is that, whereas the old Case Study was designed to be sat alongside the Final Level strategy papers (where knowledge was tested), the TOPCIMA is a concluding stand-alone assessment of all your professional capabilities and competencies.
>
> The 'syllabus' for the TOPCIMA is the whole of the CIMA qualification. This means that 'knowledge' includes your knowledge of numerical techniques as well as your knowledge of theories and approaches. This is another difference between this assessment matrix and the previous one (where numerical skills were treated as a separate criterion). However, rather than knowledge being less highly rewarded in the TOPCIMA than the old Case Study, the opposite is true. There are now three criteria looking at different aspects of knowledge (see B and C below).
>
> Notice that 'relevant' is a word that appears in each of the pass level assessment matrix descriptions for this criterion. You should not try to cram every knowledge area into one case study. The idea is to use only those knowledge areas that clearly apply – either to your analysis of the pre-seen and unseen material, or to the options you are considering. If the examiner thinks that you are trying to 'force' knowledge into your answer, you will not gain credit on this criterion because the knowledge is not relevant. You will also find it difficult to gain marks for 'application', as it is not possible to apply irrelevant knowledge.

2.2 Interpretation / exam technique

The way to score highly for technical skills is to use at least three, but preferably, five different techniques or models in your answer.

In practice you may not feel that it is appropriate to show a Porter's five forces analysis, say, explicitly and would rather put just the key issues identified through such a model into your report. However, in the TOPCIMA exam, it is vital that you show the marker that you are using a range of techniques, with their appropriate labels.

A typical report should thus contain the following:

- a SWOT analysis, summarising the strategic position of the firm
- key ratios calculated and discussed
- three other techniques, specially selected for their relevance to the case (see Chapter 4 for a revision of such techniques).

Assuming a total of 5 marks for technical skills in the matrix, you could expect to score a mark per technique for appropriate (i.e. relevant) use.

3 Application skills

The aim of this part of the assessment matrix is to test whether you have the ability to 'apply technical knowledge in an analytical and practical manner'.

Marks will be awarded for the way in which technical knowledge is used in application to the case study and the requirements of the question(s).

3.1 CIMA Student Guide 12 *Understanding the assessment matrix*

The CIMA Student Guide 12 *Understanding the assessment matrix* gives the following guidance on application skills:

> It is not enough simply to have the technical knowledge – you must be able to apply it. This means application to the specific organisation, situation and facts given in the pre-seen and unseen materials. This criterion looks at how well you are able to process the given data into useful information by application of your knowledge. This also includes the use of relevant financial and numerical data in your calculations.
>
> It is important to recognise that much of the knowledge gained from textbooks does not apply perfectly to real world situations. Sometimes such application will be limited, due to weaknesses and limitations in the model or calculation.
>
> Other times, such application would be simplistic, and possibly misleading, due to the context of the case.

3.2 Interpretation / exam technique

To some degree, the marks you earn here will be dictated by how many techniques and models you have used. If you have only used two techniques, say, then you are limited to only two techniques' worth of application.

Assuming a total of 10 marks, for application you should expect to be able to score up to 3 marks per technique for good application to the case.

To ensure that you get 3 marks rather than 1, ensure that you link the analysis to the key issues in the case. For example, you should interpret any ratios calculated rather than just leaving them as figures in an appendix.

If performing calculations, then try to keep them as simple as possible without trivialising them. While the marks they earn will impact different parts of the assessment matrix, it is unlikely they will be worth more than 10 marks in total.

4 Diversity

The aim of this part of the assessment matrix is to test whether you have the ability to 'extract from various subjects the knowledge required to solve many-sided or complex problems'.

You will be awarded marks for the breadth of knowledge you demonstrate in your answer.

4.1 CIMA Student Guide 12 *Understanding the assessment matrix*

The CIMA Student Guide 12 *Understanding the assessment matrix* gives the following guidance on diversity:

> The TOPCIMA is designed as a multi-disciplinary case study. You should try to look at a range of different viewpoints when applying your knowledge. A good Chartered Management Accountant is a manager first and an accountant second. This means taking a broad business or commercial view.
>
> The syllabus for the TOPCIMA is the whole of the CIMA qualification. However, if there is a 'core' syllabus for the TOPCIMA, it must be Management Accounting – Business Strategy.
>
> All TOPCIMA case studies will look at the strategic issues within an organisation and industry so, of all the papers, P6 is the one to concentrate on. The other strategy papers (P3

and P9) will, of course, feature regularly in the TOPCIMA, as they look at more specialised aspects of strategy. However, material from the Managerial Level papers (and even, occasionally, Certificate) may also feature in a TOPCIMA case study.

It is not necessary to try to study the entire syllabus again, as you will be able to identify any relevant knowledge areas from the pre-seen material.

When evaluating a situation, and formulating your arguments, it helps to deliberately think about different viewpoints. There are two ways you might do this:

- Think carefully about issues relating to the three Strategic Level knowledge areas: business strategy, financial strategy and risk & control strategy. Make sure that you try to identify issues in each of these three areas.
- Think about the issues from the point of view of each different stakeholder, or functional manager, mentioned in the case. Take time, for example, to consider HRM, marketing and quality issues, not just financial ones.

4.2 Interpretation / Exam technique

As well as including different technical areas, most students can earn extra diversity marks by incorporating two aspects in your answer:

- Incorporate three facts you have researched regarding the industry concerned. These could include the activities and strategies of real-life firms, recent trends and critical success factors.
- If the unseen material suggests a possible strategy, then bring in pre-learnt details of the practicalities of such strategies. For example, if a joint venture is put forward as a possible strategy for the firm, then you could suggest something along the lines of: 'In situations such as this, the key areas of negotiation are normally the sharing out of risks and rewards,...'

5 Focus skills

The aim of this part of the assessment matrix is to test whether you have the ability to 'solve a particular problem by distinguishing the relevant information from the irrelevant in a given body of knowledge'.

You will be rewarded for your ability to focus on the issues in the question, and use what is relevant but ignore what is not relevant.

5.1 CIMA Student Guide 12 *Understanding the assessment matrix*

The CIMA student Guide 12 *Understanding the assessment matrix* gives the following guidance on focus:

> Necessarily, with about 20 pages of information contained in the pre-seen and unseen material, a significant proportion of this will turn out to be irrelevant to the key issues. This criterion looks at your ability to 'sift through' the mass of data provided, and pick out only those facts that should be used in order to formulate a valid argument.
>
> Information may be relevant for a number of reasons:
>
> - It is a fact required as an input to a theoretical model or calculation.
> - It forms part of an argument, or evidence to support it.
>
> Information may also be irrelevant for the following reasons:
>
> - It is contradicted or negated by another fact.
> - It is not required to support an argument.
> - It relates to a relatively minor issue, which you choose not to deal with.

5.2 Interpretation / exam technique

The main mistake students make with focus is to confuse it with prioritisation, below. Focus does not mean that only your top five key issues are discussed in the report. Rather you should discuss each of your ten, say, issues. The less important issues can be dealt with using a section titled 'other issues'.

Within each issue discussed you must ensure that only relevant information is included.

This is particularly important with calculations where you should state why certain figures have been excluded.

6 Prioritisation skills

The aim of this part of the assessment matrix is to test whether you have the ability to 'in multi-problem situations, identify the problems and rank them in the order in which they need to be addressed'.

Rewarding candidates for their ability to prioritise the issues, and to recognise what problems are more important than others, was a regular feature of the case study under the 'old syllabus' and remains important.

6.1 CIMA Student Guide 12 *Understanding the assessment matrix*

The CIMA Student Guide 12 *Understanding the assessment matrix* gives the following guidance on prioritisation:

> There are many different ways that issues can be prioritised, but there are two things that you must do to gain good marks against this criterion in the TOPCIMA case study:
>
> Your issues must be 'clearly prioritised in a logical order', so you must choose some appropriate rationale for your prioritisation, bearing in mind the situation described in the scenario. The basis used to prioritise issues might be timescale (short-term to long-term), scale of impact (most significant to least significant), degree of risk (highest risk to lowest risk), or anything else that you feel to be most appropriate.
>
> You must present your answer 'based on a clear rationale', so you must explain the basis on which issues have been prioritised, and justify why you feel that basis is appropriate.
>
> This is a difficult skill to master, and you should practise prioritisation of issues in as many case studies as possible. You might find it useful to use group work, either in class or in study groups. After discussing a case study, each member of the group can identify and prioritise what they believe to be the most important issues, then give a short presentation explaining their rationale. The group can then vote on which approach seemed the most appropriate, and which rationale was most clearly expressed.

6.2 Interpretation / exam technique

Prioritisation is possibly the most important skill within the matrix, so ensure you spend sufficient time thinking about your answer.

- Start by identifying your top five issues. This should be based on a mixture of criteria including urgency, size and impact on the strategic goals of the organisation.
- With issue number 1 describe it as your 'top priority' and justify why it is the most important. Repeat with the rest of your top issues.
- Ensure that the order within each section of your report reflects your prioritisation.
- Ensure that you devote more time and space to your discussion of issue 1 than to issue 2 and so on.
- If you have done the prioritisation early enough or are sitting the computer-based case, then order your SWOT to reflect the order of prioritisation.

7 Judgement

The aim of this part of the assessment matrix is to test whether you have the ability to 'appreciate that there can be alternative solutions and understand the role of judgement in dealing with them'. Judgement' might be defined as 'informed common sense'.

7.1 CIMA Student Guide 12 *Understanding the assessment matrix*

The CIMA Student Guide 12 *Understanding the assessment matrix* gives the following guidance on judgement:

> In order to satisfy this criterion, there are two things that you must do:
>
> - You must recognise that, in any strategic situation, there is a range of alternatives available to the organisation. You should identify, evaluate and rank these options.
> - Having done this, you must then exercise professional judgement in selecting what you think to be the optimal solution.
>
> In identifying the options available, you might develop clues provided in the case, or you might use strategy models such as Ansoff's product/market matrix or Porter's generic strategies.
>
> In evaluating and ranking options, you might use the tests of suitability, feasibility and acceptability. This might involve SWOT analysis (suitability), cost-benefit analysis (feasibility) or stakeholder mapping (acceptability). All of these, if relevant, could also gain credit for 'knowledge', 'application' and 'diversity'.

7.2 Interpretation / exam technique

Judgement marks are likely to focus purely on the identified top five issues. For each of these your analysis should incorporate the following:

- alternatives to the suggested course of action and why they have been discounted
- arguments for and against each option.

When doing this, try to incorporate any key figures and real-life business awareness points as well as points extracted from the material.

8 Integration

The aim of this part of the assessment matrix is to test whether you have the ability to 'integrate diverse areas of knowledge and skills'.

A CIMA spokesperson has said that 'this is about the "balance" in the script and how "holistic" the answer is'.

8.1 CIMA Student Guide 12 *Understanding the assessment matrix*

The CIMA Student Guide 12 *Understanding the assessment matrix* gives the following guidance on integration:

> Obviously, with all these different skills being tested, there is a temptation to write content into your answer specifically to satisfy certain criteria. This criterion checks whether you are able to integrate the various skills and knowledge areas into a cohesive answer. There should be a balance between the various skills, so that overall the report feels professional, rather than contrived.

8.2 Interpretation / Exam technique

Many students struggle to understand what integration is really looking for. The marker will be looking at the report as a whole, rather than at just one section and will be concerned that:

- Final recommendations are consistent with the main body of analysis, which in turn is consistent with key prioritised issues, which in turn are consistent with the SWOT analysis. For example, if a key issue discussed later on is not in the SWOT then you will be marked down on integration.
- The report flows well.
- All key issues identified are discussed in sufficient detail and result in recommendations being made.

  For example, some students identify five key issues but only make clear recommendations on three of them. This is usually due to poor time allocation. It is better to discuss issues in less depth if it results in a better balanced report that is 'finished'.

The higher-skills aspect of integration is to look at each of the key issues and consider the overall balance and fit of the strategies concerned. For example, three strategies may be proposed, each of which has sufficient merit to recommend accepting them. However, the firm may be experiencing capital rationing and so could only undertake one. Identifying this problem and discussing how to proceed would score highly on integration.

Note that, due to the nature of this skill, markers' views will tend to be polarised so your script is either good or bad with few scripts earning middle marks.

9 Logic

The aim of this part of the assessment matrix is to test whether you have the ability to 'communicate effectively with users by formulating realistic recommendations in a concise and logical fashion'.

The ability to think logically is a prime quality in a management accountant, and you will be awarded marks for your ability to demonstrate logical thinking and a logical approach.

9.1 CIMA Student Guide 12 *Understanding the assessment matrix*

The CIMA Student Guide 12 *Understanding the assessment matrix* gives the following guidance on logic:

> This is an important criterion, and you will notice that it is weighted more highly on the sample assessment matrix. The reason for this is that there are two different aspects to the logic of your answer:
>
> - You should demonstrate good communication skills. This means that the language you use should be professional and appropriate, avoiding slang and being appropriately formal. You should also produce a business document, normally a report or a presentation, which has the appropriate format and content. This is a type of business communication criterion, and will reward you for preparing a report that follows all points logically through, from identification of a weakness to the selected and recommended course of action.
> - Throughout your answer, the content should be structured in such a way that the arguments you put forward lead logically to your conclusions and recommendations. Failure to provide recommendations really makes your answer a waste of time, and would not to gain much credit on this criterion.

9.2 Interpretation / exam technique

There are two keys to scoring high logic marks:

- Ensure that clear, well-argued recommendations are made for each key issue and brief recommendations made for each of your 'other issues'.
- Ensure that your report is set out in the required format with all sections completed appropriately (see Chapter 3 for details on report writing).

Note that the skills of judgement, integration and logic are very much linked and are essentially marks for your ability to reach a professional judgement and communicate your views in a realistic and logical manner.

You are also encouraged to communicate in a 'concise' manner. The marker will not give you credit for writing at unnecessary length. The suggested solutions provided later in this text are probably longer than most students would be able to manage in a three-hour examination.

10 Ethics

The aim of this part of the assessment matrix is to test whether you have the ability to 'identify ethical dilemmas'.

This is a new feature of the case study examination. We might expect a variety of 'conflict of interest' types of problem in case study scenarios.

10.1 CIMA Student Guide 12 *Understanding the assessment matrix*

The CIMA Student Guide 12 *Understanding the assessment matrix* gives the following guidance on ethics:

> To all strategic decisions there is an ethical dimension. Business is about compromise and, necessarily, someone must benefit at the expense of another. This criterion rewards you for recognising the ethical issues and, if appropriate, recommending action. Ethics is a broad topic, and you should consider whether the following different aspects are relevant to the case:
>
> - Personal and professional ethics, as you will often be acting the role of a newly qualified Chartered Management Accountant and manager.
> - Business ethics, as you will be acting as part of an organisation, or as an advisor to it.
> - Corporate Governance, as strategic decisions have an impact on the stakeholders of the organisation.
> - Social responsibility, as strategic decisions often impact on the world outside the organisation's boundary.

10.2 Interpretation / exam technique

Some students make the mistake of only discussing ethics if it is considered to be a key issue in the case. Rather ethical issues should be included for **all** cases.

To score high marks for ethics you should thus do the following:

- Identify at least three ethical issues using the types mentioned in the CIMA Student Guide above – personal and professional ethics, business ethics, corporate governance and social responsibility.
- For each issue, explain why it has an ethical dimension.
- For each issue, suggest what could be done to resolve it.

Ethics now features in Paper P3 of the syllabus but, if you have not studied this area in depth, or have forgotten your earlier studies, a chapter on the CIMA Ethical Guidelines is provided in this text (Chapter 5).

11 Summary

The above comments can be summarised into the following generic grid. Note: the distribution oof marks is variable.

Matrix heading (marks)	What you need to do
Technical (5)	Prepare appendices or use key techniques. A SWOT should be the starting point. Other examples: ratios, Ansoff, PEST, Porter's five forces, Porter's generic strategies, BCG, Product lifecycle, balanced scorecard, suitability/feasibility/acceptability, etc.
Application (10)	Use/apply the above techniques / technical knowledge. Prepare relevant calculations.
Diversity (5)	Show business awareness for both the industry dealt with in the scenario and situations and events that impact a business in general e.g. franchising, acquisitions, etc.
Focus (15)	Select relevant key information for discussion. This should start with your five prioritised issues but can be expanded to other strategic areas.

	These issues will mainly be from the unseen information.
Prioritisation (10)	Using your SWOT, identify five key issues. Following the approach: • Clearly identify the issue • Justify the prioritisation of the issue. You must ensure it is CLEAR that you have prioritised: 'The following key issues identified from the SWOT analysis identified in Appendix x have been prioritised in the following order.' 'The main priority is……'
Judgement (15)	Discussion of the five key areas in greater detail. Evaluate any options and consider alternative solutions or actions. Some other area you identified should also be expanded upon, time allowing.
Integration (10)	Does the report cover the main issues and flow from identification to recommendation? Prioritised Discussed Evaluated Recommendations
Logic (20)	Did you follow the CIMA guidelines on report structure? Clear recommendations should be given for the five key areas first and then any other areas discussed in the report. Avoid recommendations without prior discussion.
Ethics (10)	Identify an ethical issue. Explain/justify the issue. Offer advice. To highlight this area show ethics as a separate section of the report and do the recommendations here rather than in the recommendations section.

chapter

3

REPORT WRITING

Contents

1 Report contents

The unseen information usually asks you to prepare a report that

- prioritises, and
- discusses the issues facing the company, and
- makes appropriate recommendations.

It is thus vital that your report is structured to clearly separate these three steps.

While many different report formats are used in practice, we recommend that you use the following format unless you have strong reasons to do otherwise.

1.1 Front sheet

All reports have a front sheet. Yours should contain the following information:

- The word 'report' large and clear on it somewhere
- The recipient of the report e.g. 'To the Directors of X'
- The producer of the report
- Date
- The title of the report
- The status of the report e.g. 'draft', 'confidential'.

1.2 Contents page

A contents page shows the marker how you have structured your report and should help towards integration and logic marks.

A typical report could have the following contents:

1.0 Introduction

2.0 Terms of reference

3.0 Key issues

4.0 – 8.0 Analysis of issues

9.0 Ethical considerations

10.0 Recommendations

11.0 Conclusion

Appendices 1, 2,...

1.3 Introduction

The introduction sets the scene for the report and, to some degree, reveals why the report has been requested. A good introduction can be constructed using three short paragraphs covering the following:

- performance to date, possibly incorporating a key ratio from the very start (e.g. declining margins)
- future prospects, possibly incorporating key ratios (e.g. growth rates)
- key challenges facing the firm (note: evidence of prioritisation from the beginning).

1.4 Terms of reference (TOR)

The terms of reference section usually answers the 'who, what, why?' of report writing:

- **Who** has asked for the report and who are we?
- **What** have we been asked to do?
- **Why** have we been asked to do it? This looks at the strategic context of the case and has already been partly covered in the introduction

In the real world the terms of reference would also contain any disclaimers the writer wishes to make, for example:

- 'This report is for the sole use of the recipients and no liability is accepted for any losses incurred by any other persons acting upon any information contained herein.'
- 'We have relied on figures provided by the Board of X and our recommendations may have to be revised should any of the figures used prove to be materially inaccurate.'

In the exam these can be ignored to save time.

1.5 Identification of key issues

In this section you identify the key issues and explain the basis of your prioritisation. You do not discuss the issues beyond that – detailed analysis and recommendations will be made elsewhere.

Some students get confused by the term 'issues'. This does not necessarily mean problems only but could equally refer to possibilities.

This section could begin with a statement linking the key issues to a SWOT analysis. For example:

'A detailed SWOT analysis of the firm has been carried out and is summarised in Appendix 1. Based on this analysis we have prioritised the key issues facing the firm as follows.'

For each key issue you should aim to do the following:

- Identify the issue and explain why it is an issue.
- State the need for a management decision (in the case of a proposal being evaluated) or for management action to develop a plan (in the case of an identified problem).
- Justify the basis of your prioritisation. As stated above, this assessment could include reference to the issue's urgency, size and impact on the strategic objectives of the firm.

Ensure that:

- issues are discussed in order of priority
- all key issues appear in the SWOT analysis in Appendix 1.

1.6 Main body of the report – analysis of issues

Each of the prioritised issues should have a section of their own. For example:

4 Franchising

5 Loss of major customer

6 etc

Your approach to each section will depend on whether the issue is a proposal to evaluate or a problem to solve.

Problems

- The opening paragraph needs to explain the **extent** of the problem with reference to theory or real-world examples. Numbers should be used to substantiate the extent where applicable.
- Subsequent paragraphs should then deal with what **could** be done i.e. provide alternative solutions, starting with 'do nothing' (used sparingly) and then moving onto other possibilities. No recommendations should be made at this stage.

Proposals

- With proposals the opening paragraph should explain the theoretical backdrop to the proposal – e.g. market development within Ansoff's matrix – and how it applies.
- In addition you could include an explanation of what the proposal is e.g. what franchising involves.
- Numerical references (e.g. possible valuations) can also be included here.
- Subsequent paragraphs could include the advantages and disadvantages of the proposal or an analysis using the suitability/feasibility/acceptability model.
- Again, no recommendations should be made at this stage.

Once these are completed you should have one further subsection to cover 'other issues'. For each of these, one or two lines should suffice to identify the issue, briefly explain it and make an action point.

1.7 Ethical considerations

One approach for dealing with ethical issues is to discuss them within the context of contrasting stakeholder views (e.g. higher profits may beat the expense of poor working conditions, in which case there is a conflict between shareholcers and employees). The ethics section should thus contain the following:

- An opening paragraph explaining ethics in the context of stakeholders.
- For each ethical issue identify the nature of the issue, highlight the specific nature of contrasting stakeholder views and make reasonable recommendations.

1.8 Recommendations

As with the main body of the report, each of the prioritised issues should have a subsection of their own here.

For each key issue you should aim to write one major paragraph or three short ones.

Either way you should aim to address the following:

- What you actually recommend the firm does – don't sit on the fence here!
- The key issues supporting your recommendation.
- The next step that is needed to be taken, possibly referring to timescales, implementation issues, etc.

Remember to incorporate bigger issues at this stage.

For example, preliminary conclusions may be that all proposals are attractive, but you could then bring in issues of capital rationing and suggest which strategy should be undertaken.

1.9 Conclusion

The conclusion is really just finishing off the report in a professional manner. One approach is as follows:

- Start by restating the key issue(s) facing the firm, as outlined in the introduction.
- Briefly summarise the main recommendations.
- Make a brief comment on the future.

For example:

'In conclusion, the main issues facing X are dealing with competitive rivalry and managing growth. Once the publicity and HR issues are resolved, X should again have a platform for high future growth.'

The conclusion could also be a useful place to mention any further information required and possible further work.

1.10 Appendices

Appendices should be at the back of the report and clearly labelled.

Typically:

- Appendix 1 will be a position analysis using a SWOT.
- Appendix 2 will give key ratios.
- Appendices 3 to 5 will cover other techniques used / calculations.

With calculations you should comment on the method used and any assumptions / limitations of your analysis.

2 Writing style

2.1 Introduction

Writing style is something that develops over time. It is influenced by your education and experiences. To some it comes easily, they enjoy words – but you are not looking to win any prizes in literature.

It's about putting facts, ideas and opinions in a clear, concise, logical fashion.

Some students get very worried about their writing styles. As a general rule you try to write as you would talk.

2.2 Logical flow

A typical point starts with a statement of fact, either given in the case or derived from analysis – 'what?'

This can then be followed by an interpretation – 'so what?'

This can then lead to an implication – 'now what?', or 'what next?'

For example:

1 What? – The NPV is positive.

2 So what? – Suggesting we should go ahead with the project.

3 Now what? – Arrange board meeting to discuss strategic implications .

A similar structure can be obtained using the Socratic approach – what, why, how?

- So what?
- Why should we use it?
- How does it work?

2.3 Who is reading the report?

Failure to pitch the level correctly will inevitably result in failure to communicate your ideas effectively, since the reader will either be swamped with complexity, or bored with blandness.

The recipients of the report should also dictate the level of tact required.

Tactless	Tactful
The directors have clearly made errors	There were other options open to the board that, with hindsight, would have been beneficial
The marketing director is responsible for this disastrous change in strategy	The board should consider where this went wrong? It would appear that the marketing department may have made some mistakes

2.4 Making your report easy to read

To ensure that the marker finds your report accessible and easy to read, you should try to do the following:

- Use short words, short sentences, short phrases and short paragraphs. If you are adopting the 'what, so what, what now' approach, then you could have a paragraph containing three sentences. The next point can then be a new paragraph, also containing three sentences.

- Use the correct words to explain what you mean! For example, students often get confused between:

  recommendations (what they should do – actions) and options (what they could do – possibilities)

  objectives (what we want to achieve – the destination) and strategies (how we intend to achieve them – the route).

- Avoid unnecessary repetition. Some students fall into the trap of thinking that writing a professional report means simply writing more words to say the same thing! The issue is quality not quantity.

  For example, compare the following:

'I, myself, personally'	OR	'I'
'export overseas'	OR	'export'
'green in colour'	OR	'green'

- Spelling – this may seem a small and unimportant point, but poor spelling makes a document seem sloppy and may convey an impression that the content is as loose as the general appearance! Poor spelling interrupts the marker as they read your report, so there is the danger that they conclude that it did not have a logical flow.

chapter

4

TOOLS FOR TECHNICAL ANALYSIS

Contents

1 Why a detailed analysis is important

It is extremely important that you should have studied the pre-seen material thoroughly before you go into the examination. There are two main reasons for this:

- It will save time in the examination itself if you are already familiar with the pre-seen material.
- It enables you to develop a view of the situation facing the organisation in the case study, and in particular its strategic and financial position and prospects.

You will not be able to answer the examination question itself from the pre-seen material alone, and the unseen material given to you in the examination will present significant new information that will alter the situation substantially. Even so, a major step towards success in the examination is a careful study and exploration of the pre-seen material.

2 Our recommended approach – outline

It would be wrong to suggest that there is a unique method of analysing the pre-seen material. However, it is important that you should have an organised approach to the analysis. The approach described and illustrated in this text is as follows:

- **Read the pre-seen material from beginning to end without making any notes**, simply to familiarise yourself with the scenario. Read the material again, as many times as you think necessary, without making notes. You can do this over a period of several days, if you wish. When you think you are reasonably familiar with the situation described by the material, you should start to make notes.
- **Start to make notes.** By making notes, you will become more familiar with the detail of the scenario. We recommend that you make notes on each paragraph (or each group of short paragraphs) in the pre-seen material. Think about what the paragraph is telling you, and consider how this information might be of interest or relevance.
- **Do some simple calculations.** You will almost certainly be given some figures in the pre-seen material. These might relate to the company's profits or losses, or product profitability. There might be income statements and balance sheets for previous years, future business plans, cash flow statements, capital expenditure plans, EPS and share price information and so on. Do some simple calculations, such as financial ratio calculations or a cash flow analysis. These might give you a picture of changes in profitability, liquidity, working capital management, returns on capital, financial structure or cash flows over time.

- **Revise any 'technical' topics that might be relevant.** The pre-seen material might make a reference to a particular 'technical' issue, such as the balanced scorecard approach, corporate governance requirements, internal controls, the use of derivative instruments, company valuations, and so on. If you have forgotten about any topic that might be relevant, go back to your previous study materials and revise it.
- **Find out what you can about the industry in which the case study organisation operates.** Carry out some research into the industry in which the organisation described in the case study operates. You can use a search engine such as *Google* or *Yahoo* to find information on the Internet. If you can identify the name of one or more companies that actually operate in the industry, visit their websites and find out what you can about them. Occasionally, the case study might relate to an industry that has been in the financial news, and you might therefore find useful articles in the newspapers, such as the *Financial Times.*

  You might think that the case study is describing an actual company (under a different name). However, this will not be the examiner's intention. Although it will help you to be familiar with what is happening in the industry, the case study should avoid 'real-world' examples.
- **Use 'formal' techniques to analyse the pre-seen material**, using your notes and your background understanding of the industry. A number of formal techniques are suggested later in this chapter. The aim of this analysis is to identify, if possible, the strategic and financial position and prospects of the organisation in the case study.
- **Summarise your analysis.**
- **Give yourself more time to think.** You should now spend some time thinking about the case study, as much as you can. You don't have to be sitting at a desk or table to do this. You can think about the case study when you travel to work or in any spare time that you have for thinking.

  – When new ideas come to you, jot them down.

  – If you think of a new approach to financial analysis, carry out any calculations you think might be useful.

3 Techniques for analysis

You can use any techniques for analysis with which you are familiar. The aim of analysing the pre-seen material, however, should be to identify any strategic or financial issues, or possibly operational and management issues or ethical issues, that could be of relevance.

You might be familiar with the following techniques:

- 7-S framework analysis
- value chain and supply chain analysis
- McFarlan's grid analysis for IT systems
- a resources audit (5 M audit)
- Porter's five forces model analysis
- PESTEL analysis
- Porter diamond analysis
- identifying critical success factors
- financial analysis
- SWOT analysis.

We recommend in particular that you use at least one technique for strategic position analysis (such as SWOT analysis) and that you carry out some financial analysis of the figures in the pre-seen material.

4 Operations and management

The pre-seen material is likely to give you a lot of information about the management and the operations of the organisation in the case study. Some of this information might seem unimportant (or of doubtful importance). You can use a number of techniques to consider what issues seem important, and what issues seem more significant than others.

4.1 7-S framework analysis

This approach was developed by McKinsey and others to help understand the factors that determine the effectiveness of an organisation. You should consider each of the '7 Ss' and make a note of any factor that could be of some importance.

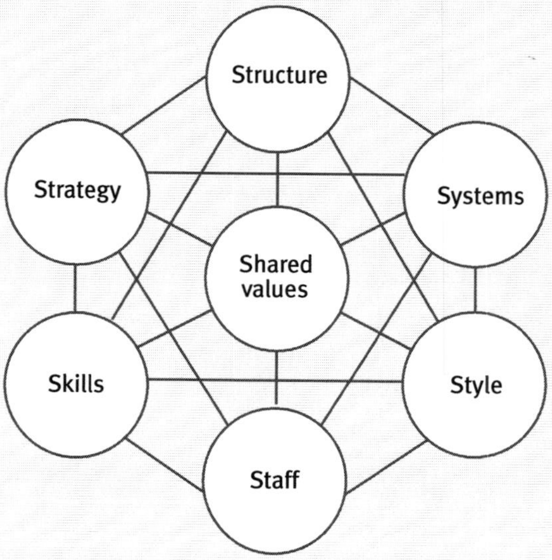

Systems. Systems are the formal and informal procedures that govern day-to-day operational activity. Do these appear to operate effectively, or have there been problems? For example:

- a company might have experienced problems with the procurement of key materials from suppliers, thus suggesting difficulties with its procurement systems
- there might be problems with the IT systems
- there might be problems with the fulfilment of orders (despatch to customers).

Style. This refers to how management spends its time and presents itself to staff. Does management style help to create greater efficiency, or is there a problem with management style that has created some resentment amongst employees?

Shared values. These are the fundamental values and aims that guide an organisation. They can be particularly strong in a small company, but might be difficult to sustain as a company grows bigger. When there is a strong sense of shared values, there is often a strong motivation for achieving success.

Skills. What are the distinctive capabilities or competences of the organisation? Are these being fully exploited? Is a lack of skills affecting the efficiency of the organisation?

Staff. Staff can contribute to the efficiency of an organisation, or can be inefficient. In some cases, there might be a shortage of staff. In a case study scenario, you might be given a short description of the experience and personality of several key members of staff, such as divisional managers. Are there any key individuals? Are they easily replaceable? Does the pre-seen material suggest that there is a problem (or potential problem) with any individual? Are there bad personal relationships between any key individuals?

Structure. Structure refers to how the firm is organised. What is the management and organisation structure of the company? Do there appear to be any strengths or weaknesses in this structure? Who makes the decisions? Who should be making the decisions?

Strategy. Strategy can be defined simply as the route chosen by the firm to achieve success. Your analysis of the pre-seen material will almost certainly need to include a detailed analysis of strategy.

4.2 The value chain and the supply chain

The value chain

It might be helpful to look at what the pre-seen material tells you about the value chain within the organisation. The concept of the value chain was developed by Porter. He argued that management should see the operations within their organisation as sequences of activities delivering value to the customer. Management should consider how each activity can be made to provide greater value.

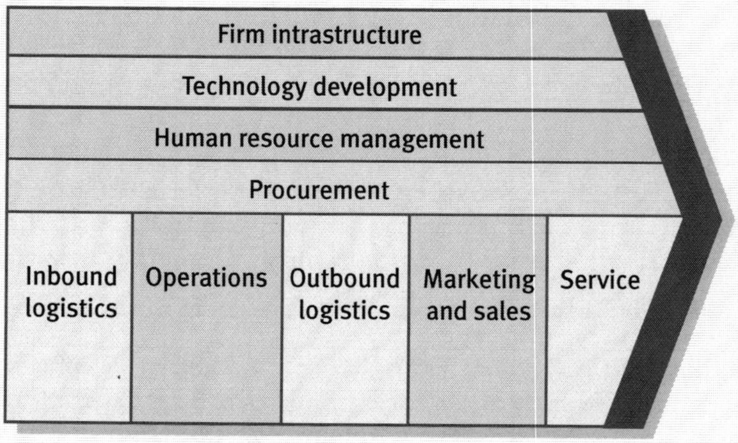

Each activity in the value chain is a source of:

- costs to the firm: these reduce profits and render it vulnerable to competitive attack by lower cost rivals. Value can be increased by reducing costs
- benefit to the customer: these generate revenue and, if superior, can justify higher prices. Value is increased by creating more benefits in excess of the costs of providing them
- benchmark comparison: if the firm performs an activity less well than a rival, it will suffer adverse comparison to rivals and excessive costs.

The supply chain

The supply chain describes the links from the production of raw materials for a product or service to the delivery of the final product to the end-consumer. An organisation has a position in the overall supply chain. Value delivered to the end-consumer can be increased by making improvements at any point in the supply chain, and an organisation often relies on its suppliers to add value.

Procurement policy and the management of supplier relationships can be a key operational issue. You might find it useful to think about the supply chain of the company in the case study, and the effectiveness of the company's relationships with its suppliers.

4.3 McFarlan's grid

The pre-seen material might give you data about the IT systems or management information systems currently used by the organisation. McFarlan's grid is a simple technique for identifying the way a firm uses its information systems and the likely scale of future investment needed.

		Future strategic value Low	High
Current strategic value	Low	Support	Turnaround
	High	Factory	Strategic

It might be useful to consider the following issues:

- Does the IS adequately support current operations?
- Are there internal changes (such as new working practices, production techniques or competitive strategies) that demand a change in IS provision?
- Are there external changes (such as e-commerce, IT/IS innovations or adoption of new methods by rivals) that demand changes to the firm's IS?
- What is management's support for IS and is it likely that the necessary changes will get approval and funding?

5 Resources audit

Another approach to analysing the strategic, financial and operational position of a company is to carry out a resources audit, also called a '5 M audit' because the main categories of resources are men, money, machinery, markets and materials. The matters identified by a resources audit might duplicate many of those that would be revealed by a 7-S analysis. It is therefore unlikely that you will benefit from doing both a 7-S analysis and a resources audit. Select the approach that you prefer.

To carry out a resources audit for the purpose of analysing the pre-seen material, you should go through the pre-seen material, making a note of any information that might seem relevant in relation to that category of resources.

The table overleaf suggests the type of information you might be able to extract.

Resource	Matters covered	Things to look out for
Men	• Characteristics of work force (age, skill) • Characteristics of managers (age, experience, track record) • Costs of labour • Staffing levels and labour turnover • Organisation culture • Organisation structure	Details of named individuals. They could feature in the unseen material in scenarios such as: • being available for a new project or promotion • precipitating a crisis by leaving • being the person you write your report to. People whose opinions or agendas are detailed as: • a source of conflict • a progressive force for change • resisting change.
Money	• Profitability of business • Liquidity and solvency of the business • Availability of capital for expansion • Relationship with shareholders: shareholder returns/dividends • Value of the business in event of sale or merger	If the company has falling profits, a strategy might be required to halt the decline and turn the company round. If the company has too little capital to fund its expansion, you might need to consider whether additional funding is possible. If not, the company will have to restrict its expansion plans.

Machinery	• Quality of capital assets (premises, machines, vehicles) • Methods of operations • Quality of IT • Quality control; process quality	Are some assets in need of replacement and can the company afford to replace some/all of them? Opportunities to improve financial returns by improvements to assets, technology or operating methods.
Markets	• Competitive positioning and market share • Brand recognition, strength and values • Quality and position of product(s) in product life cycle • Customers served and their potential profitability • Route to market (e.g. relationship with sellers; use of e-commerce)	Assess whether sales of the product are likely to grow or contract in the future. Vulnerability to competition. Power exercised by buyer/customer could depress profits. Products reaching the decline stage or late maturity stage of their life cycle will need replacement. Does brand/reputation limit the business?
Materials	• Relations with suppliers • Costs of materials • Quality of inputs • Purchasing policy and methods • Security of supplies of key inputs • Extent of collaboration or reliance on suppliers	Check cost of sales and gross margins for evidence of supplier power. Consider ways to reduce input costs by: • greater supplier choice • collaboration in JIT arrangements/ strategic supplier relationships.

6 Environmental assessment

Environmental assessment is the evaluation of factors in the environment of an organisation that could have a significant influence or effect on its future. Techniques of assessment that can be used are:

- Porter's five competitive forces analysis or five forces model
- PESTEL
- Porter diamond.

6.1 Porter's five forces model

Porter has argued that the long-term profitability of companies within an industry is reduced by the presence of one or more strong competitive forces. The profitability and survival of any company in the industry will depend on countering these five forces.

For the purpose of analysing the pre-seen material, you can assess the apparent strength of any of these five factors and whether they might be relevant to the future strategic direction that the organisation should be taking.

Force	**This force is strong if:**
Buyer power This is the power of buyers in the industry – the organisation's customers. Strong buyer power: • forces down prices • exerts pressure for expensive quality improvements and service improvements.	The industry or company depends on a small number of buyers/customers. The company's product is unbranded or undifferentiated, so that buyers have no particular reason to select the company for its supplies. The company has excess capacity or the industry is in recession. There are no costs or few costs involved for buyers in switching from one source of supply to another. The buyers have information on prices of alternative producers in the industry.

Supplier power This is the power of suppliers to firms in the industry. Strong supplier power: • reduces profits by raising prices • reduces the pressure on suppliers to provide a high quality product and service • increases the risk of unreliability in supply.	The product/service provided by the supplier is unique or differentiated, and buyers have no alternative choice of supply. There are few suppliers in the industry, and possibly a monopoly supplier. The cost of switching from the current supplier to a new supplier would be high.
Threat of entry This is the threat that new competitors will enter the market and increase the competition. When the threat from new entrants is strong: • long-run profitability in the industry will be low • companies in the industry may reduce prices to deter entry by new competitors, forcing down short-term profitability.	The industry has good long-run market potential, giving new entrants opportunities to enter and gain a competitive position. There are low set-up costs. New entrants can enter the industry without incurring high costs. A company in the industry has a good market share but poor financial position, making it a potential takeover target for a more powerful new entrant.
Substitute technologies When there are substitute technologies, customers in the industry have the option of switching from buying one product to buying the substitute/alternative. The existence of a substitute technology: • reduces demand for the product • forces manufacturers of the product to keep their prices low.	The substitute technology or product can perform the same function just as well or even better. The substitute technology is reasonably priced. It is easy for customers to transfer to the substitute technology and the costs of transferring would be low.

Competitive rivalry	
The strength of rival firms in the industry is clearly a major competitive force. Strong competition: • forces down prices • forces firms to make costly quality improvements to be competitive • creates a risk of takeovers in the industry.	Competitive forces can be particularly strong when: • the rate of growth in the industry is slowing down • customers are prepared to change to a lower price supplier • companies in the industry have high fixed costs that must be absorbed and covered by sales income.

6.2 PESTEL analysis

PESTEL analysis is an extension of PEST analysis. It involves the analysis of environmental influences on a company or an industry, within the six categories: political, economic, social, technological, ecological/ethical and legal. These are regarded as six categories of environmental influence that might be significant.

Factor	Examples to look for
Political	Government policy affecting the industry or firm Stability of government in firm's main countries of operations Potential trade wars Change of government and possibility of change in taxation or attitudes to industry and the economy
Economic	Whether the economy is wealthy or poor Growth rate of the economy and potential for recession Level and trends in interest rates and effects of firm's markets and costs of borrowing Exchange rates and the risk of a rise or fall in key exchange rates

Social	Trends in buying behaviour Demographic changes (location, age of customers) Distribution of income between social groups Lifestyle changes
Technological	Changes in the technologies of consumption (e.g. buying methods) Changes in the technology of production Changes in the technology of organisations (e.g. applications of IT to improve efficiency and effectiveness)
Ecological/ethical	Impact of the industry on natural environment: pollution, waste, sustainability issues Impact of the firm's activities on the community
Legal	Competition policy Regulation of wages and prices Regulation of employment (e.g. rules on discrimination)

6.3 Porter diamond

The purpose of the Porter diamond model is to assess to what extent the firm (or its potential foreign rival) gains world-class advantages as a consequence of having operated in its home country. This model might be useful for analysis in a case study where:

- the firm is considering developing businesses outside its home country, or
- the firm is likely to be subject to competition from outside its home country.

Factor	What to look for	Implications
Demand conditions	Are home demand patterns for the firm's goods/services in advance or behind foreign demand patterns? How similar are home customers' demands to those of foreign customers? Will high levels of home demand confer cost advantages in the foreign market?	Where home demand is broadly similar but ahead of foreign countries, the firm will have an advantage over foreign rivals. If economies of scale can be exported, it will provide the competitive advantage of lower costs.
Factor conditions	Does the firm have access to resources not generally available to foreign rivals? Will the resources in the foreign market be similar to those of which the firm has experience?	These advantages apply better to manufacturing than services. If resources are not similar, the firm may have problems transferring its competitive strategy to the foreign market.
Related and supporting industries	Does the firm depend on particular key suppliers or partners for success in the home market? Will these be available in the foreign market? Is demand generated by the existence of a particular industry in the home country and will this be present in the foreign country?	Firm will not be competitive without establishing similar partnership arrangements in the foreign country.

Competitive rivalry	How strong is the competition likely to be? Does the firm have experience of beating similar competition at home?	Apply the five forces model analysis to the foreign market to assess this.
Culture and chance conditions	Does the current success of the firm depend on factors peculiar and unique to its home country?	These are unlikely to be available in the foreign country.

7 Product portfolio analysis

7.1 BCG matrix analysis

The BCG matrix is an all-in-one strategic planning tool that not only performs position analysis but also generates strategies.

The matrix simplistically considers market share to assess competitive strength and market growth to assess market attractiveness. Once classified, products can be managed as follows:

Market share	***Market growth:*** *Low*	***Market growth:*** *High*
High	**Cash cow** • Strong position in a low growth market • Little threat from rivals • Just keep the product ticking over and collect the cash	**Star** • Attractive market so have to reinvest heavily to defend market share and grow • Little cash surplus
Low	**Dog** • Too small to benefit from economies of scale • Market does not justify further investment • Divest	**Problem child** • Attractive market but too small to capitalise on it • Either invest heavily to gain market share or get out • 'Double or quit'

NB: Less useful for service industries where economies of scale may not exist

NB: Measurement problems e.g. which market are we looking at?

If using the matrix, try to comment on whether the firm has a balanced portfolio as far as cash flow is concerned.

7.2 Product lifecycle (PLC) analysis

Products are classified according to their position in the lifecycle:

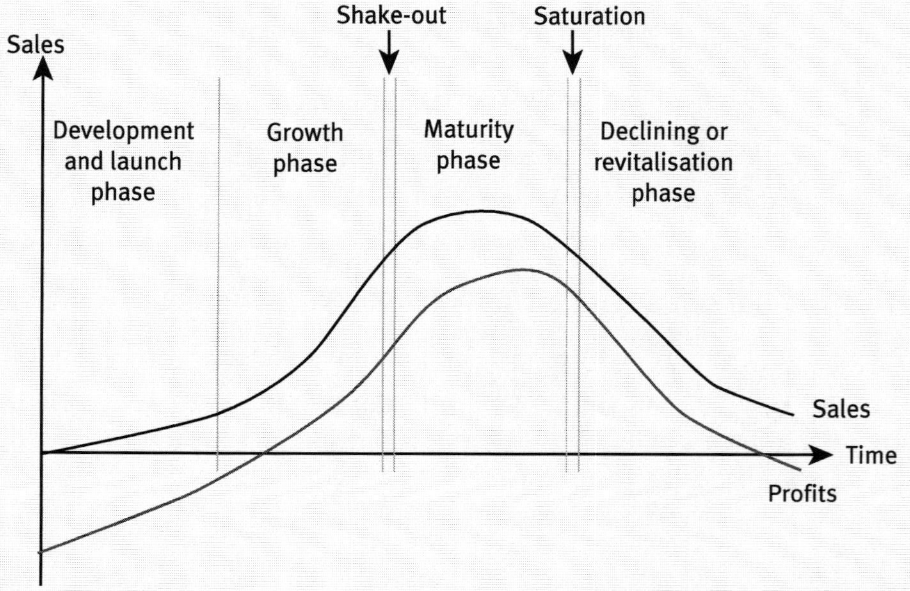

The key use of PLC analysis is to assess whether the firm has a balanced portfolio:

- Does it have new products coming through to replace older ones?
- Does it have cash-generating products to finance products that need investment?
- Does it have safe low risk products to complement high risk ones?

8 Critical success factors and performance appraisal

8.1 Critical success factors

Critical success factors (CSFs) are the factors that will determine whether a firm will be a success in its industry. CSFs vary from industry to industry.

CSFs can often be identified by answering four questions:

- What factors drive costs in the industry?
- What factors influence the revenues the firm can generate?
- What drives asset investment?
- What poses risks for the firm?

The following table expands on these by indicating what to look for.

Critical success factor	**Things to look for**
What factors drive costs in the industry?	• If fixed costs are high, this means that gaining sales volume is critical. • If product complexity is being used to gain orders (e.g. special customisation of products or width of product range), this will increase costs. Firms must understand and allow for this. • If economies of scale (volume) or economies of scope (breadth of product range) are available, this makes relative size and market share a critical success factor. • If a firm must incur high spending on advertising, research and development or asset refurbishment in order to compete, the firm must be able to afford it. • Where costs can be reduced by merger/acquisition, the firm needs to gain size and look for a merger partner or a takeover target. • If costs are affected by exchange rates or the availability of cheaper supplies from abroad, the firm might need cross-border supply chains.
What factors influence the revenues the firm can generate?	• If the firm's product commands a premium price, this means that sales promotion, brand image, meeting customer needs and technical quality are critical. • If the product competes by low prices it is critical that this market segment continues to include a substantial number of buyers willing to buy on price.

	• If revenue growth has been gained by accessing new customers and wider locations, the marketing and logistic skills of the firm are critical. • If revenue growth has been accomplished by new products and exploiting the early stages of product life cycles, it means that innovation and launch marketing are critical. • Competitors and new entrants will put pressure on revenues and so it is critical that competitive advantages are sustained and enforced.
What drives asset investment?	The CSFs in industries subject to high ongoing asset investment are: • ability to afford the costs of investment • ability to project manage and implement investment swiftly and successfully. Ensure that the firm's management (and you) appreciate that asset investment includes intangibles such as human resources and brands. • In consumer industries their rising expectations will necessitate continuous improvement and updating of premises, customer service and facilities. • In technological industries there will be need for continuous investment in R&D and production technology. • Sales growth drives asset investment if it needs extra production or distribution capacity. • Industries utilising IT strategically will need to ensure systems are kept up to date. The progress of IT applications is swift and continuous.
What poses risks for the firm?	These are events that could close the business down or severely restrict its space to operate and its earnings. **Asset risk:** factors that could result in loss of productive assets or their earning power

	(e.g. theft, destruction, legal challenges to their use). **Commercial risk:** reduction of earnings below forecast due to loss of customers, failure of new products, successful competition by rivals. **Operational risk:** breakdown in ability to provide the product or service, leading to loss of earnings and potential costs of legal claims by customer, suppliers and staff. **Financial risk:** loss of value of investments due to volatility of markets, adverse foreign exchange movements or adverse interest rate movements.

8.2 Key performance indicators

Each of the CSFs identified above should be measured by a number of key performance indicators (KPIs). If not, there is the risk that the issue concerned will not be monitored and controlled sufficiently.

A useful way of incorporating these is to use the balanced scorecard, which looks at a range of issues / factors relevant to different stakeholders:

Financial perspective	**How do we look to shareholders?**
Customer perspective	**How do customers see us?**
Innovation and learning	**Can we continue to improve and create value?**
Internal business processes	**What must we excel at?**

9 Financial analysis

To answer the questions in the case study examination, you will have to do much more than calculate and analyse some commonly used financial ratios. However, financial ratio analysis is a very useful approach to finding out about the financial position of an organisation, and its financial strengths and weaknesses. Depending on the information provided in the pre-seen material, you might be able to carry out some simple ratio analyses on historical data or on the data in a financial plan or business plan.

Here is a brief checklist of ratios and other calculations you might find useful. You should be familiar with all of them.

9.1 Analysing trends and magnitudes

Financial indicator	Things to look for
Sales turnover • Absolute figure shows the size of the company • % change per annum shows growth rate	• The company's stage in the product or industry life cycle. • Healthy companies have annual growth rate in sales in excess of the rate of inflation.
Group operating profit • Absolute figure shows the amount of profits • Annual growth in annual profit shows rate of increase	• If the company is unprofitable, or profits are falling, then the case study is probably about a profitability crisis and finding a turnaround strategy. • A high % increase in profit in comparison to % increase in sales turnover indicates a high fixed cost base. Look for increases in sales turnover that do not generate a large increase in profit. Does this indicate a problem?
Divisional sales revenue and operating profit • Absolute figure for divisional profit • % change per annum in divisional profit	• Assess the relative size and importance of the divisions. • Loss-making divisions need to be dealt with urgently. • Compare growth rates of each division to assess where strategic investment should perhaps take place.
Borrowings (loans and overdraft)	• High or rising borrowings might suggest high financial risk. • Consider why finance is debt and not equity.

Share price	
• The change in price through time • P/E ratio compared to rival companies	• An upward trend in share price is healthy. • A low or falling share price shows loss of investor confidence.

9.2 Ratios

Profitability ratios

You might find useful information from an analysis of profit/sales ratios, for:

- the company as a whole
- each division, or
- each product or service.

Profit margins can be measured as a net profit percentage and as a gross profit percentage. You can then look at trends in the ratios over time, or consider whether the margins are good or disappointing.

Analysing the ratio of certain expenses to sales might also be useful, such as the ratio of administration costs to sales, sales and marketing costs to sales or R&D costs to sales. Have there been any noticeable changes in these ratios over time and, if so, is it clear why the changes have happened?

Liquidity ratios

The two main measures of liquidity are:

- the current ratio (= ratio of current assets: current liabilities)
- the quick ratio or acid test ratio (= ratio of current assets excluding inventory: current liabilities).

The purpose of a liquidity ratio is to assess whether the organisation is likely to be able to pay its liabilities, when they fall due for payment, out of its operational cash flows.

The current ratio is probably more useful when inventory is fairly liquid and inventory turnover is fast. The quick ratio or acid test ratio is a better measure of liquidity when inventory turnover is slow.

Check these ratios for any significant change over time, or for the possibility of poor liquidity. As a very rough guide, a current ratio below 2:1 and a quick ratio below 1:1 might be low. However, the liquidity ratios are only likely to be of significance for the case study when the ratios get very low, or the deterioration in the ratios is very large. For example, if a company has current liabilities in excess of its current assets, a liquidity problem would seem likely.

Working capital ratios

Working capital ratios can be calculated to assess the efficiency of working capital management (= management of inventory, trade receivables and trade payables). They can also be useful for assessing liquidity, because excessive investment in working capital ties up cash and slows the receipt of cash.

The main working capital ratios are:

- average turnover period for inventory: slow turnover might indicate poor inventory management
- 'debtor days' or the average time that customers take to pay: the industry average might be 30 or 60 days
- average time to pay suppliers: again, the industry average might be 30 or 60 days.

You should be familiar with these ratios and how to calculate the length of the cash cycle or operating cycle.

Financial structure ratios

You might be required to consider methods of funding in your case study examination. If a company plans to expand in the future, where will the funds come from?

- Additional debt finance might only be possible if the current debt levels are not high, and financial gearing is fairly low. (The interest cover ratio is also a useful measure of debt capacity. It is the ratio of profit before interest and tax to interest costs. When the ratio is low, possibly less than 3, this could indicate that the company already has as much debt capital as it can safely afford.)
- If a company will need additional equity finding, will internally generated profits be a sufficient source of funds or will a new share issue be necessary?

9.3 Cash flow analysis or funding analysis

If the main objective of a company is to maximise the wealth of its shareholders, the most important financial issues will be profitability and returns to shareholders. However, other significant issues in financial strategy are often:

- cash flows and liquidity, and
- funding.

If the pre-seen material gives you enough data, you might be able to carry out a rough assessment of the company's cash flows, by constructing a cash flow statement. The purpose of such an analysis should be to get an idea of where the company has been getting its cash, and how it has been using the cash. A possible cash flow problem occurs whenever the cash flows from operations do not appear to be sufficient to cover all the non-operational cash payments that the company has to make, such as spending on capital expenditure items.

An analysis of future funding can be carried out by looking at the history of changes in the balance sheet. It is a relatively simple task to look at the growth in the company's assets over time, and at how the asset growth has been funded – by equity, long-term debt or shorter-term liabilities. If equity has funded much of the growth in assets, it might be possible to see how much of the new equity as been provided by retained profits, and how much has come from new issues of shares (indicated by an increase in the allotted share capital and share premium reserve).

10 Strategic position analysis: SWOT analysis

Many of the techniques of assessment described above should give you ideas about the future problems and potential of the firm in the case study. A final step in your analysis should be to draw up a SWOT analysis.

The analysis might change when you get the unseen material in the examination, but SWOT analysis is a simple technique that enables you to present a wide range of issues clearly and effectively.

You should include a SWOT analysis in your examination answer, particularly when the question asks you to present a report that discusses the issues facing the case study organisation. A SWOT analysis could be presented as an appendix to your report.

If you prepare a SWOT analysis from the pre-seen material in advance of the examination, you will find it much easier and quicker to prepare a similar analysis in the examination itself.

A SWOT analysis of an organisation is simply a listing of the following:

- The STRENGTHS of the organisation. These are internal factors that give the organisation a distinct advantage.
- The WEAKNESSES of the organisation. These are internal factors that affect performance adversely, and so might put the organisation at a disadvantage.

- The OPPORTUNITIES available. These are circumstances or developments in the environment that the organisation might be in a position to exploit to its advantage.
- The THREATS or potential threats. These are factors in the environment that present risks or potential risks to the organisation and its competitive position.

Strengths and weaknesses are internal to the organisation, whereas opportunities and threats are external factors.

A SWOT analysis can be presented simply as a list of strengths, followed by weaknesses, then opportunities and finally threats. It would be useful to indicate within each category which factors seem more significant than others, perhaps by listing them in descending order of priority.

Alternatively a SWOT analysis, if it is not too long and excludes minor factors, can be presented in the form of a 2 x 2 table, as follows:

Strengths	**Weaknesses**
Opportunities	**Threats**

With this method of presentation, the positive factors (strengths and opportunities) are listed on the left and the negative factors (weaknesses and threats) are on the right.

The analysis is improved if:

- the factors within each category are listed in descending order of priority, and
- minor factors are excluded entirely.

You should not forget that you will be assessed on your ability to prioritise the problems and issues facing the organisation in the case study, and preparing a SWOT analysis will help you to organise your thoughts.

11 Strategic options

Having completed a position analysis you can start to consider the strategic options facing the firm by answering three questions:

1 How are we going to compete – what should our competitive advantage be based on?

2 Where are we going to compete – what are the directions for growth?

3 How do we get there – organic growth, acquisition or a joint arrangement of some sort?

11.1 Porter's generic strategies

Porter argues that there are three ways to gain a sustainable competitive advantage.

Overall cost leadership

- Based on achieving the position of lowest cost producer in the industry for **standard** products and services – not necessarily inferior ones.
- The company can operate in even the most marginal segments of the market and undercut rival's prices at any time. (Price usually becomes the main weapon in competing.)
- Cost advantages come from economies of scale, large production runs, automation, learning effects, etc – use the value chain if you need more detail.

Differentiation

- Based on offering a **better** quality product than competitors.
- Customers are willing to pay extra for this differentiation.
- The difference must be valued by customers and may be real or created via advertising.

Focus/niche

- A company may find it difficult to gain a cost or quality advantage across the whole industry but can do so by focusing on a particular buyer group, market segment or a section of the product range.

'Stuck in the middle?'

- Porter argues that firms must choose between cost leadership and differentiation. Any attempt to do both will result in the firm having neither – a recipe for disaster.

Porter's generic strategies can be used in a number of ways:

- Position analysis – competitive advantage is a key part of a SWOT analysis e.g. being stuck in the middle is a major weakness.
- Prioritisation – maintaining a competitive advantage in a competitive marketplace would be considered important in most scenario.
- Strategy evaluation – competitive advantage is a useful issue to include when assessing potential strategies.

11.2 Ansoff's matrix

Ansoff's matrix analyses current and proposed strategies into four classifications:

	Existing products	**New products**
Existing markets	*Market penetration* • Price cuts? • Spend more on advertis-ing? • Small improvements to products? • Buy rivals? • Competitive strategy?	*Product development* • R&D could be critical • Acquire rights to make other firms' products • Buy in products and re-badge • Joint developments • Can use existing distribution channels
New markets	*Market development* • New customer segments • Industrial v consumer markets • New regions of the country • Foreign markets • Barriers to entry?	*Diversification* • Related diversification (e.g. vertical integration) • Unrelated diversification (conglomerate diversifi-cation)

Ansoff's matrix is very easy to use and hence score technical skills marks. As well as classifying current strategies it is particularly useful at identifying possible directions for growth.

12 Strategic choice

The pre-seen analysis may contain details of the firm's future plans, which should be evaluated. The suitability/acceptability/feasibility model developed by Tilles is particularly useful here:

Suitability – is the strategy consistent, both externally and internally?

- Does it give the firm a better fit with the environment?
- Portfolio analysis – how do new products fit with existing ones?
- Are their synergies with other parts of the business?
- Resource deployment analysis – how does the strategy match against strengths and weaknesses?

Acceptability – look at risk and return.

- Is the risk acceptable?
- Does the strategy meet the criteria for 'success' for different stakeholder groups?
- Techniques could include NPV, IRR, expected present value.
- Problems dealing with multiple objectives and non-quantifiable objectives.
- Could involve sensitivity analysis to assess risks.

Feasibility – is the strategy within the resources and capability of the organisation?

- Is the time-scale achievable?
- Do we have the critical success factors necessary to implement the strategy?

13 Thinking about the pre-seen material

When you have completed your analysis of the pre-seen material, you should still have some time before the examination to think about the case study and to re-assess the analysis you have made so far.

The examination will test your ability to appraise a situation, identify critical issues, evaluate problems and recommend a way forward. In effect, the examination is testing your ability to contribute to decision-making at a senior level within an organisation.

Thinking about the case study should give you an opportunity to exercise your potential talent. If you were a senior manager in the organisation in the case study, what would be concerning you most of all? Are there any decisions that might have to be made?

- **Strategic issues.** What do you think the company should be trying to achieve? What about the strategic direction the organisation is taking? What do you think the organisation's strategy ought to be? (But remember, the unseen material in the examination will introduce an unexpected 'twist'.)

- **Financial issues.** What is the financial position of the company, and what are its future financial prospects? What do you think about the balance sheet, profitability, sales, growth, working capital management, cash flow management and liquidity, capital investment and funding?
- **Management issues.** If you were a director of the organisation, working with the individuals in the case study, would you be aware of any problems of management? Are there any individuals who are not doing their job as well as they should? Is the organisation over-reliant on any particular individual? Is authority being delegated in the most appropriate way?
- **Ethical issues.** Do there appear to be any ethical problems? How would you want to resolve them? (The pre-seen material might hint at possible ethical problems, but you are more likely to find problems of this kind introduced on the examination day in the unseen material.)
- **Objectives.** Never forget what the objectives of the organisation ought to be. Is the current management team giving proper consideration to the organisation's objectives (probably increasing shareholder value)? How would you be expecting to increase earnings, dividends and, if the company's shares are quoted on a stock market, the share price? If the company is a private company, how might shareholders be expecting to 'realise their investment' – through an eventual listing and stock market launch, or a trade sale of the business to a competitor?

Never forget that this examination is not really testing what you have learned. It is testing your ability to analyse, assess, evaluate and apply judgement to 'realistic' business problems. Thinking about the case study allows you to exercise these abilities. We therefore recommend very strongly that you allow yourself as much time as possible for the thinking process.

Just before the examination, you should go over the pre-seen material, and your notes, again. Compare your earlier thoughts about the case study with your current thinking, which may well have changed. Make sure that your ideas are still consistent with the information in the pre-seen material.

You should now be ready to take the examination.

chapter

5

CIMA'S ETHICAL GUIDELINES

Contents

1 Ethics and the TOPCIMA examination

One criterion on which you will be assessed in the TOPCIMA examination is your ability to advise on or resolve ethical dilemmas. You should therefore be aware of CIMA's Guidelines on ethical conduct. You can download a copy of the Ethical Guidelines from CIMA's website, if you want to read the full text.

The Ethical Guidelines are included in the syllabus for Paper P3 *Management Accounting: Risk and Control Strategy*. However, if you have not studied the Guidelines before, this chapter gives you a summary. There are lengthy quotations from the Guidelines themselves, which are reproduced by kind permission of CIMA.

The case study might present ethical issues in a different way, and you might need to apply judgement in deciding how to apply the Guidelines to the particular circumstances presented in the case study. The Guidelines state: 'It is not practical or possible to establish ethical requirements which apply to all situations and circumstances members may encounter. The objectives as well as the fundamental principles of the Guidelines are of a general nature and are not intended to be used to solve a member's ethical problems in a specific case. Members should consider the principles set out in the Guidelines as the basic principles which they should follow when performing their work.'

2 The requirement to act professionally

The Guidelines stress the point that CIMA members and students are professional accountants, and must behave professionally.

- 'As members of a profession, CIMA's members have a duty to observe the highest standard of conduct and integrity.'
- 'The Guidelines assume that, unless a limitation is specifically stated, the objectives and fundamental principles are equally valid for all members, whether they be in industry, commerce, the public sector, public practice or education.'

'A profession is distinguished by certain characteristics including:

- mastery of a particular intellectual skill, acquired by training and education
- acceptance of duties to society as a whole in addition to duties to the client or employer

- an outlook which is essentially objective
- rendering personal services to a high standard of conduct and performance.'

3 The public interest

'A distinguishing mark of a profession is acceptance of its responsibility to the public.' For a professional accountant, the public consists of:

- employers
- creditors
- clients
- governments
- employees
- investors
- the business and financial community, and
- others who rely on the objectivity and integrity of professional accountants to maintain the orderly functioning of commerce.

This reliance imposes a public interest responsibility on the accountancy profession. The public interest is defined as the collective well-being of the community of people and institutions the professional accountant serves.'

The Guidelines go on to make the crucial point that the responsibility of a professional accountant is not exclusively to an employer or client, because a public interest consideration might also apply. In other words, a conflict of interest could arise.

'A professional accountant's responsibility is not exclusively to satisfy the needs of an individual client or employer. The standards of the accountancy profession are heavily determined by the public interest, for example:

- financial managers serve in various financial management capacities in organisations and contribute to the efficient and effective use of the organisation's resources
- internal auditors provide assurance about a sound internal control system which enhances the reliability of the external financial information of the employer
- independent auditors help to maintain the integrity and efficiency of the financial statements presented to financial institutions in partial support for loans and to shareholders for obtaining capital
- tax experts help to establish confidence and efficiency in, and the fair application of, the tax system

- management consultants have a responsibility toward the public interest in advocating sound management decision making
- professional accountants have an important role in society.

Investors, creditors, employers and other sectors of the business community, as well as the government and the public at large, rely on professional accountants for sound financial accounting and reporting, effective financial management and competent advice on a variety of business and taxation matters. The attitude and behaviour of professional accountants in providing such services have an impact on the economic well-being of their community and country.'

4 Objectives of the accountancy profession

The objectives of the accountancy profession are to work to the highest standards of professionalism and also to meet the public interest requirement. The Guidelines state that, to meet these objectives, four basic requirements must be met:

- **Credibility.** There must be credibility in information and information systems.
- **Professionalism.** Employers, clients and other interested parties must recognise that accountants are professionals.
- **Quality of services.** There must be assurance that all services obtained from a professional accountant are carried out to the highest standards of performance.
- **Confidence.** 'Users of the services of professional accountants should be able to feel confident that there is a framework of professional ethics to govern the provision of services.'

5 Fundamental principles

Having stressed the need for accountants to act professionally, and for others to recognise that accountants are professionals, the Guidelines go on to list a number of fundamental principles that accountants must observe. These are:

- **Integrity.** The accountant should be straightforward and honest in performing professional services. Significantly perhaps, for the purposes of the case study examination, the Guidelines state that 'accountants should not be party to the falsification of any record or knowingly or recklessly supply any information or make any statement which is misleading, false or deceptive in a material particular'. So what should you do if your chief executive officer suggests that the financial statements should be altered to make the company's position look better, and that the external auditors should be persuaded to agree to the changes?

- **Objectivity.** 'A professional accountant should be fair and should not allow prejudice or bias or the influence of others to override objectivity.' Objectivity is considered in more detail below.
- **Professional competence and due care.** It is worth studying this principle in full. The Guidelines state that: 'In agreeing to provide professional services, a professional accountant implies that there is a level of competence necessary to perform those services and that his or her knowledge, skill and experience will be applied with reasonable care and diligence. Professional accountants must therefore refrain from performing any services which they are not competent to carry out unless appropriate advice and assistance is obtained to ensure that the services are performed satisfactorily. A professional accountant should perform professional services with due care, competence and diligence. There is a continuing duty to maintain professional knowledge and skill at a level required to ensure that a client or employer receives the advantage of competent professional service based on up-to-date developments in practice, legislation and techniques.'
- **Confidentiality.** 'A professional accountant should respect the confidentiality of information acquired during the course of performing professional services and should not use or disclose any such information without proper and specific authority or unless there is a legal or professional right or duty to disclose.'
- **Professional behaviour.** Accountants should behave in a professional way, and should not act in any way that brings discredit to the profession or CIMA. An interesting additional comment inserted in the Guidelines is that: 'A professional accountant, particularly one having authority over others, should give due weight to the need for others to develop and hold their own judgements in accounting matters, and should deal with differences of opinion in a professional way.'
- **Professional and technical standards.** The fundamental requirement that professional accountants must apply professional and technical standards to the work that they do could have some relevance to a case study examination. Again, it is worth reading the Guidelines in full on this point. 'A professional accountant is expected to present financial information fully, honestly and professionally, so that it will be understood in its context. S/he also knows, understands and follows professional standards; a professional accountant should carry out professional services in accordance with relevant technical and professional standards. They have a duty to carry out, with care and skill, the instructions of the client or employer insofar as they are compatible with the requirements of integrity, objectivity and, in the case of public practice, independence.'

6 Specific guidelines

Having stated the fundamental principles on which ethical conduct must be based, the Guidelines consider a variety of more specific issues. It is useful to look at a number of these, since the situations they envisage could easily feature in a case study.

6.1 Objectivity

The fundamental principle of objectivity imposes the obligation on accountants to be fair, intellectually honest and free of conflicts of interest. This requirement applies both to accountants in public practice and accountants who are not in public practice, who 'prepare financial statements as a subordinate of others, perform internal auditing services, and serve in financial management capacities in industry, commerce, the public sector and education'. The Guidelines state that 'all members should protect the integrity of their professional services, maintain objectivity, and avoid any subordination of their judgement by others'.

The Guidelines state that matters concerning objectivity could arise in the following circumstances:

- An accountant could be exposed to a situation in which pressure might be brought to bear on him or her, which could damage his or her objectivity.
- Reasonableness should be applied when identifying relationships that are likely to impair an accountant's objectivity.
- Relationships should be avoided that allow prejudice, bias or the influences of other individuals to override objectivity.

6.2 Resolution of ethical conflicts of interest

Conflicts of interest can arise in a variety of different ways. When a conflict of interest arises, there is a conflict between:

- the professional responsibilities of the accountant, and
- either internal or external pressure on the individual to do something different that is not consistent with professional requirements.

For example:

- There might be a danger of pressure from an overbearing supervisor, manager, director or partner.
- There might be family or personal relationships which can give rise to the possibility of pressures being exerted on the accountant.

- An accountant should not mislead his employer as to the degree of expertise or experience he possesses and, where appropriate, should obtain expert advice and assistance.
- An accountant might be asked to act contrary to technical or professional standards.
- There could be a problem of divided loyalty, between loyalty to an employer or superior and loyalty or duty to the profession.
- 'Conflict could arise when misleading information is published which may be to the advantage of the employer or client and which may or may not benefit the member as a result of such publication.'

When an accountant in employment is faced with a significant ethical issue, his first step should be to take up the matter through the established grievance procedure or similar appropriate procedure of the organisation. The procedures recommended by the Guidelines are worth noting:

- 'If following these policies does not resolve the problem or the member is unable to use such procedures, the member should consider discussing the problem with his or her immediate superior, unless that person is involved, in which case the issue should be submitted to the next higher level of management.'
- 'At higher levels of management the acceptable reviewing authority may be some or all of the board of directors, or the auditors, but contact with levels above the immediate superior should only be initiated with the superior's knowledge, assuming non-involvement.
- 'Prior to or following any of these stages, discussion with an objective adviser or the member's professional accountancy body may be useful. Such discussion should be concerned to clarify the issues involved and to identify possible courses of action without breaching the duty of confidentiality to the other parties involved.'
- If the ethical conflict still exists after fully exhausting all levels of internal review, the last resort with a significant matter such as fraud might have to be to resign and submit an information memorandum to an appropriate representative of his or her employing organisation.

6.3 Professional competence

Accountants 'should refrain from agreeing to perform professional services which they are not competent to carry out unless competent advice and assistance is obtained to enable them to satisfactorily perform such services'.

6.4 Confidentiality

A professional accountant has an obligation to respect the confidentiality of information about an employer's or a client's affairs acquired in the course of his work. This duty of confidentiality continues even after the end of the relationship with the employer or client.

- 'Confidentiality should always be observed unless specific authority has been given to disclose information or there is a legal or professional duty to disclose.'
- 'Confidentiality is not only a matter of disclosure of information. It also requires that anyone acquiring information in the course of performing his or her work will not use that information for personal advantage or for the advantage of a third party.'

7 Conclusion

This chapter has not covered the Ethical Guidelines in full, but has drawn attention to ethical issues that could arise in the TOPCIMA examination. It is quite possible that a case study will introduce a different ethical issue. If you think that an ethical issue does arise, and these notes do not seem to cover the situation, you might wish to read the Guidelines in full on the CIMA website (www.cimaglobal.com and key 'ethics' or 'ethical guidelines' into the search function).

chapter

6

ZUBINOS: ANALYSING THE PRE-SEEN MATERIAL

Contents

Scenario – Pre-seen material

Zubinos was the TOPCIMA case for both the March and May 2006 examination papers. When analysing this material and answering the examination question, you should assume that 'now' is early 2006.

What follows is the assessment matrix followed by the detailed paragraph by paragraph analysis that was carried out in the 'knowledge' publication for Zubinos.

You could try answering each of the questions before looking at the suggested answers to aid your understanding of the case.

Assessment Matrix for TOPCIMA - Zubinos

Criterion	Marks*	Clear pass	Pass	Marginal pass	Marginal Fail	Fail	Clear fail
Technical	5	Thorough display of relevant technical knowledge. **5**	Good display of relevant knowledge. **4**	Some display of relevant technical knowledge. **3**	Identification of some relevant knowledge, but lacking in depth. **2**	Little knowledge displayed, or some misconceptions. **1**	No evidence of knowledge displayed, or fundamental misconceptions. **0**
Application	10	Knowledge clearly applied in an analytical and practical manner. **9-10**	Knowledge applied to the context of the case. **6-8**	Identification of some relevant knowledge, but not well applied. **5**	Knowledge occasionally displayed without clear application. **3-4**	Little attempt to apply knowledge to the context. **1-2**	No application of knowledge displayed. **0**
Diversity	5	Most knowledge areas identified, covering a wide range of views. **5**	Some knowledge areas identified, covering a range of views. **4**	A few knowledge areas identified, expressing a fairly limited scope. **3**	Several important knowledge aspects omitted. **2**	Many important knowledge aspects omitted. **1**	Very few knowledge aspects considered. **0**
Focus	15	Clearly distinguishes between relevant and irrelevant information. **13-15**	Information used is mostly relevant. **9-12**	Some relevant information ignored, or some less relevant information used. **8**	Information used is sometimes irrelevant. **5-7**	Little ability to distinguish between relevant and irrelevant information. **1-4**	No ability to distinguish between relevant and irrelevant information. **0**
Prioritisation	10	Issues clearly prioritised in a logical order and based on a clear rationale. **9-10**	Issues prioritised with justification. **6-8**	Evidence of issues being listed in order of importance, but rationale unclear. **5**	Issues apparently in priority order, but without a logical justification or rationale. **3-4**	Little attempt at prioritisation or justification or rationale. **1-2**	No attempt at prioritisation or justification. **0**
Judgement	15	Clearly recognises alternative solutions. Judgement exercised professionally. **13-15**	Alternative solutions or options considered. Some judgement exercised. **9-12**	A slightly limited range of solutions considered. Judgement occasionally weak. **8**	A limited range of solutions considered. Judgement sometimes weak. **5-7**	Few alternative solutions considered. Judgement often weak. **1-4**	No alternative solutions considered. Judgement weak or absent. **0**
Integration	10	Diverse areas of knowledge and skills integrated effectively. **9-10**	Diverse areas of knowledge and skills integrated. **6-8**	Knowledge areas and skills occasionally not integrated. **5**	Knowledge areas and skills sometimes not integrated. **3-4**	Knowledge areas and skills often not integrated. **1-2**	Knowledge areas and skills not integrated. **0**
Logic	20	Communication effective, recommendations realistic, concise and logical. **16-20**	Communication mainly clear and logical. Recommendations occasionally weak. **11-15**	Communication occasionally unclear, and/ or recommendations occasionally illogical. **10**	Communication sometimes weak. Some recommendations slightly unrealistic. **5-9**	Communication weak. Some unclear or illogical recommendations, or few recommendations. **1-4**	Very poor communication, and/or no recommendations offered. **0**
Ethics	10	Excellent evaluation of ethical aspects. Clear and appropriate advice offered. **9-10**	Good evaluation of ethical aspects. Some appropriate advice offered. **6-8**	Some evaluation of ethical aspects. Advice offered. **5**	Weak evaluation of ethical aspects. Little advice offered. **3-4**	Poor evaluation of ethical aspects. No advice offered. **1-2**	No evaluation of ethical aspects. Unethical, or no, advice offered. **0**
TOTAL	100	* **Note:** The number of available marks a llocated to each criterion will normally be as shown.					

1 Case and commentary – Zubinos

1.1 Market overview

The number of chains of coffee shops in the UK has increased four-fold in the last five years, with thousands of branded coffee shops now operating around the UK. The total turnover for all branded coffee shops in the UK exceeded £1 billion (£1 billion is equal to £1,000 million) during 2005. Over the last few years a number of UK-based branded coffee shops have emerged to compete with the internationally recognised coffee shop brands.

A further shift in the market growth is that the coffee bar culture has extended beyond the UK's major cities and is now successfully penetrating smaller towns. This has mainly been driven by the larger of the coffee shop brands. Consumer awareness of branded coffee shops has also increased in the last few years.

The range of products offered has also changed over the last few years and branded coffee shops are now meeting customer demand for a larger range of foods and better quality products by using premium ingredients. Furthermore, branded coffee shops are able to command a higher average price for their products by using quality and service as differentiators, as price appears not to be a particularly sensitive factor.

In addition to the branded coffee shops, there is a large number of non-specialist food and beverage outlets including department stores, supermarkets and bookshops, which continue to expand their own cafés. They are enjoying the success of the 'coffee culture' that has been established by the branded coffee shops.

Market research is very important in this fast-moving consumer-driven marketplace. The over-riding factor that continues to be the most important reason that consumers select a coffee shop is its convenience of location. There were over 500 branded coffee shops in London at the end of 2005.

Questions and comments on Section 1.1 – market overview	**Response**
The case is about a coffee shop chain based in the UK. This is of particular interest because most cases sat by CIMA so far have been based in imaginary countries. Name as many UK coffee shops as you can. Read the session on 'Industry Awareness' in Chapter 7 and explore some of the websites mentioned before continuing.	• The 'big 3' in the UK market are Starbucks, Costa Coffee and Caffé Nero. • Others include Coffee Republic and Caffé Ritazza.
Why did 'coffee culture' start in big cities?	• Population density. • Affluence. • Large number of businesses so would catch lunchtime trade. • People may be more influenced by trends.
Why do you feel the range of products offered has changed?	• Any innovations appear to be quickly copied, so new products are developed to try to keep ahead of competitors.
Branded coffee shops appear to be competing using Porter's generic strategy of differentiation. How is this being achieved and what are the main threats to such a strategy?	The main areas of differentiation are: • quality of coffee • range of options offered • quality of food • comfortable surroundings • extras – Starbucks offers internet access in some shops. The problem with all of these is they can be copied so, in addition, many firms are trying to enhance their brand names to create customer loyalty.
Evaluate the threat from non-specialist food and beverage outlets.	High – especially if the store is considered up-market. Starbucks, for example, often has its outlets within bookshops, and for good reason.

How important do you think brand name is in this market?	Debatable – Starbucks expansion has been mainly driven by word of mouth suggesting that brand loyalty is high. Also, brand recognition and loyalty do appear to be increasing. On the other hand, most customers will look for coffee quality first, so a few bad experiences will result in customers moving to the competition.

1.2 Zubinos' personnel

The career histories of Zubinos' Directors and key employees are shown in Appendix 1.

Questions and comments on Section 1.2 and Appendix 1 – key personnel	Response
Luis Zubino (Chairman and MD)	• Governance issue – should separate chairman and CEO • No formal qualifications but an entrepreneur
Vivien Zubino (Director)	• Perhaps best to view Luis and Vivien as a team
Jane Thorp (Marketing Director)	• Has relevant experience (phone company would have targeted similar clientele) • Shares should increase motivation
Maria Todd (Procurement Director)	• Good experience • Shares should increase motivation • Text highlights control problems with procurement and the extent to which it should be centralised
Anita Wiseman (HR Director)	• Relevant experience • Coffee shop mangers hire staff – no mention here of training

Questions and comments on Section 1.2 and Appendix 1 – key personnel	Response
George Shale (FD)	• Has management consulting experience as well as knowledge of accountancy • Should provide good financial control
Bob West (Business Planning Manager)	• Good experience of start-ups
Jack Rayfield (shop management and security)	• Good practical manager but role needs clarifying
Val Pline and Sally Higgins (Area Managers)	• Shows good policy of promoting staff from within • Relationship with Anita re HR issues? • Bonuses linked to turnover and net margins – not directly under their control – main job seems to be HR?
Carl Martin (KPE)	• Not been hands on … yet. There to protect KPE's investment, so potential for conflicts of interest in the future
Comment on the overall balance of the board.	• A good mix of formal qualifications, experience and enthusiasm • Ideally, want a separate chairman
Outline and evaluate the arguments for and against centralising procurement.	For: • Economies of scale re purchasing • Better quality control to ensure product consistency • Should get better stock management Against: • Ignores local expertise • Prevents local ordering to prevent stock-outs • May demotivate local managers On balance: • Centralise to ensure consistent quality

1.3 The first Zubinos coffee shop

On returning to the UK in early 2001, Luis Zubino, the founder of Zubinos, bought a flat in London and set about locating suitable premises for his new business venture. His original plan was to have over five coffee shops opened within five years and he wanted the cash generated from each coffee shop to finance the opening costs for the next coffee shop. He had put together a business plan to get a personal loan, which was secured on both his own flat and his parents' house. This loan, together with his savings, was used to acquire £300,000 of equity in Zubinos.

Zubinos was formed in March 2001 with 2 million authorised shares of £1 each, of which 300,000 shares were allocated to Luis Zubino and these shares were fully paid up at par value in March 2001. At the time these shares were issued, £1 per share at par value was considered a fair value.

Luis Zubino opened the first Zubinos shop in June 2001 in London, in rented premises. He fully understood that it was location and convenience that would be critical to the success of the coffee shop. He had been lucky in being able to rent a large corner shop on a busy junction, which was surrounded by offices and on the route to nearby public transport, thereby having the benefit of many passers by. Luis Zubino hired a large number of staff to ensure good customer service and to minimise waiting times during peak busy periods such as lunch breaks.

Most coffee shops only serve a selection of hot and cold drinks and a small range of snacks and cakes. What distinguished Zubinos from many of the other branded coffee shops back in 2001, was that Zubinos also sold a range of freshly made sandwiches, with high quality fillings and other food items. Zubinos also sold a specialised brand of ice cream, which Luis Zubino imported from Italy, as he considered that the quality and taste was far superior to many other ice cream brands available in the UK. He was convinced that ice cream, which is a product that is kept frozen, could generate high margins, as it would have very little waste and none of the problems associated with the short shelf-life of other foods.

Within six months, the first Zubinos shop was generating a high turnover and had established a high level of repeat business. Zubinos became a popular meeting place. The level of profitability was below plan as more staff had been employed to meet demand and Luis Zubino considered that he did not want to lose customers' goodwill by increasing waiting times to be served. By December 2001, he handed the day-to-day management of the shop to Val Pline, who had proved herself to be the hardest working and most trustworthy of all the staff employed at the coffee shop.

Luis Zubino briefed Val Pline on his plans for the shop for the next few months and agreed to pay bonuses to her when the turnover reached a certain level and again when net profit (after staff and fixed costs) reached £100,000 in any financial year. Val Pline was impressed with the business plan and her new responsibilities. Only six months previously, she had joined a coffee shop with limited experience and now she found herself running the coffee shop with the possibility of earning bonuses when it became even more successful.

Questions and comments on Section 1.3 – the first coffee shop	Response
What were the keys to success with the first coffee shop?	• Location, location, location! • Quality service, e.g. employing more staff to reduce waiting times • Food range offered – especially sandwiches and ice cream • Motivated staff

1.4 The growth of Zubinos

Within two and a half years, by the end of 2003, Luis Zubino had opened a further five coffee shops, which was twice as fast as his original business plan had envisaged. All five shops were in rented premises to reduce the initial set-up costs, but Luis Zubino had not reduced the level of expenditure on the coffee shops design and fittings. The atmosphere that the coffee shop design had created was good, and was attractive to the target market of young people. Early on, from his market research, and from personal experience in his parents' business, Luis Zubino wanted his coffee shops to appeal to the 20-to-35 year old age range. This was for several reasons:

- The target age range market segment has more time and more disposable money.
- They attracted other people of similar ages into the coffee shops, as they become the place to meet up.
- The target age range would be attracted to the 'trendy' atmosphere that Luis Zubino has created at Zubinos.

Luis Zubino wanted to expand the number of Zubinos coffee shops, but could not find suitable premises to rent in the locations he wanted. By mid-2004 he appointed a management consultancy firm for financial planning advice on how he could expand the business. Zubinos had only been in existence, at that stage, for fewer than four years.

The consultant with whom he dealt with was George Shale, and the two quickly established good rapport and worked well together. It was George Shale's idea to open only a few more Zubinos coffee shops in the London area where sites were difficult to obtain and rent very expensive. George Shale recommended that Zubinos should start to expand into towns and cities elsewhere in the UK where shop location would not be such a problem, rather than continue to expand within the fiercely competitive London market.

When Jane Thorp joined Zubinos in early 2003, she could immediately see the large potential of the Zubinos brand. By the end of 2003, Zubinos had six shops operational with plans for four further shop openings in 2004. Eight further shops were opened in 2005, resulting in eighteen coffee shops in total operational by the end of 2005. The geographical split of Zubinos coffee shops was ten in London and eight coffee shops outside of London. Zubinos has not had any problems with building up its customer base after each new shop opening in the smaller towns and cities into which it had expanded.

George Shale also suggested that Zubinos could consider opening Zubinos coffee shops on the premises of another retailer. He undertook to try to locate a chain of retailers who would rent out part of their shop space. This has been done with other coffee shop chains, which have coffee shops located in motorway service areas and chains of bookshops. Luis Zubino liked the idea of a Zubinos coffee shop in a chain of other shops and a search for a suitable retail chain started in May 2004. However, with the expansion of Zubinos into eight provincial towns and cities, Zubinos has not yet pursued the identification of a suitable retail chain into which it could open Zubinos coffee shops.

The Zubinos business has a high turnover. However, profitability was still lower than some of its competitors, for several reasons as follows:

- high rental costs for three of the ten London coffee shops
- high staff costs, as good customer service remains a high priority for Zubinos
- lower than average gross margins on some products due to the higher than average procurement cost of the quality ingredients that Luis Zubino has selected

- lower margins on coffee products as over 80% of its coffee beans are procured from suppliers who deal only with 'Fair Trade' coffee producers.

Questions and comments on Section 1.4 – the growth of Zubinos	Response
What were the key elements of the ongoing growth of Zubinos?	• Rental properties to reduce setup costs. • Consistent design, targeting young people. • Being willing to accept advice and move out of London.
Assess the reasons given for lower margins than competitors.	• Higher rental costs – have competitors already got the best VFM sites? Are larger competitors better at negotiating? Has the demand from larger competitors pushed up rents? • Higher staff costs – having more staff is seen as part of Zubinos' competitive advantage. • Cost of quality ingredients – alternatives should be reviewed but quality has been key to Zubinos' success so should not be compromised. • Cost of Fair Trade coffee – to be commended on ethical grounds but to what extent does Zubinos advertise this? Should be contributing to their competitive advantage.

1.5 Staffing issues and performance-related bonuses

Luis Zubino was kept very busy with expanding the Zubinos business and left each of the coffee shop managers alone to run each Zubinos coffee shop. Most management responsibilities were devolved to the shop managers, who were responsible for local procurement of food supplies, staff recruitment and day-to-day staff management.

Vivien Zubino, Luis Zubino's wife, managed one of the London Zubinos coffee shops after they married in 2002. She also undertook much of the procurement of coffee supplies, together with Jane Thorp, until the full time Procurement Director, Maria Todd, joined Zubinos in September 2004. However, there were often duplication of orders or gaps in delivery of supplies as both Jane Thorp and Vivien Zubino were constantly busy with other responsibilities.

Payroll was operated by an outsourced agency centrally and Luis Zubino managed all other staff issues. It was only with the appointment of Anita Wiseman in November 2004 that human resource (HR) matters were undertaken centrally. Zubinos employed over 360 staff (some part time) by 31 December 2005.

Anita Wiseman wants to formalise job responsibilities and recruitment and ensure that staff are offered promotion in newly opened branches of Zubinos. Following on from the dismissal of three employees during 2005 for minor thefts, of both produce and cash, she also suspected that staff management and the required control procedures were not in place in the coffee shops. Coffee is a high value product and one employee was dismissed for selling stolen bags of coffee beans. This theft was only identified because he had been foolish enough to steal, and then sell, the bags of coffee beans on the premises of the Zubinos coffee shop in which he worked. A fellow employee had reported the incident to Luis Zubino.

Anita Wiseman has introduced quarterly performance-related bonuses for all employees based on the sales revenue and the net margin for each coffee shop. The bonus is paid quarterly to recognise the previous quarter's results and to motivate staff to stay with Zubinos, so reducing the high staff turnover. However, the bonuses paid for the last two quarters of 2005 were lower than previously paid, as the targets were more challenging. Some coffee shop managers and other employees were disappointed with their reduced bonus payments despite working as hard as ever over the Christmas 2005 period.

Questions and comments on Section 1.5 – staffing issues	Response
Comment on the problems between Vivien and Maria.	Again highlights the need to clarify roles and improve communication lines – see comments on Section 1.2 above.
Comment on the thefts and staff dismissals.	Highlights the need for suitable stock control procedures. However, Zubinos must be careful not to create a culture where staff no longer feel valued.
Assess the bonus system introduced.	The general view is that bonuses should motivate staff. However, there are a number of concerns in this case: • While staff may see how their actions contribute to turnover (e.g. by increasing customer loyalty), they may not be able to see the link with margin and will thus not be motivated by it. • The quarterly approach may encourage staff to stay but could prove problematic if there is a 'bad' month at the start of a quarter as staff may give up trying until the next quarter.

1.6 Fair Trade produce

Luis Zubino, having a strong social conscience, felt that the coffee beans used by Zubinos coffee shops should be bought from suppliers of Fair Trade coffee. Additionally, from his initial research into the industry, he was convinced that Zubinos could charge a price premium for the use of Fair Trade coffee.

Fair Trade benefits 800,000 farmers worldwide selling a wide variety of products. Farmers are organised into small co-operatives, whereby products are procured at an agreed minimum price, which is above the price that some small independent farmers would be able to achieve for their crops on the open market. Fair Trade produce is successfully breaking the cycle of poverty for farmers in many countries and the coffee industry is one where Fair Trade has been very successful. Luis Zubino felt strongly that, in today's world where consumers are demanding more humane and more environmentally sensitive products, the use of Fair Trade coffee in Zubinos coffee shops is a responsible and sensible choice of supply.

From the opening of the first Zubinos in 2001, Luis Zubino bought 100% of all coffee from Fair Trade suppliers. As the range of coffees expanded in Zubinos coffee shops, he found that some coffee and cocoa beans were unavailable through Fair Trade suppliers. On average, Zubinos procures over 80% of its produce from Fair Trade suppliers. Luis Zubino would still like this to be 100%. When Maria Todd joined in September 2004, Luis Zubino requested her to increase the proportion of coffee supplies procured from Fair Trade suppliers. This necessitated a change from some of its current suppliers to achieve this objective. The extensive use of Fair Trade coffee is used in some of Zubinos' marketing literature, and it has raised the profile and awareness of Fair Trade with some of its customers.

Questions and comments on Section 1.6 – Fair Trade produce	**Response**
Assess the emphasis on Fair Trade coffee.	All the large chains claim to treat coffee farmers fairly: • Starbucks and Costa Coffee usually have Fair Trade coffee available • Caffé Nero does not use the trade mark 'Fair Trade' (they disagree with minimum prices for farmers) but insist they are being fair. Zubinos needs to be seen to be treating farmers fairly or they might lose some customers to competitors. The Fair Trade route is probably the best. However, whether Zubinos should only sell Fair Trade coffee is more debatable. Consumer interest in Fair Trade products has been increasing as indicated by the recent Growth in visibility of the Fair Trade mark.

1.7 IT development

Jane Thorp commissioned an IT company in early 2005 to completely update the Zubinos website. The total cost of this IT work was forecast to be £220,000, but the final cost was a little over £300,000 including new hardware equipment. The new website has helped to create stronger brand awareness. The new Zubinos website also has an online communications area which allows users to 'chat' online. Since November 2004, a range of Zubinos merchandise can also be ordered online. This range of merchandise includes coffee machines and coffee supplies, which have been selling well, despite little direct publicity.

George Shale is continuously frustrated by the lack of financial and business information in a usable format. The company had grown fast and he has prepared several proposals requesting that a new database financial forecasting system is implemented. He also wants the shop managers to be more involved in sales and profit forecasting and the system that he had proposed would allow shop managers to input their data for consolidation. However, Luis Zubino felt that the shop managers are already under a heavy workload and that the quality of the data that they could input into the proposed system would be little better than that currently submitted by e-mail to Zubinos Head Office. The current standard of forecasting by shop managers is not very good and has generally underestimated the growth in sales. The database proposal has been turned down previously on cost grounds, as Luis Zubino considers that the cost does not justify the slightly improved level of forecasting.

However, a new IT system to capture sales and product analysis data at source, which will also help with stock control, was commissioned in October 2005. This project has been scaled down from the original specification and is forecast to cost £110,000.

Questions and comments on Section 1.7 – IT development	Response
Comment on the new website.	The move by Zubinos puts it ahead of the competitors' actions: • Starbucks' UK website gives information but does not allow online ordering. Its US website allows you to buy coffee and music. • Caffé Nero's website sells coffee, clothing, books and cups. • Neither Coffee Republic nor Costa Coffee's sites have online sales. • No competitor seems to offer online chat areas or coffee making equipment (though selling the latter could be seen as a way of losing customers!)
Comment on the new IT system.	• Poor information is often a problem for growing firms, so it is vital that Zubinos gets full feedback from stores. • The proposed system makes sense in that it seeks to reduce the burden on managers. • It is questionable whether shop managers are the best people to be forecasting future sales.

1.8 Introduction of a business investor

By summer 2004, Zubinos had eight coffee shops open and had found suitable locations for two more. However, Zubinos' bankers, Kite Bank, were reluctant to increase the level of loans. At the end of June 2004, Zubinos had three loans in place, totalling £600,000. All loans were at 12% interest per year. These were:

- an initial five-year loan for £300,000 taken out in December 2001
- a second five-year loan for £200,000 taken out in December 2002 to fund further expansion

- a third five-year loan taken out in April 2004 for £100,000, to cover a shortfall in working capital due to all cash resources being used for expansion.

Instead, the bank introduced Luis Zubino to the manager of the bank's private equity provider, who is Carl Martin. Carl Martin and Luis Zubino established a good working relationship early on in their business meetings and Carl Martin was impressed with the business plan and the growth of the Zubinos business in the last few years. He felt confident that, if Kite Private Equity (KPE) were to invest in the Zubinos business, the additional private equity finance, together with less expensive loan finance, would allow the Zubinos business to expand far more rapidly.

After many discussions and the preparation of additional, more detailed business plans, KPE agreed to invest in the Zubinos business in January 2005.

KPE invested £2.4 million in equity finance initially, but the agreement was to also provide loan finance when required by expansion plans. The agreed value of loan finance was up to £5.0 million over the next four years at an annual interest rate of 10% per annum, secured against Zubinos assets. KPE appointed Carl Martin as its representative on the Board of Zubinos.

The balance sheet, income statement and statement of changes in equity for Zubinos for the last two financial years are shown in Appendix 2.

Questions and comments on Section 1.8 – introduction of a business investor	**Response**
Comment on the bank loans obtained prior to the KPE investment.	• Having to raise a five-year bank loan just to cover working capital (loan 3) showed that Zubinos needed a larger injection of long-term finance. • Repayments needed in 2006/7/9.

Questions and comments on Section 1.8 – introduction of a business investor	Response
KPE is performing the role of venture capitalists – providing high risk finance for growth until the firm is large enough to consider flotation. What are the objectives of KPE likely to be?	• High overall return (taking into account interest, dividends and ultimately selling the shares, KPE may expect a return in excess of 25 to 30% per annum). • An exit route. There is no mention of this in the pre-seen information but private equity firms often look to exit in five years, either through flotation or a trade sale. • Good financial control – it has insisted on a board member to represent them but has made demands concerning information systems and cashflow targets.

Note: A more detailed analysis of Zubinos' financing arrangements is covered in 'Financial Strategy Perspective'.

1.9 Shareholdings at December 2005

Since the formation of Zubinos in 2001, other Directors have purchased shares in Zubinos. They have paid between £2 and £5 per share, based on the agreed fair value at the time they acquired shares.

Luis Zubino and the rest of the Zubinos' shareholders welcomed KPE into the business. KPE purchased 400,000 shares at £6 each (£1 each plus a share premium, based on an agreed fair value, of £5 per share). The shareholdings at 31 December 2005 are shown below.

	Number of shares	% shareholding
Luis Zubino	300,000	30.0%
Vivien Zubino	120,000	12.0%
Jane Thorp	30,000	3.0%
Maria Todd	24,000	2.4%
Anita Wiseman	36,000	3.6%
George Shale	90,000	9.0%
KRPE	400,000	40.0%
Total shareholdings	1,000,000	100.0%

The Zubinos Board comprises the above six shareholders plus Carl Martin, KPE's nominated representative. Luis Zubino is Chairman of the Board in addition to his role as Managing Director.

Questions and comments on Section 1.9 – shareholdings	Response
Comment on the shareholdings.	• KPE is the majority shareholder. • The Zubino family does not have overall control of 'their' company. • The votes of the other directors (especially George Shale) could be very important if a disagreement arises between KPE and the Zubinos.
Assuming a share value of £6 per share, calculate the market value of the firm and comment. (Note that the £6 share price was used for the KPE investment over a year ago.)	• One million shares worth £6 each would value the company at £6 million. • This makes the company too small for a Full Listing on the Stock Exchange but big enough to consider an AIM listing.

1.10 Analysis of gross margin

George Shale commissioned a new IT system in October 2005 that will capture and analyse sales and cost of sales data without all of the manual intervention and spreadsheet analysis that is currently required to produce management information. The system is due to be operational in early 2006.

The analysis of the gross margin across the 18 Zubinos coffee shops for the year to 31 December 2005 is shown as follows. It should be noted that the figures below are for all 18 Zubinos coffee shops, but 8 of them were operational for only part of 2005.

	Coffee products	**Other drinks**	**Sand-wiches**	**Ice-cream**	**Other foods**	**Total**
	£000	£000	£000	£000	£000	£000
SAles revenue	4,734	1,344	3,584	896	3,360	13,918
Cost of food & drinks	926	642	1,260	182	1,962	4,972
Gross margin	3,808	702	2,324	714	1,398	946
Gross margin %	80%	52%	65%	80%	42%	64%

Questions and comments on Section 1.10 – analysis of gross margins	**Response**
What difference does it make that eight of the shops were only operational for part of the year?	• Calculations per shop (e.g. average revenue per shop) are trickier. • Other than that, not much. Most of the cost of sales will be variable costs (food, coffee) or fixed per shop (any salaries). Any company-wide fixed costs in cost of sales (central purchasing costs?) will result in the gross margin improving as company sales grow.

Questions and comments on Section 1.10 – analysis of gross margins	Response
Comment on the relative margins.	• To assess gross margins you really need a basis for comparison. Caffé Nero achieved an overall gross margin of 24.3% in their 2005 accounts. Zubinos appears to have done much better but that could be down to differences in cost classification. Caffé Nero's operating margin was 8.56% compared with Zubinos' 9.10%, so the difference is perhaps not as marked as it first seems. • Other foods and other drinks seem to be the weak links – perhaps Zubinos needs a clearer strategy on these products (e.g. better quality teas brewed correctly, organic snacks, etc).

1.11 Zubinos' expansion plans

The current five-year plan was approved by KPE, and subsequently the Zubinos Board, in December 2005. This plan includes the expansion of Zubinos to 75 coffee shops by the end of 2010. An extract from this current five-year plan is shown in Appendix 3.

Much of the expansion planned is due to be financed by cash generated by operations, as well as additional loan finance from KPE. The amount of loan finance will be determined by whether the new openings will be in rented premises or whether the company will be required to purchase the site. Much will depend on the location selected and the alternatives available in each town or city targeted for expansion.

During 2005, eight new Zubinos coffee shops were opened. Up to the end of 2004, all coffee shops, except one, were in rented premises. Zubinos has previously purchased one property in London in 2003, in which it has its head office above the coffee shop. During 2005, two of the newly opened Zubinos coffee shops were in large premises that had been purchased, as Luis Zubino was unable to locate a suitable site that could be rented. The cost of the two coffee shops that were purchased were over £1 million each, including the shop fitting costs.

Jane Thorp uses a number of criteria for the selection of new sites for future Zubinos coffee shops. These include:

1 **Competition** – the strength of the competition in the proposed market place and whether the competition will stimulate growth, but not be too strong so as to restrict profits.

2 **Resources.** Whether there are adequate resources, staff and supply links to set up a new coffee shop.

3 **Consumer** demand. Is there sufficient demand for a Zubinos coffee shop and what is the current level of demand and how is it being met? A further issue is whether the area has the income to create profitable demand for Zubinos.

Some relevant factors in Zubinos' expansion plan are the population size and the population density. When population becomes concentrated it often tends to take on a different character. Urbanisation produces the need for a higher level of products and services. Jane Thorp uses a number of easy measures such as the presence, or absence, of well-known chains of clothes retailers, to determine the potential for a new coffee shop location.

Jane Thorp had prepared a paper for the December 2005 Zubinos Board meeting, proposing that each Zubinos coffee shop should have a few computers available for customers' use, for browsing on the internet or for passing business people to send e-mails. The proposal is for the computers to be available free of charge for all customers. The Board considered the proposal, but decided against it for several reasons, not just on cost grounds, but on space considerations and also concerns over damage or theft. Luis Zubino stated that Zubinos did not need to offer its customers such facilities, as Zubinos coffee shops already were very busy at peak times. Jane Thorp is confident that this innovative free service is a good way of retaining customer loyalty and for attracting new customers.

Questions and comments on Section 1.11 – Zubinos' expansion plans	Response
Comment on the rent/buy strategy to date.	• Rental avoids the high initial outlay of buying, though this will be financed in some way, such as a mortgage • Buying creates a larger exit barrier • Buying reduces the risk of increases in rents • The firm is exposed to fluctuations in property values if bought • Bought properties can be used as security for further finance
Comment on the criteria used to locate shops.	• On the whole, seems very good • Under 'consumer demand' they could review the number and type of local employers to get an idea of lunchtime trade as well as shoppers • Difficult to assess potential competition from new shops opening in the same locations • No mention of costs of shop /fittings /staff • No mention of shop visibility – for example, a shop on a corner can attract traffic from four directions while an in-street shop will only attract from two directions • More could be made of demographic details from the 2001 Census to assess local residents as potential customers

Assess the strategy of offering free access to computers.	Arguments for: • Might attract new customers Arguments against: • Cost • Space • Potential damage/theft • Changes the ambience of the shop • Does it encourage customers to take longer over their drinks or do they buy more? **Note:** Starbucks has a related but different approach – they offer Wi-Fi enabled internet access for customers to use their own computers. Zubinos could do likewise as it offers the service without having to buy any computers. A 'follow the leader' strategy is often worthwhile.

1.12 Labelling of foods

One of the London-based Zubinos coffee shops had just broken the barrier of sales of £1 million in a rolling 12-month period. The manager at this coffee shop decided to try to increase sales further by introducing additional nutritional data for some food and drink products. The coffee shop manager decided, without consulting anyone, to display the calorie information as a ploy to improve sales. However, when she calculated and displayed the calorie content of many of the coffee products and foods, she was disappointed to find the calorie content very high. Many customers were also very surprised and switched to other drinks and did not purchase any cakes or pastries. This led to a small reduction of sales revenue.

This Zubinos coffee shop manager then started a new initiative during summer 2005 in the Zubinos coffee shop in which she manages. She introduced a small range of low fat and low calorie snacks and meals, which proved to be very popular. However, when this was discussed with Jane Thorp in Marketing, a major disagreement arose concerning the range of foods that Zubinos should be offering, and Jane Thorp's view that there should be a standard menu at all Zubinos coffee shops. The manager was furious that Zubinos Head Office had not welcomed her low calorie meal initiative.

Questions and comments on Section 1.12 – food labelling	**Response**
Assess the need for a standard menu.	Arguments for: • Better quality control • Protects / enhances the brand name • Gives rise to economies of scale in purchasing. Arguments against: • Stifles local initiative, thus demotivating managers • Prevents firms tailoring their products to local demand preferences.
Assess the plan to sell low calorie foods.	Arguments for: • Responds to trends in society • Helps differentiate the firm from competitors. • Higher margins? Arguments against: • None?
Assess the option of displaying nutritional information.	Difficult – Zubinos will want to display information for low calorie, healthy drinks / snacks but not for high calorie ones (e.g. Italian ice cream!). Customers will get suspicious if only some products are labelled! It may be preferable to advertise some products as 'low calorie' or 'low fat' without referring to these issues with the rest of the product range.

Comment on the conflict described.	Zubinos needs to create a culture where staff feel valued and motivated. Perhaps the problem here was not that the idea was rejected but the process (if any) that took place.

1.13 Other recent developments in the Zubinos business

In April 2005, Zubinos introduced its first delivery service from three of its central London coffee shops. This delivery service to local businesses provides coffee and a catering service on customers' premises. Customers place orders on-line to their local Zubinos coffee shop. Despite a few initial problems, the delivery service is working well, although sales are still very low. Customers are automatically invoiced after delivery, instead of the usual cash payments in the coffee shops. There has been some additional work caused by payments received not matching with the invoiced amounts, and shop managers have simply written off the small differences. There is no system yet in place to chase up payment for deliveries if the customer does not pay within Zubinos' 30-day terms.

Zubinos wants to continue to be innovative and to be ahead of its competitors in terms of the types of foods offered. Jane Thorp and Maria Todd are in contact with a number of food manufacturers to explore offering a wider range of foods. They need to ensure that any new food ranges fit in with Zubinos' current pricing and food quality levels.

Questions and comments on Section 1.13 – other recent developments	Response
Assess the strategy to deliver.	Arguments for: • Increases turnover • May attract new customers to try the shop. Arguments against: • May lose customers from the shop at lunchtimes • Doesn't capitalise on shop ambience • Up against cheaper competitors who don't have the overheads of a luxury shop • Slow to take off.

Assess the current payment system.	Seems unnecessary – why can't customers pay online when they make their orders? This would reduce delays and eliminate matching problems. It is unlikely that customers would object as long as the website is secure.

1.14 Proposed expansion of Zubinos overseas

Jane Thorp and Luis Zubino believe that, during 2007, when Zubinos plans to have over 26 shops open in the UK, it will be in a position where it could consider expanding overseas. Already, a number of contacts of Luis Zubino, who live in Europe, are keen to operate Zubinos coffee shops in Europe.

The current five-year plan, which was approved by KPE and the Zubinos Board in December 2005, is based on operating 50 coffee shops in the UK by 2010 and 25 coffee shops in Europe.

However, Luis Zubino would like to have more than 25 coffee shops operating in Europe by 2010. There are a number of reasons why Zubinos should consider expanding abroad and these include:

- Saturated home market where competition is so intense that it can no longer gain any significant market share improvement.
- Competition may be less intense in a different market.
- Comparative advantage in product against local competition, particularly in areas dominated by British people living and holidaying abroad, which is becoming increasingly popular in some areas of Europe, especially Spain.

Questions and comments on Section 1.14 – overseas expansion	Response
Assess the three reasons given for expanding overseas.	Saturated home market? • Most analysts agree that London is saturated but there are still opportunities in the regions. Less intense competition? • Some larger competitors have already expanded into continental Europe – Starbucks, for example, has 20 shops in France and 44 in Spain. While this is much lower than in the UK, there is still a threat. • Caffé Nero is considering expanding overseas but has yet to do so. • In countries such as France and Italy, they will be competing against traditional coffee shops that gave rise to the Starbucks model in the first place! (Note: Starbucks has no shops in Italy) Targeting local British residents? • Ex-pats will be more familiar with UK brands, so the approach should work. Whether they are familiar enough with Zubinos is another matter.

1.15 Appendix 1 – Zubinos' personnel

Luis Zubino – Chairman and Managing Director

Luis Zubino, now 29, had worked in his parents' café for two years after he left school. He did not want to go to university and instead saved enough money to travel extensively. He is an intelligent man, who has his father's entrepreneurial spirit. After spending several years abroad, he returned to the UK in 2001 and established Zubinos.

Vivien Zubino – Director

Vivien Zubino, now aged 30, married Luis Zubino in 2002, after the opening of the first Zubinos shop. She is a director of Zubinos and now works part time at one of the Zubinos coffee shops in London. She has assisted her husband in achieving his ambitious plans and has helped to create the designs for the Zubinos coffee shops and also some of the innovative menus available at Zubinos coffee shops. She has always supported her husband and his ideas, which has contributed to the high growth achieved to date. Vivien Zubino purchased shares in Zubinos during 2002.

Jane Thorp – Marketing Director

Jane Thorp was the first professional appointment that Luis Zubino made in early 2003. He knew by then that Zubinos had the potential to be successful, and understood the importance of branding, and the company needed a strong Marketing Director. Jane Thorp had previously worked in marketing for a mobile phone company and more recently for a leading high street fast food chain, which she did not like. Jane Thorp, aged 32, relished the challenges that Zubinos posed and was determined to help both Luis and Vivien Zubino to create a successful business. She invested personal funds into the company in 2003 when she bought 30,000 shares, which was then nearly 7% of the issued share capital.

Maria Todd – Procurement Director

Maria Todd, now 35, had worked in procurement for an international food retailer and was frustrated with the lack of initiative she was allowed to use. She had extensive procurement and contract experience and welcomed the challenges that a growing company, such as Zubinos, could offer her. Maria Todd invested £120,000 of personal funds to buy shares in the company.

Maria Todd joined Zubinos in September 2004 and is based in its Head Office, which is located above one of the London

Zubinos coffee shops. The first floor above the shop accommodates around 28 employees including two junior procurement staff. Prior to Maria Todd joining Zubinos, most of the procurement decisions were made by a variety of people. She is frustrated by the lack of discipline in the company, as many coffee shop managers still order some supplies from local food wholesalers to meet demand. The coffee shop managers state that they need this flexibility to provide customers with the foods in demand. However, Maria Todd considers that the coffee shop managers are simply not planning their food ordering very well and are continuously running out of a variety of products. One shop even ran out of the specially mixed Zubinos coffee beans recently.

Anita Wiseman – Human Resources Director

Anita Wiseman, now 29, has known Luis Zubino since their school days. She has a degree in human resource management and has worked in human resources (HR) for a chain of department stores before joining Zubinos in November 2004. Prior to Anita Wiseman joining the company, much of the HR management work had been out-sourced or handled by Luis Zubino, who had delegated authority for hiring new employees to each coffee shop manager.

George Shale – Finance Director

George Shale, aged 39, had worked for a leading audit group for over 10 years before he moved into management consultancy. Zubinos appointed the consultancy firm that George Shale worked for in mid 2004 for financial planning advice. George Shale was the consultant in charge of the Zubinos case and worked closely with Luis Zubino on a new five-year plan. George Shale was so convinced by the business plan that he had helped to produce, and in Luis Zubino's ability to grow the Zubinos business, that he joined Zubinos in December 2004. He bought 90,000 shares in Zubinos. Prior to George Shale joining the company, much of the finance work was managed by Zubinos' external auditors, and supplemented by temporary finance staff. Since joining Zubinos, George Shale has recruited a small team and has taken all accounting and finance matters in-house.

Bob West – Business Planning Manager

Bob West, aged 35, used to work for George Shale at the management consultants and was recruited by George Shale to fill the new post of Business Planning Manager at Zubinos in June 2005. Bob West has always worked as a consultant and been involved with many young start-up business ventures, and has a lot of experience. However, he has not been involved in the food retailing business before joining Zubinos.

Jack Rayfield – Shop management and security

Jack Rayfield, aged 52, joined Zubinos in 2003 having worked in retail management for the past 20 years. He was recruited by Luis Zubino who considered him to be a reliable hard working manager who could take care of the day-to-day operations involved with the shops. Since Jack Rayfield joined, he has introduced many new procedures and tightened up some poor business practices. One of the procedures that he has introduced is daily banking of cash and reconciliations to records of revenue for each shop.

Jack Rayfield is very good on HR matters and has played an active role with shop managers in the recruitment of staff, particularly for new Zubinos coffee shops. However, recently he has clashed with Anita Wiseman over many issues.

Val Pline and Sally Higgins – Zubinos' Area Managers

Both Val Pline and Sally Higgins had originally joined Zubinos in junior supervisory roles in its early days and then progressed to coffee shop managers. In September 2005, they were both appointed to the new roles of area managers. Val Pline is responsible for all London and the South East-based Zubinos coffee shops and Sally Higgins has responsibility for all other UK coffee shops.

They have both received management training and have been rewarded with performance-related bonuses linked to sales revenue and net margins. They are now responsible for the recruitment and management of all staff for the coffee shops that they manage. Due to high staff turnover, which is not unusual in this business sector, they have spent much time on staff recruitment and on staff training issues.

Carl Martin – Investment Director, Kite Private Equity (KPE)

Carl Martin, aged 39, is the liaison manager at KPE who is responsible for a range of clients into which KPE has invested equity and loan finance. The companies that KPE has invested in vary greatly and are operating in a wide range of industries, including manufacturing, service and retail sectors. Carl Martin was appointed to the Zubinos Board in January 2005, to manage KPE's shareholding.

Due to Carl Martin's demanding role in many other companies, he has left the Zubinos' management team to manage the Zubinos business. He is content that the monthly sales and profits that had been achieved during 2005 were ahead of the agreed forecast. Therefore, he has not been as 'hands on' as he would have been if targets had not been met. Carl Martin gets on very well with Luis Zubino, and they both have much mutual respect for each other's roles. Luis Zubino appreciates that Zubinos would not have been able to grow as quickly without the KPE finance and is very pleased that Carl Martin has not really interfered with the way that Zubinos is run.

Note: The analysis of Appendix 1 was carried out in paragraph 1.2 above.

1.16 Appendix 2 – financial statements

Zubinos' Balance Sheet, Income Statement and Statement of changes in equity

Note: All data in this Appendix is presented in international financial reporting format.

Balance Sheet	As at 31 December 2005		As at 31 December 2004	
	£000	£000	£000	£000
Non-current assets (net)		7,0205		2,958
Current assets				
Inventory	420		395	
Trade receivables and rent prepayments	209		124	
Cash and short-term investments	391		85	
		1,020		604
Total assets		8,045		3,562
Equity and liabilities				
Equity				
Paid in share capital	1,000		600	
Share premium reserve	2,630		630	
Retained profits	1,751		854	
		5,381		2,084
Non-current liabilities				
Loans:				
Bank loan at 12% (repayable in 2006)	300		300	
Bank loan at 12% (repayable in 2007)	200		200	
Bank loan at 12% (repayable in 2009)	100		100	
KPE loan at 10% (repayable in 2010)	300		-	
		900		600
Current liabilities				
Trade payables	1,367		689	
Tax	283		160	
Accruals	114		29	
		1,764		878
Total equity and liabilities		8,045		3,562

Note: Paid in share capital represents 1 million shares of £1.00 each at 31 December 2005.

Income Statement	Year ended 31 December 2005	Year ended 31 December 2004
	£000	£000
Revenue	13,918	7,962
Total operating costs	12,651	7,225
Operating profit	1,267	737
Finance costs	– 87	– 69
Tax expense (effective tax rate is 24%)	– 283	– 160
Profit for the period	897	508

Statement of changes in equity	Share capital	Share premium	Retained earnings	Total
	£000	£000	£000	£000
Balance at 31 December 2004	600	630	854	2,084
New shares issued during 2005	400	2,000	-	2,400
Profit for the period	-	-	897	897
Dividends paid	-	-	-	-
Balance at 31 December 2005	1,000	2,630	1,751	5,381

Note: For the purpose of the case, it should be assumed that the accounts for the year ended 31 December 2005 are final and have been audited.

Question 1 on 1.16 Appendix 2

Produce an outline cash flow statement from this information and comment.

Response

Cash flow statement for 2005

	£000
Operating profit	1,267
Less: increase in inventory (420 – 395)	(25)
Less: increase in trade receivables (209 – 124)	(85)
Plus: increase in trade payables and accruals (1,367 + 114 – 689 – 29)	763
Net cash inflow from operating activities	1,920
Dividends paid	0
Tax paid (2004 bill)	(160)
Finance costs (2005 figure)	(87)
Increase in non-current assets (7,025 – 2,958)	(4,067)
Net cash outflow before new financing is considered	(2,394)
New finance raised – equity (1,000 + 2,630 – 600 – 630)	2,400
New finance raised – debt (KPE loan)	300
Increase in cash and short-term investments (391 – 85)	306

Comments

- The key drain on cash is the expansion into new premises – over £4 million spent in 2005.
- Healthy net cash flow from operating activities.
- Finance raised in 2005 was really only enough to cover 2005 expansion – what about future plans?

Question 2 on 1.16 Appendix 2

Do a ratio analysis of the figures and comment (try to bring in some figures from real-world companies).

Ratio analysis

	2005	2004	Caffé Nero y/e 5/05	2005 working	2004 working
Profitability					
Growth in turnover	74.8%	N/A		13,918/7,962	
Growth in operating profit	71.9%	N/A		1,267/737	
Capital employed	6,281	2,684		5,381 + 900	2,084 + 600
ROCE	20.2%	27.5%	18.9%	1,267/6,281	737/2,684
Return on equity	16.7%	24.4%	31.4%	897/5,381	508/2,084
Operating profit margin	9.10%	9.26%	8.57%	1,267/13,918	737/7,962
Asset turnover	2.22	2.97	2.21	13,918/6,281	7,962/2,684
Liquidity					
Current ratio	0.58	0.69	0.47	1,020/1,764	604/878
Quick ratio	0.34	0.24	0.43	(1,02 – 420)/1,764	(604 – 395)/878
Total inventory days	12	20	4	(420/12,651) × 365	(395/7,225) × 365
Trade receivables days	5	6	11	(209/13,918) × 365	(124/7,962) × 365
Trade payables days	39	35	51	(1,367/12,651) × 365	(689/7,225) × 365
Length of operating cycle	–22	–9	–36	12 + 5 - 39	20 + 6 - 35
Investor ratios					
Gearing - Debt/Equity – using book values	0.17	0.29	0.98	900/5,381	600/2,084
Interest cover	14.6x	10.7x	6.6x	1,267/87	737/69
Dividend cover	N/A	N/A	N/A		
EPS	89.7p	84.7p	7.5p	897/1,000	508/600

Comments

Profitability

- Revenue and operating profit have both increased dramatically (revenue by 75% and operating profit by 72%). High growth is welcomed but usually brings potential problems re working capital and control – these are discussed below.
- ROCE has fallen, presumably because of the recent large increase in capital employed due to store openings and because new stores have only been open part of the year. However, it is still higher than Caffé Nero, for example.

- Return on equity has fallen significantly. Partly this will be the effect of high growth and using year end figures in the calculations but the main factor is the large amount of equity injected in the year.
- Operating margins have weakened slightly but are still better than Caffé Nero, for instance. At first sight this does not seem to be a cause for concern. However:
  - One would normally expect margins to improve with growth due to the presence of fixed costs. Here there will be many costs that are variable (e.g. coffee, food), some that are fixed per store (e.g. rents, salaries) and some that are fixed overall (e.g. directors' salaries).
  - Operating costs have actually risen by £5.4 million or 75.1%, so good operational cost control is vital.
- Asset turnover has weakened, again due to the high recent investment in non-current assets. It will take time for the newer stores to get up to speed. The current figure is comparable with Caffé Nero.
- Overall the growth is impressive but there are some concerns over the falling margins.

Liquidity

- Both current and quick ratios are less than 1, which would normally indicate a problem. However, the nature of the business model is that it should be cash rich (as shown by the negative operating cycle) so it is perhaps not such a problem here.
- Current ratio has worsened but the quick ratio has improved, suggesting that stock levels have not risen in line with the rest of the business. This is further supported by the fall in inventory days. Zubinos needs to ensure that it has adequate stock levels to prevent stock outs, as happened in one store.
- Trade payables days have worsened, which again is probably due to using y/e figures for a growing business.
- The main issue for liquidity is whether sufficient funds have been raised for new store openings – both to set up new stores and to meet working capital requirements.

Gearing

- Gearing has decreased as there has been more new equity raised than debt. The overall level of gearing looks very low by market standards so there should be scope for using more debt finance in the future to aid expansion and reduce the WACC.
- Interest cover has risen and is high enough not to be a cause for concern.
- EPS has risen – a good sign if more equity is wanted. The current figure is also considerably higher than that of Caffé Nero.
- Overall the balance sheet looks healthy.

Note: A more detailed analysis of Zubinos' financing arrangements is carried out in the session on Financial Strategy.

1.17 Appendix 3

Extracts from Zubinos' five-year plan

	Actual	Plan				
	2005	**2006**	**2007**	**2008**	**2009**	**2010**
Number of coffee shops:						
Start of the year	10	18	26	36	48	60
New openings	8	8	10	12	12	15
End of the year	18	26	36	48	60	75
Average number of coffee shops for the year	14	22	31	42	54	68
Analysis of new shop openings:						
UK	8	8	9	5	5	5
Overseas	-	-	1	7	7	10
	£000	£000	£000	£000	£000	£000
Coffee shops revenue	13,498	22,176	37,072	57,378	82,553	110,751
Revenue from new product launches in each year	420	1,560	2,200	2,900	3,800	4,800
Total revenue	13,918	23,736	39,272	60,278	86,353	115,551
Pre-tax operating profit	1,267	2,160	3,613	5,606	8,203	10,977
Capital expenditure	4,800	2,700	3,400	3,800	4,100	5,000

Note: The extracts from the five-year plan shown above were approved by KPE and the Zubinos Board in December 2005.

Question on 1.17 Appendix 3

Analyse the above figures in terms of:

- growth
- operating margins
- revenue per store, using the average number of stores in the year
- Capex per new store opened.

Please comment on your figures.

	2005 Actual	2006	2007	2008	2009	2010
Growth – turnover	75%	71%	65%	53%	43%	34%
Growth – no. of shops	80%	44%	38%	33%	25%	25%
Operating margin	9.10%	9.10%	9.20%	9.30%	9.50%	9.50%
Capex per new shop (£000)	600	338	340	317	342	333
Revenue per store (£000), using average no.	994	1,079	1,267	1,435	1,599	1,699

Comments

It is easy with any high growth plan to dismiss it as being unrealistic. However, Zubinos did achieve growth in turnover of 75% in 2005 so they are doing something right. The issue is whether the high growth is sustainable into the future.

- While future growth is forecast to slow, it is difficult to see how the high figures are possible given the following:
  - industry growth of 4.1% per annum is forecast in the UK (Zubinos is including overseas growth but the figures still seem high)
  - larger competitors will also be expanding, so there will be intense competition for every suitable location
  - even Starbucks is looking to get 20% annual growth.
- It is difficult to see how margins will increase when:
  - they have been falling
  - they are still already higher than major competitors, such as Caffé Nero.
- Presumably the new products will have high margin?
- The future cost of new shops is much lower than that achieved in 2005. This could be due partly to lower costs overseas (depends where, though) and partly because 2005 was not typical, with Luis buying two large sites.

Future plans need to be clarified regarding how many stores will be bought and how many rented (much lower Capex).

- The large increases in average revenue per shop also seem very high – for example, the average revenue will increase by 17% from 2006 to 2007.
- Overall the plan looks 'ambitious' or 'unrealistic', depending on who you are writing to! It is interesting, therefore, that KPE were happy with them, possibly because targets have been beaten before.

1.18 Appendix 4

UK National News

TUESDAY DECEMBER 20 2005

ZUBINOS is winning a share of the coffee wars

THE coffee shops chain, Zubinos, renowned for its choice of coffees and fresh foods, today opened its eighteenth coffee shop and is now expanding nationwide.

Managing Director, Luis Zubino, commented 'our customers are very important to us and we provide them with the coffees that they want and a wide variety of top quality foods in an appealing atmosphere'.

Zubinos has eight coffee shops outside the capital. They are much larger than many of its competitors' coffee shops. Zubino stated, 'our customers want to feel as if they are at home and we have created the authentic European coffee house atmosphere. Our sales are growing rapidly, which confirms to us that our customers like what we provide.'

It is forecast that sales for 2005 will be over £14 million, which is nearly 75% up from sales of around £8 million during 2004.

Zubinos appears to have managed to compete effectively against the many coffee shops chains, most of which have nationwide coverage. However, as Zubinos expands, the market expects there to be some consolidation. A leading UK coffee shop chain, Café Café, recently bought 12 coffee shops from the global coffee shop chain Whistle.

When asked about Zubinos expansion plans, Luis Zubino stated, 'it is our intention to continue to expand within the UK and to open Zubinos coffee shops overseas in the next few years'.

KPE, the private equity arm of Kite Bank, is financing much of the Zubinos expansion. KPE is quoted as being 'very pleased with Zubinos operational and financial performance to date'.

Questions and comments on 1.18 - Appendix 4 - UK National News	Response
Comment on the strategy of having larger shops than competitors.	One must always question when a firm seems to buck the industry trend – genius or a mistake waiting to happen? Arguments for: • There always seem to be lengthy queues at the most popular coffee shops. Larger shops could allow Zubinos to gain customers from competitors. Arguments against: • The queues suggest that customers would rather wait then get inferior coffee. Would Zubinos' customers wait if shops were smaller?

chapter

7

ZUBINOS: INDUSTRY AWARENESS

Contents

1 Introduction

The case concerns a chain of coffee shops based in the UK so students were expected to research the industry. What follows is an example of the type of analysis that could have been done.

2 Market overview

In 2005, the UK-branded coffee chain market continued to expand rapidly, exceeding £1.1 billion in turnover for the first time.

The market is set to grow by a compound annual rate of 4.1% in size and 8.9% in terms of number of outlets over the next three years to reach £1.4 billion in turnover and 3,427 outlets by December 2008.

Coffee bar culture has extended well beyond the UK's major cities into smaller towns and the provincial areas due to:

- high consumer demand, and
- rapid opening programmes by coffee bar chains such as Starbucks, Costa Coffee, Caffé Nero and others.

While parts of London may be over-saturated with coffee shops, there are still significant opportunities in the regions.

3 Key players

The main players in the UK market are:

- Starbucks – http://starbucks.co.uk/en-GB/
- Costa Coffee – http://www.costa.co.uk/
- Caffé Nero – http://www.caffénero.com/ (**Note:** While all of the companies mentioned here are much bigger than Zubinos, it shares more characteristics with Caffé Nero than many others so is a reasonable comparator. The web-site is also more accessible than most.)
- Caffé Ritazza – http://www.compass-group.co.uk/ourbusiness/foodservicebrands/brands/caffé-ritazza.htm. (Compass also owns Harry Ramsdens and Upper Crust.)
- BB's Coffee and Muffins – http://www.bbscoffeeandmuffins.com/
- Coffee Republic – http://www.coffeerepublic.co.uk/

Starbucks Coffee Company is the market leader in the coffee-focused segment with 466 UK outlets, followed by Costa Coffee with 405 outlets and Caffé Nero with 248 outlets.

70% of new coffee-focused outlets are opened by the top three players.

Costa Coffee is currently the fastest growing operator.

BB's is the largest shopping centre operator.

The branded segment represents approximately 30% of the defined market at present, and is forecast to grow to 35% by 2008-2009.

Independent coffee operators, however, have experienced declining sales due to growing competition from the chains, with the majority of independent coffee shop owner/managers surveyed in Greater London believing that they had been adversely affected by the chains. Another concern is that rents in key locations have been driven up by the chains.

The focus of expansion by the main chains remains on London suburbs and small regional towns and provincial areas. London growth strategies now centre on expanding in suburban London and 'in-filling' certain pockets of Central London.

4 Competition from non coffee-focused operators

The largest non-specialist players are:

- Bakers Oven (Del Rico)
- O'Brien's Sandwich Bars
- Prêt A Manger
- Benjys
- EAT.

Prêt A Manger has revitalised its product range and has increased store numbers by 6% in the 12 months to December 2005. Similarly, EAT increased store numbers rapidly.

Benjys Sandwiches has introduced its 'Love the coffee' range at reduced prices – at around 60% of the price for a regular cappuccino compared to Starbucks.

5 Basis of competition

The main aspect emphasised by all coffee-focused operators is the superior quality of their coffee. This is derived from the following:

- careful selection of the best coffee beans, which are ground on site

- investment in the best machines
- highly trained operatives ('baristas').

Maintaining the quality of coffee while expanding rapidly is seen as a key challenge. Non-specialists have also seen the need to develop their own coffee to compete. Most firms stress that they pay fair prices to coffee growers and some use Fair Trade coffee – see http://www.cafedirect.co.uk/ for more information on Fair Trade coffee.

Coffee-focused chains have further developed their food ranges to increase average spend and to cater for increasingly time-poor consumers who seek greater convenience and one-stop shops.

In addition, each chain tries to offer a 'lifestyle experience' with comfy sofas, carefully selected music, etc. The aim is that coffee shops become the most popular places to meet and relax, after home and work.

Companies also seem keen to stress how socially responsible they are. Part of this is the emphasis on Fair Trade mentioned above, but some firms go beyond this:

- Starbucks has linked up with TimeBank, a national volunteering charity, and the National Literacy Trust.

6 Market trends

Results from more than 7,500 face-to-face customer interviews in coffee shops reveal that:

- UK consumers are visiting branded coffee chains more frequently.
- 'Convenience of location' remains the most important reason consumers select a specific coffee shop.
- Visiting coffee bars to relax and to meet friends and colleagues were important reasons for visiting coffee bars.
- Brand recognition increased 22.9% between June 2004 and December 2005 and customer loyalty is on the rise.
- Average customer spend increased 6% due to price rises and increasing food spend within coffee shop outlets.
- Price sensitivity on coffee has declined.
- 58% of customers surveyed mention that they are concerned and more aware of the importance of healthy eating, although this does not always translate into healthy eating patterns.

There also appears to be an increasing awareness of Fair Trade products.

7 Growth strategies

Starbucks is the best known player in the world market, so some aspects of its strategy are considered first. Different directions and vehicles for growth are then outlined.

Starbucks

The key aspects to Starbucks growth strategy are as follows:

- Starbucks does not franchise but owns all of its stores 'in order to manage the quality standards and customer experience'. It has, however, used joint ventures in countries such as Japan and China.
- Rather than trying to capture all the potential markets as soon as possible, Starbucks goes into a geographic market and tries to dominate it completely before setting its sights on further expansion.
- Starbucks will blanket an area completely, even if the stores cannibalise one another's business. A new store will often capture about 30% of the sales of a nearby Starbucks, but the company considers that to be a good thing.
- The Starbucks-everywhere approach cuts down on delivery and management costs, shortens customer lines at individual stores, and increases foot traffic for all the stores in an area.
- Very low marketing costs – Starbucks typically spends just 1% of its annual revenues on advertising. (Retailers usually spend around 10% of turnover.)
- Vertical integration – Starbucks owns multiple roasting and distribution facilities.

Franchising

Most firms have adopted similar strategies to Starbucks. The emphasis on having the best coffee is a common theme throughout the industry. Most firms have sought to develop their coffee range:

- Starbucks offers rare Black Apron Exclusives™, coffees in the US.
- Caffé Nero offer soya milk options and Swiss water decaf.

However, one main area where there is disagreement between firms is in franchising.

Like Starbucks, Caffé Nero does not franchise. Other firms, including Costa Coffee, BB's and Café Ritazza have preferred franchising as their vehicle for expansion. The main reasons given for this are:

- rapid expansion
- shared financing costs
- strength of brand name.

Coffee Republic is an interesting example to consider. Having seen profits decline (£8.9 million loss in 2003), it sold some shops to competitors (e.g. eight stores to Caffé Nero in 2004), switched to a 'deli' style approach focusing more on food and now plans to use franchising to capitalise on its name. The company had more than 100 coffee bars three years ago and is now looking to sell off around 30 sites to franchisees, retaining ownership of only 10 to 15 stores.

Product development

Many operators have developed the food side of their business to include sandwiches, bagels, Italian wraps, paninis, soup, pasta, muffins and pastries. As mentioned above, Coffee Republic is moving towards a New York style deli approach.

While there may be a regional emphasis (e.g. Caffé Nero stresses an Italian flavour), most of the major operators simply claim that their food is of the highest quality to match their coffee.

Some operators have also developed their non-coffee drinks range e.g. Starbucks has a more complete range of teas (Tazo® Teas) and iced drinks.

Market development

Most of the larger firms have looked to expand internationally, usually via franchising as detailed above e.g. Starbucks now has over 6,000 locations in over 30 countries.

The logic of reproducing the best of Italian and French coffee culture throughout Europe and North America is self-evident, but Starbucks has even made significant inroads into traditionally tea-drinking countries such as China. (Partly this is due to the attractiveness of Western Culture to the emerging middle class.)

chapter

8

ZUBINOS: FURTHER DETAILED ANALYSIS

Contents

1 Introduction

As well as a detailed paragraph by paragraph analysis, it is a good idea to perform more detailed analysis under the following headings:

- Business strategy
- Financial strategy
- Risk and control
- Ethics

This is a chance to use standard techniques, such as SWOT, along with more specific analyses.

Finally, you should précis the case study.

2 Business strategy analysis

2.1 Consolidate your understanding of the strategic position of Zubinos using a SWOT analysis

Strengths

- Established competitive strategy of differentiation based on quality coffee, more staff and FairTrade coffee
- Strong balance sheet
- Directors have a good mix of relevant expertise and experience
- KPE's willingness to invest further debt finance
- Performance-related pay, together with directors owning shares, should result in more motivated employees
- Cash rich business model (negative cash operating cycle)
- The board is looking to the future, wants to grow the business and has a five-year plan in place. A clear strategy exists
- A clear focus on customers and their importance is driving the business, not just financials
- Little conflict evident at board level although the centralisation has caused some problems

Weaknesses

- Not listed – making equity finance harder to raise
- Higher costs than competitors due to higher staff costs
- Falling margins
- Small player in the UK so may lack the economies of scale of larger rivals
- May be trying to grow too quickly – in particular Zubinos may not have the control systems in place to manage the growth properly
- Role ambiguity – especially in the areas of centralisation and standardisation
- Poor information systems
- Poor control systems
- Relatively low margins on 'other drinks' and 'other foods'
- Some staff discontentment among shop managers
- Yet to pay a dividend – how long will KPE be happy with this?
- Not yet clear what the exit strategy is for KPE
- Luis Zubino's social conscience results in a conflict with commercial best practice. Could alienate KPE
- Decision making does not appear to have a sound academic framework i.e. no evidence of NPV

Opportunities

- Opening more shops in the UK – especially outside London
- Shop within shop outlets
- Motorway services
- Overseas expansion
- Greater public awareness of Fair Trade issues
- AIM listing
- Significant capital gains may be made on acquired properties
- Franchising is a popular means of expansion in practice. This is an option not yet considered

Threats

- Intense competitive rivalry
- Coffee drinking is a luxury, what happens in recession? With a higher cost base Zubinos is not well positioned to survive a recession
- Decline in market growth / market saturation
- Coffee may cease to be as fashionable
- Owning two premises exposes Zubinos to risks in the property market. This will affect Zubinos' debt capacity and may create exit barriers if prices fall
- The business is very dependant on Luis Zubino – could the business survive his death/resignation or desire to sell? His shares alone are worth £6m x 0.30 = £1.8m at January 2005

Out of these, the key issues for Zubinos are as follows:

- Highly competitive, risky industry.
- Whether the industry will continue to grow at the rate experienced to date.
- Zubinos tries to succeed through a competitive strategy of differentiation based on quality Fair Trade coffee and higher staff levels. The extent to which the firm can maintain its competitive advantage could be a key issue in the case.
- Structure, information reporting and role ambiguity need to be improved to facilitate growth.

2.2 Assess the coffee shop industry using Porter's five forces analysis

Competitive rivalry – very high

- Major quoted companies – Starbucks, Caffé Nero, etc.
- Large number of smaller independent operators.
- Increasing competition from non coffee-focused operators.
- It is difficult to differentiate your product – competitors can quickly match any innovation.
- BUT – high industry growth to date has reduced the extent of rivalry. If the market is reaching saturation, as some analysts predict, then rivalry will intensify.

Threat of entry – high

- For new firms entering the industry the main barriers are as follows:
  - Obtaining suitable premises – location is seen as a key success factor and competition for prime locations has driven up rents.
  - Brand name – debatable how significant an issue this is.
  - Expertise to make a quality cup of coffee – e.g. buying quality beans, training for baristas – not a key issue as easily available.
  - Overall these barriers are not significant, though are likely to be higher in cities such as London and lower in the regions.

Threat of substitutes – low

- Main threat is that coffee loses its fashionable, trendy image – for example, if customers become more concerned over Fair Trade issues, or if quality teashops become the new trend.
- Unlikely to be a major problem but such trends should be monitored.

Power of suppliers – lower for coffee, higher for premises

- Owners of prime retail sites have significant power to increase rents.
- Coffee growers have low power but only the biggest firms (e.g. Starbucks) deal directly with them. Most coffee beans go via distribution channels involving exporters, buyers, roasters and distributors.
- Coffee growers have very little power, despite the efforts of the FairTrade Foundation.
- The industry is dominated by the 'big four' multinational buyers/roasters – Nestlé, Kraft, Procter & Gamble and Sara Lee.
- These large buyers have medium power over their customers (coffee shops, other roasters, etc) – few suppliers, differentiated products.

Power of customers – low

- Customers have low power in the sense that an individual customer does not purchase enough coffee to be able to influence a firm on their own.
- However, there are few switching costs to prevent customers voting with their feet and going to competitors' shops if unhappy with the quality or cost of products offered.

- Firms have been trying to boost brand strength and customer loyalty.

Summary: A very competitive and hence very risky industry, stressing the need for careful positioning and a clear competitive strategy.

2.3 Analyse the coffee industry using a PESTEL/PEST/SLEPT style analysis

Political factors

- The main political issue is the heightened awareness of the plight of third-world farmers and public pressure for governments to act. If this gets translated into better terms for coffee growers, then there will be a price increase for the raw coffee.
- Also, governments in the countries where coffee is grown could also act more to protect their farmers.

Economic factors

- Coffee shops have seen huge growth in the UK over the last ten years. A significant factor here is the growth and stability of the UK economy. If there were an economic downturn, then many customers may decide to switch to cheaper sources of coffee.
- Exchange rates could also affect the cost of imported coffee.

Social factors

- Visiting coffee shops is currently seen as a vital ingredient of an affluent lifestyle. At some stage this could change towards a different beverage / style of meeting place – French-style cafés or traditional tea shops, for example.

Technological factors

- Improvements in the quality of home coffee machines may reduce demand for visiting coffee shops. This is unlikely to be a major issue as most people go to coffee shops as a meeting place, not just for the coffee.
- Improvements in the quality of commercial coffee machines has made it easier for other firms to try to match the quality of the specialist coffee shops.

Environmental/ethical factors

- The main ethical concern in the coffee industry is the welfare of coffee growers. The growth of FairTrade reflects increasing public awareness of these issues and is likely to produce more demand for coffee shops that can demonstrate that they are more socially responsible.
- **Note:** Starbucks has also been targeted by anti-globalisation protesters, despite its well-advertised focus on social responsibility!

Legal factors

- Employment and food safety legislation will affect coffee shops but are unlikely to be major issues.

2.4 Competitive advantage

Zubinos is trying to compete on the basis of differentiation. Assess each of Porter's generic strategies as options within the coffee shop industry.

Differentiation

Many firms claim that their coffee is the best quality. This can be based on a combination of the following:

- choice of beans (e.g. aribica v robusta, geographical location, type of roast, blends used, etc)
- training of baristas
- machinery used
- variations offered.

Other areas of differentiation include:

- food offered
- comfort / luxury / atmosphere of surroundings
- ambience created by specially selected music
- speed of service
- extras e.g. access to the internet.

The main problem with all of these factors is that they can be copied by competitors. The ongoing success of this strategy is down to ongoing innovation (e.g. food lines) and because customer opinions differ on which coffee tastes best.

Cost leadership

There are some economies of scale available to larger players in the industry:

- lower cost coffee due to bulk discounts on purchasing
- lower cost machinery due to bulk discounts on purchasing
- backwards integration into coffee roasting may reduce costs.

Whether these are sufficient to underpin a strategy of cost leadership is more questionable. If the quality of the coffee and the premises can match competitors, then the firm with the lowest costs will 'win'. Porter suggests that this often occurs when a market becomes mature.

Focus

The bulk of the industry targets younger customers. Firms can try to focus further by the following:

- location e.g. BB's operate mainly in shopping centres
- ethnic slant e.g. Italian, French, etc.

Whether such firms are more competitive than the bigger players is questionable.

Summary

Differentiation looks set to stay as the strategy of choice but increasing maturity and saturation within the industry will force a greater emphasis on cost aspects.

2.5 Using Ansoff's matrix outline possible directions for growth for Zubinos

Ansoff's matrix – product / market mix

	Existing products	**New products**
Existing markets	*Market penetration* The UK market could be penetrated further by: • further expansion outside London • buying a smaller competitor • shop within shop outlets • developing FairTrade aspects further to enhance differentiation.	*Product development* Margins are lower on 'other drinks' and 'other foods'. Both could be developed: • develop low calorie, healthy food options further • develop quality teas side of business (e.g. offer 'afternoon tea' on a level comparable with quality hotels) • move into the quality deli market (cf Coffee Republic). Other product developments could include: • selling music (cf Starbucks) • offering access to the internet.

	Existing products	New products
New markets	*Market development* New markets could include the following: • motorway services • shopping centre outlets • further online sales • overseas expansion – whether through organic growth or acquisition.	*Diversification* Related diversification: • e.g. backwards vertical integration into coffee roasting. Unrelated diversification (conglomerate diversification): • e.g. anything!

2.6 List the main issues for Zubinos to consider if looking at shop within shop operations

The main issues to consider are as follows:

The host store

- Reputation of the host.
- Typical clientele of the host store – do they have the right economic and sociological mix? Do they appeal to younger more affluent customers?
- Location of the host store – is it in the type of location that Zubinos would have chosen normally for a shop?
- Number of customers that typically visit the host.
- How many customers visit the host during lunch.
- Financial strength of the host.

The arrangement

- Location of Zubinos within the host store – is it in a prominent position?
- Nature of charges – does the host charge a fixed rent and take a share of profit?
- Level of typical costs – what would the breakeven point be? How do costs compare to normal outlets?
- Advertising – will the host include Zubinos' name in any advertising? (**Note:** This is a recent development with motorway service stations.)
- Minimum rental term, notice period – what exit barriers will there be should Zubinos want to close the operation?

2.7 List the main issues for Zubinos to consider if looking at expansion overseas

The main issues to consider are as follows:

- Location – best to start in major metropolitan centres.
- Competition e.g. too much competition from traditional Italian coffee shops in Italy!
- Resources e.g. staffing – where would training take place?
- Setup costs.
- Financing e.g. foreign loans, KPE, etc.
- Local culture – would Zubinos have to develop a coffee culture or is it already there?
- Legal aspects – separate companies, differences in employment law.
- Forex risk.
- Organisational structure – would the overseas operations be run from the UK or set up as separate divisions?
- Structure of deal e.g. lease v buy premises.
- Organic growth v acquisition v joint venture.

3 Financial strategy analysis

3.1 Analyse the financing arrangements used by Zubinos to date and comment on the options available for raising finance in the future

Financing to date

The financing history of Zubinos is typical for the start up and growth stages of a company:

- Initial seed capital was put in by Luis Zubino using a personal loan secured on his flat and his parents' house.
- Luis has always tried to use internally generated funds to finance expansion.
- Key staff were invited to buy shares and input more equity.
- Bank loans were used when needed – even for working capital (2004 loan). Normally one would try to match the life of finance to the life of the investment so it could be argued that a five-year loan is not appropriate for working capital, unless on takes the view that working capital is long term.
- Eventually the firm had grown to the point where it needed a more substantial equity investment and KPE was brought on board.

Current position

As discussed in the analysis of the financial statements in the section 'case and commentary', the balance sheet looks healthy:

Investor ratios	2005	2004	Caffé Nero
Gearing – Debt/Equity – using book values	0.17	0.29	0.98
Interest cover	14.6x		6.6x
Dividend cover	N/A	N/A	
EPS	89.7p	84.7p	7.5p

- Gearing is low and interest cover high. One could argue that the gearing level is too low and that the firm is failing to take advantage of the tax benefits of debt finance.
- Earnings per share has increased from 2004 to 2005, despite the large injection of equity in 2005.

Future financing needs

Taking the business plan in Appendix 3, we can get a rough idea of financing needs.

£000	2006	2007	2008	2009	2010
Pre-tax operating profit (Note)	2,160	3,613	5,606	8,203	10,977
Tax at 24% (given)	(518)	(867)	(1,345)	(1,969)	(2,634)
Net inflow	*1,642*	*2,746*	*4,261*	*6,234*	*8,243*
Capex	(2,700)	(3,400)	(3,800)	(4,100)	(5,000)
Repayment of bank loans	(300)	(200)	-	(100)	(300)
Net cash flow	*(1,358)*	*(854)*	*461*	*2,034*	*2,943*

Note: This assumes for simplicity that pre-tax operating profit = cash inflow.

This would indicate that approximately £2.2 million of further finance is needed over the next two years – more if the growth in profit is not as high as the plan forecasts.

The figures are very different if we assume (reasonably) that the profit figure given is after depreciation and then try to reverse out the depreciation. For illustration suppose we assume that depreciation is approximately 10% of opening NBV each year. Based on the Capex plans and the current balance sheet, this would give depreciation as follows:

£000	**2006**	**2007**	**2008**	**2009**	**2010**
NBCV of fixed assets b/f	7,025	9,022	11,520	14,168	16,851
Depreciaition @ 10%	(703)	(902)	(1,152)	(1,417)	(1,685)
Capex	2,700	3,400	3,800	4,100	5,000
NBV of fixed assets c/f	9,022	11,520	14,168	16,851	20,166

The financing estimate would then become:

£000	**2006**	**2007**	**2008**	**2009**	**2010**
Pre-tax operating profit (Note 1)	2,160	3,613	5,606	8,203	10,977
Tax at 24% (given)	(518)	(867)	(1,345)	(1,969)	(2,634)
Net inflow	*1,642*	*2,746*	*4,261*	*6,234*	*8,243*
Add: depreciation	703	902	1,1512	1,417	1,685
Capex	(2,700)	(3,400)	(3,800)	(4,100)	(5,000)
Repayment of bank loans	(300)	(200)	-	(100)	(300)
Net cash flow	*(655)*	*48*	*1,613*	*3,451*	*4,628*

This would suggest that internally generated funds are sufficient to finance expansion except for 2006 when further finance (presumably extra loans from KPE) are required.

Raising debt

- KPE has already agreed to invest up to £5 million in loans over the next four years. This should cover the financing needs of the business plan.
- Two premises were bought in 2005 for over £1 million each. They are likely to already be included in the security for the 2005 KPE loan of £300,000, which should leave enough to go some way towards the security for the new loans. The loan is for £300,000, so there should be scope for at least another £1 million loan without the need for further assets.
- Zubinos' other assets are less likely to be seen as attractive to lenders. Most shops are rented and shop fittings would not be considered as quality assets for security purposes.

- If new premises are bought, then they could also offer some security.
- Low gearing and high interest cover would indicate that other debt should be relatively easy to raise, except for the security issue discussed above.

Raising equity

- The existing directors may be willing to invest more equity but are unlikely to be able to afford the sums required.
- KPE may be willing to invest more equity but this may be resisted by the other shareholders if KPE's share were to go above 50%.
- At some stage the firm will consider a flotation. At present the market value (see below) does not support a full stock exchange listing in the UK but AIM could be a consideration. This would give an exit route for KPE, allow the directors to realise gains and would make raising further equity easier.

3.2 Calculate the market value of Zubinos using earnings, assets and dividend approaches

Tutorial note: Zubinos has experienced high growth to date, like many firms in the real world. Unfortunately this can make it very difficult to apply standard valuation models without getting strange answers. What follows should be seen as an application of techniques, highlighting problem areas, rather than producing definitive answers.

1 Earnings approach

Zubinos is unquoted, so the main problem here lies in obtaining a P/E ratio.

(i) *Using a P/E ratio derived from the share issue to KPE*

One approach is to go back to the start of 2005 when shares were issued to KPE at a price of £6, valuing the company at £6 million in January 2005.

Using this there are two ways of getting a P/E ratio:

1 Look backwards at 2004 earnings ('historic').

2 Look forwards at 2005 earnings ('forecast').

Either approach is valid as long as you are consistent with applying the result. Most published P/E ratios are backwards looking but Merchant Banks prefer to use forward looking P/Es for valuation purposes. Some websites show both. To get a market value at the start of 2006, the two approaches would give:

1 MV = 2005 earnings × backwards looking P/E, or

2 MV = 2006 projected earnings × forwards looking P/E.

Applying these two approaches gives the following:

Type of P/E ratio used	Backward looking	Forward looking
Earnings to calculate Jan 2005 P/E ratio	508	897
P/E at Jan 2005	6,000/508 = 11.8	6,000/897 = 6.7
Earnings to calculate MV at Jan 2006	897	2,160 × 0.76 = 1,642
MV at Jan 2006	11.8 × 897 = 10.6m	6.7 × 1,642 = 10.9m

Note that the results are not dissimilar.

If the unseen information does not give any further useful data for valuation, then these figures for P/E ratio and market value should be used.

(ii) *Using the P/E ratio of similar quoted companies*

In practice it is more usual to value an unquoted company by finding similar quoted companies. This is not as easy as it seems as most comparable companies are part of larger groups – Whitbread owns Costa Coffee and Compass owns Café Ritazza, for example. As for Starbucks, it is not even quoted in the UK!

By looking at their websites, the following figures can be obtained

P/E ratios:	Café Nero	32 historic, 39 forecast
	Starbucks	51 historic, 47 forecast

Again, the high P/E ratios are due to high growth expectations in the market (Caffé Nero's PBT grew by 200% last year!).

For illustrative purposes, the P/E of Caffé Nero will be the starting point here. Obviously you would be looking for a figure to be given in the unseen information.

Given that Zubinos is unquoted, it is standard procedure to reduce the P/E ratio of the quoted donor by around 25 to 35%. This would give a P/E for Zubinos of 20, say. Using the P/E of 20 obtained above and 2005 earnings, this gives a market capitalisation of:

MV = 20 × 897,000 = £17.9 million

The difference in the two approaches is probably due to a mixture of the following:

- Caffé Nero is not a good match
- different growth expectations
- KPE drove a hard bargain when agreeing to inject new finance.

2 Net assets approach

Book value of equity = £5,381,000

This is substantially lower than the market value based on earnings. This is to be expected as goodwill is not shown on the balance sheet.

The main use for an asset valuation is to determine a minimum acceptable selling price by calculating a net realisable value (NRV). This would involve using the services of surveyors / professional valuers. The main problem would be in valuing shop fittings and stocks.

3 Dividend valuation model (DVM) approach

There is no evidence of any dividends having been paid or of any plans to do so. The dividend valuation model would thus value the shares at zero!

If the unseen material gives details of future proposed dividend streams (unlikely), then a minority stake could be valued using the cost of equity of a similar quoted company.

3.3 To perform further detailed calculations for Zubinos, such as NPV or SVA, we will need a suitable discount rate. Calculate the WACC of Zubinos

Tutorial note: As stated under valuation, Zubinos' high growth to date makes it very difficult to apply standard cost of capital models without getting strange answers. Again, what follows should be seen as an application of techniques, highlighting problem areas, rather than producing definitive answers.

Cost of debt (kd)

Zubinos' debt finance is made up of bank loans so the cost of debt can be quickly calculated using:

k_d = Bank loan rate x (1 – tax rate)

The tax rate is given in Appendix 2 as 24%.

12% loans k_d = 12 x (1 – 0.24) = 9.1%

10% loan k_d = 10 x (1 – 0.24) = 7.6%

Cost of equity (k_e)

Estimating the cost of equity is much more difficult as Zubinos is not a listed company. There is also the complication that the directors and KPE may have different costs of equity due to their own risk positions – KPE is probably well diversified while the directors may have put all their spare funds into Zubinos.

(i) *Dividend valuation model*

One approach would be to use the dividend valuation model and a market value calculated above:

$k_e = \{D_1 / MV\} + g$

However, the lack of any dividends, whether past or future makes this difficult!

A way round this slight hitch is to use profit after tax instead of dividend. This is justified on the grounds that the wealth of shareholders is unaffected whether profits are paid out or not (à la Modigliani and Miller), as long as they are distributed eventually.

Post tax earnings in 1 year's time = pre-tax × (1 – 0.24) = 2,160 × 0.76 = £1,642,000

A growth figure can be estimated from the plan in Appendix 3. (**Note:** This may be ambitious but as long as the shareholders believe it, it should correlate to their required returns and the value they place on the business.)

Compound average future growth can be calculated from:

$1,267 \times (1 + g)^5 = 10,977$, given growth of 54% pa

The problem with this figure is that it is unlikely to be sustainable in the long run as it clearly exceeds overall industry growth. The formula is based on growth into perpetuity! An industry growth rate could be used but that would underplay the high growth expected in Zubinos for at least the short-term future.

For illustrative purposes we shall use the 54% here:

$k_e = \{D_1 / MV\} + g = \{1{,}642 / 10{,}600\} + 0.54 = 0.695$ or approximately 70%

This figure seems absurdly high and is due primarily to the growth estimate used.

If long-term industry growth of 4% is used, then a more sensible, but not necessarily more reliable, cost of equity of 20% is obtained.

(ii) *CAPM*

If given the beta of a similar quoted company, then it could be adjusted for gearing (if necessary) and put into the CAPM equation to calculate a cost of equity. A search on the internet gives the following betas:

Caffé Nero 0.3, Coffee Republic 0.6, Starbucks 0.61

All of these seem incredibly low and would suggest a k_e of less than 10%, completely different from the previous estimates. The key is to discuss your method and results without relying too much on the accuracy of your answer. The methodology used is much more important than the answer you obtain.

Tutorial note: A k_e this low causes problems if anticipating growth higher than 10% – try using DVM with $k_e<g$.

WACC

Weighting according to market values:

Finance	Cost	MV	WACC
	(%)	(£000)	(%)
Equity	69.5	10,600	64.0
12% loans	9.1	600	0.5
10% loans	7.6	300	0.2
Total		11,500	**64.7**

For discounting purposes a figure of approximately 65% can be used.

3.4 The five-year plan in Appendix 3 makes it possible to apply the Shareholder Value Analysis (SVA) methodology to the case. Use SVA with a WACC of 20% and long-run growth of 4%, say, to value the company

We can use the figures in Appendix 3 subject to the following adjustments:

1 We need to insert the tax flows. These have been put into the year concerned for simplicity. Obviously they could be delayed by one year.

2 We would want to reverse out depreciation and other non-cash flows from the profit.

3 We want free cash flows so want to reverse out any interest payments included in the derivation of pre-tax profit in Appendix 3.

4 We need figures for working capital and replacement fixed capital investment. Replacement fixed capital investment is often equated with depreciation but the growth would necessitate incremental working capital investment.

With all of the above, the key question is how complicated do you want to make it? For illustrative purposes items 2 to 4 will be ignored. Obviously, if asked to do such a calculation, then you should read the unseen information carefully for further detail.

£000	**2006**	**2007**	**2008**	**2009**	**2010 onwards**
Pre-tax operating profit	2,160	3,613	5,606	8,203	10,977
Tax at 24% (given)	(518)	(867)	(1,345)	(1,969)	(2,634)
Net inflow	1,642	2,746	4,261	6,234	8,243
Capex	(2,700)	(3,400)	(3,800)	(4,100)	(5,000)
Net free cash flow	*(1,358)*	*(854)*	*461*	*2,034*	*2,943*
Discount factor at 20%	1	0.833	0.694	0.579	3.619
PV	*(1,358)*	*(711)*	*320*	*1,178*	*10,650*

Workings

Discount factor for cash flows from 2010 onwards = 0.579 × 1/(0.20 – 0.04) = 3.619.

	£000
Total PV of free cash flows	10,079
Less: value of debt	(900)
Value of equity	9,179

This gives a market value of approximately £9.2 million.

Note: This calculation was performed with a totally made-up WACC so do not rely on it! The idea here was to rehearse the method. It also highlights how critical the future growth estimates are to the market value.

4 Risk and control analysis

4.1 Identify and assess the risks facing Zubinos

Risk area	Zubinos
Business risks	• Very competitive industry • Risk of major competitors opening new shops in locality of Zubinos • UK market approaching saturation in London • Fluctuations in the price of coffee, due to weather conditions, Fair Trade pressure, etc • Low level risk of staff theft due to a lack of control systems
Financial risks	• Declining margins could indicate cost control problems • Low financial gearing so far • Foreign exchange risk if expand overseas (see below) • Growth is causing some problems (see below)
Political and legal risks	• Governments may act to improve the fortunes of coffee growers, putting up prices
Technology risk	• Need to get online sales on website secure • Risks if implement access to internet plans
Economic risk	• Demand for expensive coffee is linked to the state of the economy • State of the commercial property market will affect value of two properties currently owned
Reputation risk	• Zubinos' reputation could be damaged by events such as customer poisoning, which hopefully are unlikely

Overall the key risks are business risks, in particular, competitive rivalry.

4.2 What evidence is there to suggest that Zubinos may be in danger of trying to grow too quickly? In particular is Zubinos in danger of overtrading?

Arguments that Zubinos is growing too quickly

- Poor information systems.
- Role ambiguities.
- In 2004 a bank loan of £100,000 was needed just to cover working capital requirements.

Arguments that the growth should not be a problem

- Cash operating cycle is negative i.e. tend to pay suppliers after cash has already been received from customers.
- KPE has agreed to invest further debt finance for expansion.

Overtrading

Overtrading is a serious problem into which rapidly expanding businesses can easily fall. Signs of overtrading are:

- A rapid increase in stock levels, matched by a large increase in trade creditors or bank overdraft.
- Deteriorating current and quick ratios.
- A significant slow-down in the average time for paying trade creditors
- Sometimes, a large increase in debtors, with debtors also taking longer to pay. (Rapidly growing businesses might sell on easy credit terms to win new customers.)
- Overtrading firms usually see a sharp increase in the asset turnover ratio as output increases are often obtained by more intensive utilisation of existing fixed assets, and growth tends to be financed by more intensive use of working capital.

Applying this checklist to Zubinos we see the following:

A rapid increase in stock levels	**No** – Inventory up 6% v turnover growth of 75%
A large increase in trade creditors	**Yes** – Trade payables up 98%
A large increase in bank overdraft	**No** – Cash in hand (though only because of an injection of £2.4 million by KPE in 2005)
A deteriorating current ratio	**Yes** – has fallen from 0.69 to 0.58
A deteriorating quick ratio	**No** – has improved from 0.24 to 0.34

A significant increase in creditor days	**No** – up but only from 35 to 39 days
A large increase in debtors	**Yes** – debtors up 69% v growth in turnover of 75%
Debtors also taking longer to pay	**No** – down from 6 to 5 days
A sharp increase in the asset turnover ratio	**No** – down from 2.97 to 2.22

This suggests that Zubinos is not showing the classic signs of overtrading.

Summary

Overall Zubinos does not seem to be seeing too many problems with the high growth. The main issue is whether Zubinos can implement better control and information systems to manage the growth better.

4.3 Suggest some KPIs that could be used to monitor operations, using the balanced score card as a framework

Financial perspective • Turnover – in total and by store • Operating profit – in total and by store • Margins – overall and by product line, in total and by store • Number of stores • Sales mix variances
Customer perspective • Level of repeat business • Average spend per customer • Average wait time to be served • Satisfaction surveys
Internal business perspective • Brewing the perfect coffee – implementing quality control procedures is more important that KPIs here. Managers could visit shops 'incognito' to observe practices and see if recommended procedures are being complied with • Thefts could be discouraged by performing monthly reconciliations of actual stock levels to purchases / sales figures • Staff empowerment – % of management roles filled internally

Innovation and learning perspective

- Staff turnover
- % of staff who are 'qualified' baristas
- Number of suggestions made by staff and % implemented

4.4 Outline the specific risks relating to the proposed overseas expansion plan using Ohmae's 5Cs model and outline how Zubinos could manage such risks

Ohmae's 5Cs model can be used to discuss the risks faced by Zubinos as follows:

Customers

- Zubinos needs to ensure that it is opening shops in areas with enough potential customers. Existing methods of selecting locations by looking at population size, population density, presence of well-known retailers, etc can still be used to help here but the culture of the country concerned also needs examining to ensure that a demand for coffee shops exists.
- Zubinos also needs to ensure that targeted customers are affluent enough to afford the high prices it will want to charge. This will affect the choice of country as well as city.

Currency

- Whichever 'European' country is chosen, shop revenue will not be in Sterling, exposing the company to fluctuations in exchange rates, if/when profits are remitted back to the UK.
- Local costs such as salaries will be in the local currency, mitigating the risk to some degree. Whether coffee is purchased and paid for in the local currency or centrally in the UK will also affect the overall risk exposure.
- The net exposure could be hedged by forward contracts based on budgeted remittances.
- The choice of currency for financing will also affect risk exposure. Particularly if premises are to be bought, it might be advisable to finance the purchase in the local currency to match assets and liabilities.

Competitors

- A key issue is finding locations with sufficient demand without excessive competition. Choice of country and city is vital here and Zubinos should look in detail at the local competition and any details of larger competitors' expansion plans, especially Starbucks.
- Competition is not just from large chains – in Italy, for example, there are already thousands of small family-run coffee shops. The Starbucks model was in some respects

an attempt to copy such shops and it should be noted that Starbucks has not opened any shops in Italy, presumably for this reason. Similarly local cafés will be strong competitors in parts of France.

Company

- Does Zubinos have the resources required to make the expansion work? For example, how/where will training be done? How will shop managers be monitored?
- Will a focus on overseas markets detract from managing the UK side properly? For example, if Jane Thorp is busy examining potential overseas sites, will UK marketing suffer?

Countries

- As mentioned above, the choice of country is vital. If coffee culture is already well established, then there is the likelihood that the market is already well served by competitors. However, if the country has yet to pick up on coffee culture, then the opportunity would be bigger but the risk of failure higher. The best approach would be to pick a country where the market is already growing but still at the early stages.
- Spain is mentioned in the pre-seen as a possibility. Spain already has a widespread 'cortado' culture of small cafés yet Starbucks has so far opened 44 shops in Spain (compared to over 330 in the UK), mainly along the south coast where foreigners live. For many – particularly women – Starbucks offers an attractive alternative to the smoky, loud, dirty cafés which have been the only choice until now. Zubinos' strategy would thus appear to be 'following the leader' in the same way it did in the UK. This should be a lower risk strategy than pioneering elsewhere.

4.5 Assess Zubinos' organisational structure

As most firms grow they move through a series of structures from entrepreneurial to functional to divisional to matrix.

Zubinos started as entrepreneurial and currently has a predominantly functional structure:

- Directors are in charge of functional aspects such as marketing, HR, procurement, etc.

However, there are a number of ambiguities:

- Val Pline and Sally Higgins are area managers who supervise shop managers. In particular they are responsible for recruiting and managing all staff in their coffee shops, presumably meaning that they report to Anita Wiseman (HR) on such issues. However, their bonuses are linked to revenue and margins, so presumably they are held responsible for encouraging shop managers in these respects. If so, then they must report to George Shale (FD) as well.

Does this suggest more of a matrix structure or a poorly defined one?

- Shop managers run different shops but their authority is unclear regarding menu design and ordering. What they are definitely not doing well is forecasting stock levels.
- Jack Rayfield's role is also unclear as it includes HR issues such as recruitment. He seems to be doing Anita's job at times.

A clearer structure with much better defined responsibilities is vital to facilitate growth. A matrix would be sensible as it allows a geographic emphasis (within UK, Europe, etc) and a functional one.

Another aspect of structure that needs changing is the lack of segregation between the roles of chairman and chief executive, currently both performed by Luis.

4.6 Assess Zubinos' information and reporting systems

Zubinos seems to analyse new locations in detail, so the information obtained here should be fairly comprehensive.

The current system of forecasting is weak:

- Shop managers email figures to head office.
- Sales figures are usually underestimated.

Potential improvements outlined:

- George Shale wants a new database forecasting system – so far rejected on cost grounds.
- George wants shop managers to be more involved in sales and profit forecasting – but Luis feels that shop managers do not have time to do much more than they currently do.
- A new IT system to capture sales and product analysis data at source has been commissioned.

Comments

- Luis seems to undervalue information systems, particularly regarding forecasting.
- A better system is essential for predicted growth.
- It is surprising that KPE has not demanded better information systems. It may start to do so.
- There is no indication of the detailed KPIs Zubinos sets, how they are monitored (e.g. variance analysis) and what follow-up procedures are in place. Do not assume that they are not happening!

5 Précis of case study

Zubinos is a small unquoted company operating 18 coffee shops in the UK – 10 in and 8 outside of London.

5.1 The industry

The UK coffee shop industry has been characterised to date by the following:

- High growth – fourfold growth in the number of shops over the last five years.
- Overall turnover exceeding £1 billion per annum.
- Intense competition – major operators (Starbucks, Caffé Nero, Costa Coffee, etc) and many smaller ones.
- Critical success factors are location, quality of coffee and shop ambience/comfort. Food may become increasingly important as a differentiator.
- London may be approaching saturation but opportunities still exist in the 'provinces'.
- The market is forecast to grow by a compound annual rate of 4.1% in size and 8.9% in terms of number of outlets over the next three years to reach £1.4 billion in turnover and 3,427 outlets by December 2008.

5.2 Zubinos' approach

- Detailed research of suitable locations.
- Premises usually rented, though two were bought in 2005 at a cost of over £1 million each.
- Employs more staff than is absolutely necessary to reduce waiting times, though this does affect margins.
- Sells freshly made sandwiches and other foods.
- Sells specialised Italian ice cream.
- 80% of produce is from Fair Trade suppliers.

5.3 Key financials

- High growth.
- Healthy balance sheet.
- £13.9 million revenue in 2005 (up 75%).
- £1,267,000 operating profit in 2005 (up 72%).
- Operating margin down from 9.26% to 9.10%.
- Best gross margins on coffee (80%) and ice cream (80%). Worst margins on other drinks (52%) and other foods (42%).
- Shares valued at £6 in January 2005, giving P/E ratios of 11.8 (historical) or 6.8 (forward looking). This would suggest a current market value of between £10.6 and £10.9 million.

5.4 Financing

- Mainly retained profits and equity from staff in the early years.
- Variety of bank loans – one for £100,000 taken out in 2004 was purely to alleviate cash flow problems. Need to repay from 2006 onwards.
- KPE invested £2.4 million equity (40% stake) and £300,000 loan in January 2005.
- KPE willing to invest up to £5 million loan finance over the next four years.
- Low financial gearing.
- No dividends paid to date.

5.5 Current operational problems

- Role ambiguity e.g. duplication of orders, HR issues.
- Staff discontent over bonuses.
- Problems implementing standard menu.
- Slow start up of delivery service.
- Forecasting and information systems.
- Some thefts by staff.

5.6 Current plans / initiatives

- Major expansion – to have 50 shops in the UK and 25 in Europe by 2010.
- Luis wants a greater emphasis on Fair Trade products, even though they are more expensive.
- Website has been updated – better brand awareness, chat room, online sales.
- Luis is keen on shop within shop outlets – none sourced yet.
- Jane Thorp wants computers available in shops for customers to access the internet.
- Jane Thorp and Maria Todd are investigating new food ranges.
- One shop manager wanted to introduce healthier foods but this was rejected as it was not part of the standard menu.

5.7 Other

- Good mix of experience, initiative and expertise on the (relatively young) board.

chapter

9

ZUBINOS: MARCH 2006 – TAKING THE EXAM

Contents

1 Introduction

On the day of the exam the material is presented in two parts:

- the question requirement
- further detailed information on the firm.

2 Exam question requirement

'You are the consultant appointed by the Zubinos Board.

Prepare a report that prioritises and discusses the issues facing Zubinos and makes appropriate recommendations.'

Note: This general requirement has been used for the last four sittings.

3 Unseen material

Zubinos coffee shops – Unseen material provided on examination day

Read this information before you answer the question

Bad publicity for Zubinos

There have been several adverse national newspaper reports, as well as a national TV consumer programme, reporting that several of Zubinos' healthy food options are not what they seem. It has been reported that some of these foods, which have a low calorie count and are low in fat, contain high levels of salt, sugar and some additives which have had bad press over possible health concerns. Additionally, the calorie count on some foods sold at Zubinos has been shown incorrectly on its food label. The press has carried various reports from Zubinos' public relations (PR) company stating that 'the adverse comments about Zubinos' healthy foods are mainly incorrect and minor problems have been vastly over-stated'. Luis Zubino is also concerned that one of Zubinos' competitors could be trying to counter the success of Zubinos, by spreading incorrect rumours.

Zubinos outsources its quality control to a leading food agency, QAIF, which has an excellent reputation. This agency also advises Zubinos' suppliers on the food labelling requirements and assists them with labelling when Zubinos procures food items for the first time.

The UK's Food Standards Organisation (FSO), which is responsible for all foods sold in the UK, is currently sampling a number of Zubinos food items following the recent bad press.

The FSO has recently visited several Zubinos coffee shops and identified that there were several items being sold that did not have any food labels on and other food items that had incorrect or misleading data for ingredients and calorific values. Luis Zubino spoke very harshly to Maria Todd about these problems.

Maria Todd has been working very long hours and has been struggling to identify new suppliers for the planned shop openings in 2006, and was very upset by the way Luis Zubino reprimanded her over the food labelling problems. She feels that she can no longer cope with her growing role and is considering resigning.

A further embarrassing event for Zubinos occurred in early February 2006. Jane Thorp had approved each of the adverts in a routine advertising campaign promoting Zubinos. One of the adverts had stated, 'All coffee sold in Zubinos is Fair Trade coffee'. However, a former Zubinos Head Office employee, who had been dismissed for theft, recently stated in the national press that only around 60% of Zubinos coffee was procured from Fair Trade suppliers. Even though the ex-employee's claim was not totally correct, as Zubinos use around 82% of Fair Trade coffee, the press picked up on the story. The employee also claimed that he was wrongly dismissed. His story had led to much negative publicity for Zubinos. The Advertising Standards body has investigated the false claim in Zubinos' adverts and Zubinos has had to admit that the claim that all of its coffee was Fair Trade coffee was incorrect. However, the damage has been done and in February 2006, sales across all Zubinos shops were down by around 7%.

Offer to operate Zubinos coffee shops in Jibbs stores

Jibbs plc (Jibbs) is a listed company, which operates 140 do-it-yourself (DIY) retail stores in the UK and around Europe. Most of Jibbs stores in the UK are located on large out-of-town retail parks. For a number of reasons, Jibbs has seen its revenue and its EPS decline slightly over the last few years. The Jibbs Board has decided on a number of innovative ways to try to stop the decline in its business and improve the outlook for the future. This has included selling some of its smaller stores, and it also has plans for a major refit of its stores, which will be followed by advertising campaigns. Jibbs is trying to make its stores more appealing to its customers. The Jibbs Board has also decided to rent out space in its stores to a small number of other retailers and it has approached Zubinos with a proposal to open Zubinos coffee shops in some of its stores.

Jibb's Marketing Director, Jenny Wright, has put the following proposal to Zubinos, inviting it to open Zubinos coffee shops in a minimum of 20 stores, over the next six months. The proposal is to open Zubinos coffee shops for a two-year trial period, at a fixed rental fee of £50,000 per store per year. Zubinos' average rental costs are over £100,000 per annum, but the rental space on offer in Jibbs' store is about 30% smaller than most of the existing Zubinos coffee shops, which would preclude Zubinos from offering its full range of foods and drinks.

At the end of the two-year trial period, Jibbs will decide whether to invite Zubinos to open more coffee shops in its other stores. However, Jibbs reserves the right to decline to renew the rental agreement, which would result in Zubinos having to remove all of its equipment and fixtures and fittings. It was also agreed that the rental cost would not be increased by more than the rate of inflation after the two-year trial, assuming that the trial were successful. Jibbs would not take any share of revenues, but would only charge for rent. All other costs, such as water charges and electricity, would be separately billed directly to Zubinos.

The forecast capital expenditure would be lower than currently spent on new Zubinos shops, and is forecast to be £180,000 per Jibbs store. The forecast market value of fittings at the end of the two-year trial is £90,000 per Jibbs store.

Jane Thorp has prepared the following post-tax cash flow forecast, based on 20 Zubinos coffee shops. These figures exclude capital expenditure.

Based on a total of 20 Zubinos coffee shops in Jibbs' stores	**Year 1**	**Year 2**
	£000	£000
Post-tax operating cash flows	1,250	1,500

Note: These post-tax operating cash flows include the rental fees of £50,000 per store per year.

George Shale considers a suitable risk adjusted cost of capital, for this particular proposed project, to be 14% post-tax. Jack Rayfield considers that the proposed expansion into Jibbs' stores is an easy way for Zubinos to expand its number of outlets, and could save management time that is currently spent on locating and negotiating rental agreements for High Street rented premises. Also the cost of the rent is lower. Luis Zubinos has expressed his doubts as to the validity of the cash flow forecasts prepared by Jane Thorp, which are based on throughput data provided by Jibbs.

Recent events

New HR Director

In December 2005, Anita Wiseman, Zubinos' HR Director resigned and left Zubinos at the end of January 2006. She had been with the company for only a little over one year. She resigned following a series of disagreements with Luis Zubino and her frustrations with developing a workable HR policy for the company. Also, she found the overlap with the roles of the Area Managers to be conflicting with her overall HR responsibilities. She has not yet disposed of her shares in Zubinos, but only other Directors have a right to buy the shares from her, at a negotiated price. Until she has sold her shares in Zubinos, she has voting rights.

Zubinos has recruited a new HR Director, Kingsley Nu, who joined Zubinos in the middle of February 2006, but he has not yet bought any shares in Zubinos. Kingsley Nu immediately met with all of the coffee shop managers in the London area and is due to meet the remaining shop managers in March 2006. Kingsley Nu is impressed by the loyalty and hard work put in by almost all employees, which in most cases is far in excess of their job contracts.

He proposes that a company share ownership scheme is launched and that a monthly reward scheme for outstanding customer service is commenced. He considers that the working environment, the lack of rest periods and the poor facilities for staff should be improved immediately. He has presented Luis Zubino with a draft of some of his proposals, in advance of preparing a paper for the April 2006 Zubinos Board meeting. The proposals include the recruitment of additional staff (to reduce the hours worked by existing staff, many of which are unpaid hours worked in addition to their contracted hours). He also wants to improve staff facilities. The forecast annual cost of the proposals presented is estimated by Kingsley Nu to be around £300,000 per year, at current staffing levels. Luis Zubino's immediate reaction was that some of the proposals are a luxury that a small company like Zubinos simply cannot afford. He also considers this cost to be similar to the amount required to open a further Zubinos coffee shop, and he does not want to spend finance on staff issues which could slow down the expansion programme.

Zubinos loyalty card

Following Zubinos Board approval in January 2006, Jane Thorp is planning to shortly launch a Zubinos loyalty card. This scheme will award customers points each time they spend money at Zubinos shops and present their loyalty card to the cashier. When a regular customer has saved enough points they can be redeemed against purchases. This scheme is forecast to cost Zubinos 2% of its revenues for those customers who regularly use their loyalty card. It is expected that less than 50% of Zubinos' revenue will be generated by customers with a loyalty card.

Expansion into Europe

With the successful opening of three new Zubinos shops in cities around the UK in January and February 2006, Luis Zubino is enthusiastic about opening the first Zubinos coffee shop in Europe. One of Luis Zubino's contacts has located a prime city centre site in a European city and wants to operate the shop for Zubinos. The rental agreement for this shop is currently being negotiated. The first European Zubinos coffee shop opening has been brought forward and is now forecast to open in July 2006, which is an advance of its current five-year plan.

Proposed acquisition of Zubinos

The Whistle Coffee Bar (WCB) has 180 coffee shops in the UK and 140 in Europe and is trading profitably with a P/E ratio of 18. It is listed in the UK and has a current share price of £16.80.

WCB's Business Development Director for the UK, Matt Jenkins, has contacted Luis Zubino and requested a meeting. At first, Luis Zubino thought that WCB wanted to meet to discuss the site selection for new Zubinos coffee shops. Zubinos has been successful in obtaining rented sites for the most recent three Zubinos coffee shops, despite having to outbid WCB for the locations that they were also trying to secure. This has resulted in Zubinos getting the required rental location, albeit at a slightly higher rent than was originally forecast.

Luis Zubino, George Shale and Carl Martin attended the meeting with WCB, which was held at the end of February 2006. Matt Jenkins of WCB stated that they have followed the successful expansion of Zubinos with interest and that they would like to acquire Zubinos for a cash price of £15.00 per Zubinos share. Additionally, WCB stated that it would be willing to offer senior management positions in WCB (but not WCB Board positions) to many of the Zubinos management team. Matt Jenkins made a very attractive offer of a senior finance position to George Shale, if the takeover of Zubinos is successful.

Carl Martin of KPE considers this could be a possible exit route for KPE, and has taken the acquisition proposal back to his superiors at KPE.

Luis Zubino is adamant that he does not wish to sell his shares to WCB and wants to prepare a sound case to KPE to convince it (and other Zubinos shareholders) not to sell its shares to WCB either. He stated to Carl Martin of KPE that he considered that WCB had only contacted them as Zubinos had become more successful in some city suburbs and other towns than the local WCB coffee shops.

Forecast cash flows

The forecast post-tax cash flows for the next five years, based on the agreed current five-year plan, given in Appendix 3 to the pre-seen material, is as follows:

Approved five-year plan cash flows	**2006**	**2007**	**2008**	**2009**	**2010**
	£000	£000	£000	£000	£000
Operating post-tax cash flows	2,500	4,100	6,200	8,900	11,700

Note: These operating post-tax cash flows are cash generated from operations and do NOT include capital expenditure on new coffee shops and also do NOT include loan repayments.

Similar businesses to Zubinos, which are listed, have a P/E ratio of around 16. George Shale considers Zubinos' overall cost of capital, to be 12%, post-tax.

Following the meeting with WCB, George Shale and Luis Zubino met and discussed how the five-year plan could be improved. Following their discussion, George Shale has prepared a draft of a new five-year plan which Luis Zubino has now discussed with other shareholders, including Carl Martin at KPE. The updated five-year plan includes a higher growth rate in sales than in the original plan and higher gross margins, based on Zubinos' possible ability to negotiate further cost reductions from suppliers because of its increased level of purchasing. This revised plan also has a slightly higher growth of new Zubinos coffee shops, with a total of 80, instead of 75, by 2010.

However, the cost reductions factored into this forecast are rather optimistic as George Shale is aware that coffee prices are due to increase over the next year. Furthermore, George Shale is aware that Zubinos is likely to have an adverse currency exposure in 2006, due to changes in exchange rates, which have not been included in this updated forecast.

The post-tax cash flows generated by this updated forecast are shown below:

Updated five-year plan cash flows	**2006**	**2007**	**2008**	**2009**	**2010**
	£000	£000	£000	£000	£000
Post-tax cash flows	2,900	5,100	7,400	11,400	14,700

Appointment of a consultant

At the Zubinos Board meeting in early March 2006, it was agreed that a consultant would be appointed to prepare a report, which prioritises and discusses the issues facing Zubinos and makes appropriate recommendations.

4 Exam process

4.1 Reading time (20 minutes)

In the TOPCIMA exam you have 3 hours to answer the case plus 20 minutes' reading time. During the reading time you are not allowed to start writing your answer but you are allowed to annotate the question paper.

During the 20 minutes' reading time one approach would be to read through the (previously) unseen material and highlight the following:

- Matters to update your SWOT analysis, for example by highlighting and writing S, W, O or T in the margin.
- Possible issues to discuss to add to those you have brought forward from the pre-seen. In recent cases the headings used in the unseen material have generally been key issues.
- Possible ethical conflicts.

You could also be thinking about possible calculations highlighting key figures to use and which strategic tools you could incorporate.

Zubinos

In Zubinos your 20 minutes could have derived the following:

New SWOT issues

- Bad publicity re how healthy foods are (T)
- Poor control over food labelling (W)

- Staffing problems – Maria Todd considering resigning (W)
- Adverse publicity re Fair Trade claim – sales down 7% (T)
- Being sued for unfair dismissal (T)
- Plan to open shops within Jibb's stores (O)
- Anita Wiseman's resignation could indicate problems with how Luis manages his managers (W)
- Poor staff working conditions highlighted by Kingsley's plans (W)
- Luis's low regard for staffing issues (W)
- Loyalty card (O)
- European expansion (O)
- Proposed acquisition by WCB (O or T?)
- Revised plans indicate better margins and growth than before (S)

Ethical issues

- Fair Trade
- Misinforming customers – labelling and adverts
- Treatment of staff
- Conflict of interests for directors with respect to the bid from WCB

Possible calculations (not all of them – be selective which you eventually do!)

- NPV for Jibb's proposal – given discount rate of 12%
- Compare new plans with old for cash flow
- Funding implications of new plans
- Cost of loyalty card
- Valuation of Zubinos for proposed acquisition (P/Es – WCB 18, other similar companies 16)
- Evaluation of revised forecasts – are they realistic?

Strategic tools

- SWOT (always!)
- Porter's generic strategies model to discuss competitive advantage
- Ansoff to discuss growth options

4.2 Further planning time (20 minutes)

Once you are allowed to start writing your answer it is recommended that you spend a further 20 minutes planning and thinking (making 40 minutes in total).

Partly this will be spent finishing off the planning already started but, in addition, you should now focus on identifying the key issues to discuss and prioritising them. This will then allow you to structure your report and do detailed planning for each of the main issues.

A critical skill in TOPCIMA is identifying the key issues. These are usually signposted clearly in the unseen material by the use of headings.

One approach to doing this is to use a planning table with columns for

- key issues brought forward from the pre-seen material
- new issues from the unseen material
- key issues for the report.

Zubinos

For Zubinos this could look something like the following:

Key issues from pre-seen	New issues / facts	Key issues for report?
Intense competitive rivalry		
Falling margins	Revised forecasts indicate higher margins	
Expansion outside London	Jibb's shop within shop opportunity	**3** due to urgency and could be a way of dealing with rivalry
	European expansion brought forward	**4** as way of expanding where rivalry is less intense
HR problems	• Managers resigning or thinking of resigning • Poor working conditions	**5** as could undermine competitive strategy
Established competitive strategy of differentiation	Bad publicity re health aspects of food and labelling	**2** due to potential to undermine competitive advantage
Greater awareness of Fair Trade issues	Bad publicity re Fair Trade issues	

Role ambiguity		
	Being sued by former employee	
	Potential acquisition by WCB	**1** due to urgency and impact
	Loyalty card	

Notes:

- We have attempted to line up new information with issues brought forward. In some cases this is not possible – for example, intense competitive rivalry is a major issue in the coffee shop industry but does not align easily with the new information as it could relate to all of them!
- Some issues have been combined e.g. food labelling and Fair Trade are now both concerned with responding to bad publicity and competitive advantage.
- Other prioritisations are possible but the bid from WCB should feature in your top two due to the urgency of a response needed and its potential impact on the firm.

When structuring the report you have a choice whether to use issues from the pre-seen or those from the unseen material. Continuing the above discussion the heading 'dealing with intense competitive rivalry' would be very appropriate but it is better to let the unseen material drive the structure. Thus competitive rivalry could be the basis of an argument when discussing bad publicity, say, to emphasis why the bad publicity is so potentially damaging.

For each of the major issues you could then plan key arguments, bringing in real-world factors and technical knowledge.

For example, for the European expansion you might identify the following as issues:

- Rivalry – less intense? Existing competition
- Growth opportunities v saturated UK
- Control
- Forex risk
- Financing implications
- Consistent with plans of real-life firms such as Starbucks.

4.3 Calculations (20 – 30 minutes)

Depending on the case you should allocate between 20 and 30 minutes to performing calculations. The examiner has indicated that a maximum of 10 marks will be available for these, thus suggesting spending around 20 minutes. However, the discussion implications of some calculations are so important that it may be worth spending longer to get an answer to discuss.

Note that feedback from examiners indicates that valuations and other key calculations are often done very badly.

Calculations should be labelled up as appendices.

4.4 Writing (100 – 110 minutes)

You should now start to write up your report. To start with you should complete the following:

- Title page
- Contents page
- Introduction
- Terms of reference, including disclaimers
- Appendix 1: SWOT – ensuring each of your key issues is in it! (if not completed already)
- Other appendices using other selected strategic planning tools (if not completed already).

You can then write up the section prioritising key issues and then the main analysis.

4.5 Finishing it off (30 minutes)

Allow 30 minutes to write up your recommendations, pulling together your main arguments and making it very clear what action the client should take. Weaker scripts are always let down by rushed recommendations and thus appear unfinished. In some respects the recommendations section should be the high point of the report, not half a page of scribbled lines at the end.

Then conclude.

chapter

10

ZUBINOS: MARCH 2006 – SAMPLE SOLUTION

Contents

1 Introduction

What follows is a sample script for the Zubinos March 2006 exam. It does not purport to be a perfect answer and, as the discussion below reveals, has a number of deliberate flaws. As you read through it, ask yourself what you consider to be its main strengths and weaknesses.

2 Sample script

REPORT (CONFIDENTIAL)

To: The Board of directors, Zubinos Coffee Shops

From: A Consultant

Date: Today

Zubinos Coffee Shops: Current problems and future strategies

Contents

Appendices

1 Introduction

Zubinos operates in an intensely competitive industry. It is thus vital that the firm protects its competitive advantage and finds expansion opportunities in less competitive markets.

2 Terms of reference

This report has been prepared by a consultant, at the request of the Board of Directors of Zubinos Coffee Shops ('Zubinos'). It looks at how Zubinos should respond to recent problems and evaluates future expansion options.

3 Prioritisation of issues

A detailed SWOT analysis of Zubinos is shown in Appendix 1. Out of these the key points are as follows:

3.1 Priority No.1: The proposed acquisition of Zubinos by the Whistle Coffee Bar (WCB)

The Whistle Coffee Bar (WCB), a large listed competitor for Zubinos, has offered to acquire Zubinos at a price of £15 per share. Initial reactions are mixed but WCB may be successful in achieving the 51% of acceptances it needs. The directors of Zubinos thus need to formulate a response to this proposal.

This is the most important issue facing Zubinos as the proposal (if accepted) could lead to the ultimate disposal of the company. This in many ways would be the end of Zubinos as none of the directors would hold main boardroom positions with WCB. Even the brand name might disappear.

Given that shareholders are also directors (or have board representation), there we also important ethical issues regarding potential conflict of interest to resolve.

This issue is discussed in more detail in section 4 of this report.

3.2 Priority No.2: Recent bad publicity

Zubinos has recently experienced bad publicity concerning the healthiness of food sold, poor food labelling and (a perceived misrepresentation of) the amount of Fair Trade coffee used. The Board needs to formulate a response to this bad publicity.

Given that Zubinos' competitive advantage has been based on the quality of the Zubinos coffee, high quality Italian ice cream, shorter waiting times than competitors and an emphasis on Fair Trade, the bad publicity has great potential to undermine Zubinos' reputation and competitive advantage. This issue is thus prioritised second on the basis of immediacy and the scope of potential to damage the firm.

This issue is discussed in more detail in section 5 of this report.

3.3 Priority No.3: The offer to operate Zubinos shops within Jibbs' stores

Jibbs' Marketing Director, Jenny Wright, has proposed a two-year trial for Zubinos to operate coffee shops within Jibbs' stores around the country. The Board needs to make a decision whether to accept this proposal.

This issue is prioritised third on the grounds of scale, as forecast post-tax operating cash flows look to exceed £1 million each year, and strategic fit, as Zubinos is looking for lower risk growth areas.

This issue is discussed in more detail in section 6 of this report.

3.4 Priority No.4: Expansion into continental Europe

Luis Zubinos has suggested bringing forward existing expansion plans into continental Europe. This is an issue as the proposal could have serious resourcing implications. The decisions that the Board needs to make are thus whether to expand into Europe and, if so, when.

This issue is prioritised fourth on the basis that overseas expansion could be key to continuing Zubinos' high growth to date, given the saturation of the UK market.

This issue is discussed in more detail in section 7 of this report.

3.5 Priority No.5: Human resource problems

Human resource problems have come to light regarding working hours, staff responsibilities and Anita Wiseman's resignation. These all have the scope to reduce staff motivation and undermine Zubinos' competitive advantage. Management thus needs to formulate a response to these issues.

This issue is thus prioritised fifth on the basis that existing high growth plans could be compromised by low staff morale.

This issue is discussed in more detail in section 8 of this report.

4 Proposed acquisition of Zubinos by WCB

The offer to purchase Zubinos by WCB must be responded to quickly as the proposal could result in a split at boardroom level that in turn could lead to the disposal of the company.

There are some important ethical issues to clarify first before looking at the merits of the proposal.

Ethical conflicts

All shareholders have the right to vote whether to accept or reject the offer based on their own personal positions. However, given that many shareholders are also directors, they should make their decisions based on the interests of all shareholders. Their positions as directors should take priority. Any attempt to put the interests of one shareholder above the others is unethical and should be resisted.

The offer of senior management positions by WCB could be seen as shrewd business practice to keep the best directors, in line with Peter Drucker's key recommendations on successful takeovers. Alternatively they could be viewed as unethical bribes to influence the directors' decisions.

Again it is vital that each director is clear that they are voting for the best option for the wider shareholder interest, based on the commercial merits of the proposal.

Likely shareholder reaction

The likely responses to the offer are as follows (shareholdings given in brackets):

- Luis Zubino (30%) has already expressed his opposition to the bid. It is likely that Vivien Zubino (12%) will concur.
- KPE (40%) is said to be considering the deal but will be very tempted by an offer of £15 per share when it only paid £6 in January 2005. This would give an overall return of 150% in under 18 months and a simple, quick exit route.

The reaction of other shareholders/directors will depend on whether they feel that the proposal benefits shareholders / themselves, but it is not difficult to imagine a scenario with a very close vote.

A key person in this is Anita Wiseman. Although she has resigned she has not yet sold her shares. We are aware that George Shale has been made a very attractive offer and this may well influence his decision. If he were to vote along with KPE, they would have a 49% interest. Anita Wiseman's voting rights would turn this into a majority. This fact could make her shares very valuable.

The commercial merits of the deal

The key issue when deciding whether to accept the proposal is the offered share price. If the price is high enough then shareholders should be advised to sell. (Note that supporting calculations to the prices quoted below can be found in Appendix 4.)

- Using WCB's P/E ratio of 18 gives a share price for Zubinos of £16.15, whereas using the P/E of similar quoted companies (16) gives a share price of £14.35. This would suggest that the price of £15 offered by WCB is a fair price from their perspective and that they may be reluctant to raise their offer much more.

Whether to recommend acceptance thus depends on how the board views the future prospects of Zubinos. If past high growth can be continued, then the offer of £15 per share is too low but, if recent events have put a serious question mark over future plans, then the offer affords a good exit route for shareholders.

5 Dealing with recent bad publicity

Assessing the significance of recent bad publicity

To date the UK coffee shop industry has been characterised by high growth and intense competitive rivalry. Critical success factors have been identified as:

- convenience of location
- quality of coffee offered
- shop ambience / comfort.

Other important trends are as follows:

- food appears to be an increasingly important differentiator
- customers are becoming more health conscious
- Fair Trade issues are becoming increasingly important to customers.

Within this context it is clear that recent publicity will not affect the shops' location or ambience, so many customers will not change their loyalties. However, it will undermine the perceived quality of coffee and food offered at a time when these factors are becoming more important. It is thus vital that further steps are taken to counter the problem. By February 2006 sales were already down 7%.

Possible courses of action

To counter the problems described above, Zubinos should consider the following:

Improved control systems for food and labelling

Investigations must be carried out to see why some of the food sampled by the FSO had misleading labels and whether or not any of the dubious labels had been quality checked by QAIF.

If not, then Zubinos should put in place systems to ensure that all product lines are approved nationally as part of standardised menus and then checked by QAIF. This will involve the following:

- Better staff training, so all employees understand the importance of standardised menus.
- Stiffer penalties for staff who flout the rules.
- Regular spot checks to be carried out on shops to ensure no unauthorised products are being sold.

These systems should be put in place immediately and the FSO should be asked to test Zubinos' products again once the new systems are operational.

Further publicity refuting allegations

While press releases so far have helped, more is needed to convince customers. Rather than downplaying allegations, it may be more effective to admit that mistakes have been made but to reassure customers that they have been dealt with, possibly referring to QAIF and the FSO.

Ethical choices

At present Zubinos sells around 82% Fair Trade coffee. Of course it is cheaper to buy coffee that is not Fair Trade, but the reason it is cheaper is, generally, because the farmers who grow the crop get paid less. The key aim of Fair Trade is to ensure farmers get a fairer price for their produce to improve their quality of life. The decision is not just a financial one – it is an ethical one too. Recent events could be used as a springboard to switch to 100% Fair Trade coffee and then publicised accordingly.

Similarly it is common for food to be advertised to highlight its positive aspects (e.g. low fat) but avoid mentioning the negative aspects (e.g. high salt). Zubinos could take an ethical lead here by adopting more complete disclosure on its labelling. Rather than discouraging customers this could improve Zubinos' image of honesty and fairness.

6 Evaluation of the Jibbs' proposal

Jibbs has proposed a two-year trial where Zubinos would pay Jibbs a fixed rental fee of £50,000 per shop per annum to operate coffee shops within Jibbs DIY stores around the country.

This would be classified as a market penetration strategy within Ansoff's matrix. The main arguments for and against are as follows:

Arguments for the trial

- The main financial argument for accepting the trial is that the trial period has a positive net present value of £390,000 at a discount rate of 14% so should increase shareholder wealth by this amount. Details of this calculation are given in Appendix 3.
- The main strategic argument in favour is that it affords Zubinos a quick vehicle for expansion into areas with lower competition than town and city high streets.
- The nature of the proposal is a trial, giving Zubinos a relatively straightforward exit route after two years if the plan proves unprofitable, thus reducing longer term downside risk exposure.
- The rental fee proposed by Jibbs is around half the typical amount paid by Zubinos for 70% of the typical floor space. Consequently the rent per square metre is lower than usually paid.
- Zubinos can benefit from the customers who currently frequent the DIY stores.
- The sites are situated in large out-of-town retail parks, where there is often little competition from other coffee outlets. The shops may even encourage shoppers to visit the DIY stores just to have a drink.

Arguments against the trial

- An initial outlay of £3.6 million is required at a time when the rest of Zubinos is already forecast to generate a cash shortage for 2006 of £437,000 under revised plans (see Appendix 2 for details of these calculations). KPE has indicated that it is willing to loan a further £5 million over five years.
- Jibbs can terminate the agreement at the end of the trial with no recourse for Zubinos. This is particularly worrying as Jibbs could wait to see if the outlets are a success and then offer the sites at a much higher rental to a competitor.
- The size of locations precludes Zubinos from offering its full range of food and drink. However, Zubinos highest margins are for coffee (80%) and ice creams (80%), so a lack of space could be a good reason for not stocking some lower margin food lines, while ensuring a reasonable choice for customers.

7 Expansion into continental Europe

The proposed expansion into continental Europe is a market development strategy within Ansoff's classification.

The main arguments surrounding such expansion are as follows:

Arguments for expansion into Europe

- High growth potential when the UK market is becoming saturated. Despite the opening of shops by competitors, there should still be plenty of room for new coffee shops.
- A prime city-centre location should ensure suitable (i.e. young, affluent) potential customers.
- Many competitors (e.g. Starbucks) have aggressive expansion plans in Europe. Zubinos needs to expand quickly to exploit opportunities before the markets become as saturated as in the UK.

Arguments against expansion into Europe

- Depending on the country concerned, there may be significant competition from traditional cafés and bars.
- Major competitors may already have Zubinos-style outlets in the city concerned, so it vital that local competition is analysed before making a commitment.
- It will harder to manage and control the outlets from the UK.
- Zubinos would be exposed to exchange rate risk on profits in Euros.
- Increasing finance requirements in 2006, when a shortfall of around £437 thousand is already predicted (see Appendix 2).

8 Human resource problems

High growth often results in problems in working capital, control systems and human resources. In the case of Zubinos it is human resources management that is the more pressing issue.

Current problems

While most employees are generally hard-working and loyal, there are problems to address, including the following:

- Anita Wiseman resigned because she felt a lack of Board support in developing an HR plan.
- Many employees are working longer hours than required by their contracts and frequently not taking rest breaks. While such 'free labour' may be seen as advantageous, it may result in staff becoming demotivated in the longer term and leaving. It is also unethical to mistreat staff and the media could certainly interpret current practices in that light to create more bad publicity.
- Responsibilities are unclear with overlaps causing conflicts – for example, between shop managers and Maria Todd over procurement. This ambiguity was partly responsible for the problems encountered with food labelling.

Possible solutions

To improve staff motivation the following options are available:

- a new share ownership scheme for shop managers
- monthly reward schemes for all staff based on local shop profitability
- the firm's policy regarding rest periods could be clarified and shop managers instructed to encourage their staff to take the breaks they are (then) entitled to.

The issue whether or not to recruit more staff is a more complex one. Zubinos has traditionally employed more staff than rivals to improve the customer experience, albeit at the expense of lower margins. A benchmarking exercise between Zubinos and its competitors should be carried out to see if Zubinos' staffing levels are still higher. If not, then the argument for recruitment is stronger. If yes, then it is difficult to justify increasing staff levels yet further.

A change in the perspective of management is also needed. Rather than seeing HR issues as an unnecessary cost, they should be viewed as an essential resource underpinning future growth.

9 Recommendations

The proposed acquisition by WCB is a matter of some urgency to avoid management being distracted. The key issue for the board to discuss is whether the offer price is reasonable given Zubinos' growth prospects. It is our view that the current offer of £15 is attractive and should be seriously considered by the board.

Looking beyond the bid for Zubinos, the main problem facing the firm is intense competitive rivalry. The response to this should be twofold.

Firstly, Zubinos needs to protect and even enhance its competitive edge of differentiation. The key priority here involves addressing the recent bad publicity. With immediate effect, we recommend that tighter systems be introduced regarding the selection and display of food lines with accompanying publicity. Over the next year we also recommend that you consider increasing the emphasis on Fair Trade products and taking a lead with more disclosure on food labelling.

Secondly, Zubinos needs to find growth areas where rivalry is less intense. We thus concur with your existing plans to expand within the UK but outside London and would recommend that the shop-within-shop trial be undertaken, subject to the caveats discussed in section 6 above. However, we would recommend a more in-depth analysis of the overseas expansion plans, as discussed in section 7, before proceeding.

Human resource problems need to be resolved to facilitate future growth. None of the issues are very urgent but working conditions and role ambiguity need be addressed over the next year before they become critical.

10 Conclusion

In conclusion, the main issues facing Zubinos are dealing with competitive rivalry and managing growth. Once the publicity and HR issues are resolved, Zubinos should again have a platform for high future growth.

Appendix 1: Position analysis using SWOT framework

Strengths

- Established competitive strategy of differentiation based on quality coffee, more staff and Fair Trade coffee
- Strong balance sheet, profitable with high growth
- Directors have a good mix of relevant expertise and experience
- Performance-related pay, together with directors owning shares, should result in more motivated employees
- Cash rich business model (negative cash operating cycle)

Weaknesses

- Poor controls over food labelling
- Poor working conditions for staff
- Role ambiguity – especially in the areas of centralisation and standardisation
- Falling margins
- Not listed – making equity finance harder to raise
- Higher costs than competitors due to higher staff costs
- Small player in the UK so may lack the economies of scale of larger rivals
- May be trying to grow too quickly – in particular Zubinos may not have the control systems in place to manage the growth properly

Opportunities

- Shop within shop outlets e.g. Jibbs' proposal
- Overseas expansion
- Greater public awareness of FairTrade issues
- Opening more shops in the UK – especially outside London
- AIM listing
- Franchising is a popular means of expansion in practice. This is an option not yet considered

Threats

- Recent bad publicity
- Intense competitive rivalry that is increasing
- Coffee drinking is a luxury, what happens in recession? With a higher cost base Zubinos is not well positioned to survive a recession
- Decline in market growth / market saturation

Appendix 2: Analysis of revised business plans to examine financing needs.

Estimated cash flows based on revised business plan:

(£000s)	**2006**	**2007**	**2008**	**2009**	**2010**
Revised operating post-tax cash flows	2,900	5,100	7,400	11,400	14,700
Capex (Working 1)	(3,037)	(3,740)	(4,117)	(4,442)	(5,333)
Repayment of bank loans	(300)	(200)	-	(100)	(300)
Net cash flows	**(437)**	**1,160**	**3,283**	**6,858**	**9,067**

This would suggest that there is a funding gap of £437,000 in 2006 but that internally generated funds should be sufficient to finance subsequent growth.

Working 1: We have assumed that the five extra shop openings will be spread evenly – i.e. one extra each year – and have pro-rated the Capex estimates accordingly:

e.g. for 2006 estimate = 2700 × 9/8 = 3,037

Appendix 3: Evaluation of shop-within-shop opportunity

Net Present Value calculation for two-year trial

(£000s)	t = 0	t = 1	t = 2
Post-tax operating cash flows		1,250	1,500
Purchase of equipment (20 x 180)	(3,600)		
Disposal of equipment (20 x 90)			1,800
Tax re capital allowances (Working 1)		216	216
Net cash flow	**(3,600)**	**1,466**	**3,516**
DF @ 14% (given)	1	0.877	0.769
PV	(3,600)	1,286	2,704
NPV	**390**		

Working 1: Tax re capital allowances (assuming tax is paid at the year end, for simplicity)

	WDV	**Tax**	**Timing**
	(£000s)	@24%	
Initial cost	3,600		
EWDA @ 25% (assumption)	(900)	216	1
	2,700		
Balancing allowance	(900)	216	2
Disposal	1,800		

Appendix 4: Evaluation of share price offered by WCB.

WCB has offered a price of £15 per Zubinos share, valuing the company at £15 million.

To assess whether this is a fair price we have valued Zubinos using an earnings multiple approach as follows:

1 Using WCB's P/E ratio of 18

The value of Zubinos to WCB can be estimated using:

Market value = WCB's P/E ratio × Zubinos' earnings

= 18 × 897,000 (using Zubinos 2005 earnings)

= £16.15 million in total, or £16.15 per share

Applying the P/E ratio to 2006 projected earnings would give a higher figure.

Thus WCB would be looking at a gain of over £1 million, even before synergy is incorporated.

2 Using the P/E ratio of similar quoted companies

Similar quoted companies to Zubinos have a P/E ratio of 16.

Applying this to Zubinos' 2005 earnings of £897,000 gives a market value of:

Market value = 16 × 897,000

= £14.35 million in total, or £14.35 per share

This would suggest that the bid of £15 per share is reasonable.

3 Commentary

The main strengths of the sample script are as follows:

- Good structure.
- Well argued.
- Very good overall flow of argument and logic.
- Clear prioritisation of key issues.
- It addresses all (i.e. five here) of the major issues facing the firm and gives clear recommendations for each.
- The report feels finished in the sense that most managers would have been happy to send it to a client.
- Good writing style with no waffle.
- Calculations are correct and clearly explained.

The main weaknesses are as follows:

- The introduction is too brief.
- Not enough discussion of ethical considerations – it would have been better to have a separate section in the report for ethics, even though some of these are discussed in context.
- 'Other issues' have not been addressed anywhere, throwing away easy marks.
- The use of technical tools has not been made explicit enough – SWOT and some calculations are all we have in the appendices. Porter's generic strategies are referred to briefly but would be better in another appendix. Similarly for Ansoff's matrix. Again easy marks have been thrown away by not 'playing the game' and targeting the assessment matrix.
- Too many calculations – Appendix 3 calculating revised funding implications is probably over the top and time should have been spent doing more on ethics instead.
- Insufficient reference to the activities of real-world companies and market developments – Starbucks is mentioned briefly but there is little depth here.
- More could have been said on alternative courses of action and why they were dismissed.

In summary, the report looks more like one that would be sent out in practice rather than one designed to maximise the marks in the TOPCIMA exam!

chapter

11

DOMUSCO: PRE-SEEN MATERIAL

Scenario – Pre-seen material

This case study was the TOPCIMA case for the September and November 2005 examination papers. When analysing this material and answering the examination question for September 2005, you should assume that 'now' is late 2005.

Assessment Matrix for TOPCIMA – Domusco

Criterion	Marks*	Clear pass	Pass	Marginal pass	Marginal Fail	Fail	Clear fail
Technical	5	Thorough display of relevant technical knowledge. **5**	Good display of relevant knowledge. **4**	Some display of relevant technical knowledge. **3**	Identification of some relevant knowledge, but lacking in depth. **2**	Little knowledge displayed, or some misconceptions. **1**	No evidence of knowledge displayed, or fundamental misconceptions. **0**
Application	15	Knowledge clearly applied in an analytical and practical manner. **13-15**	Knowledge applied to the context of the case. **9-12**	Identification of some relevant knowledge, but not well applied.8 **8**	Knowledge occasionally displayed without clear application. **5-7**	Little attempt to apply knowledge to the context. **1-4**	No application of knowledge displayed. **0**
Diversity	5	Most knowledge areas identified, covering a wide range of views. **5**	Some knowledge areas identified, covering a range of views. **4**	A few knowledge areas identified, expressing a fairly limited scope. **3**	Several important knowledge aspects omitted. **2**	Many important knowledge aspects omitted. **1**	Very few knowledge aspects considered. **0**
Focus	10	Clearly distinguishes between relevant and irrelevant information. **9-10**	Information used is mostly relevant. **6-8**	Some relevant information ignored, or some less relevant information used. **5**	Information used is sometimes irrelevant. **3-4**	Little ability to distinguish between relevant and irrelevant information. **1-2**	No ability to distinguish between relevant and irrelevant information. **0**
Prioritisation	10	Issues clearly prioritised in a logical order and based on a clear rationale. **9-10**	Issues prioritised with justification. **6-8**	Evidence of issues being listed in order of importance, but rationale unclear. **5**	Issues apparently in priority order, but without a logical justification or rationale. **3-4**	Little attempt at prioritisation or justification or rationale. **1-2**	No attempt at prioritisation or justification. **0**
Judgement	15	Clearly recognises alternative solutions. Judgement exercised professionally. **13-15**	Alternative solutions or options considered. Some judgement exercised. **9-12**	A slightly limited range of solutions considered. Judgement occasionally weak. **8**	A limited range of solutions considered. Judgement sometimes weak. **5-7**	Few alternative solutions considered. Judgement often weak. **1-4**	No alternative solutions considered. Judgement weak or absent. **0**
Integration	10	Diverse areas of knowledge and skills integrated effectively. **9-10**	Diverse areas of knowledge and skills integrated. **6-8**	Knowledge areas and skills occasionally not integrated. **5**	Knowledge areas and skills sometimes not integrated. **3-4**	Knowledge areas and skills often not integrated. **1-2**	Knowledge areas and skills not integrated. **0**
Logic	20	Communication effective, recommendations realistic, concise and logical. **16-20**	Communication mainly clear and logical. Recommendations occasionally weak. **11-15**	Communication occasionally unclear, and/ or recommendations occasionally illogical. **10**	Communication sometimes weak. Some recommendations slightly unrealistic. **5-9**	Communication weak. Some unclear or illogical recommendations, or few recommendations. **1-4**	Very poor communication, and/or no recommendations offered. **0**
Ethics	10	Excellent evaluation of ethical aspects. Clear and appropriate advice offered. **9-10**	Good evaluation of ethical aspects. Some appropriate advice offered. **6-8**	Some evaluation of ethical aspects. Advice offered. **5**	Weak evaluation of ethical aspects. Little advice offered. **3-4**	Poor evaluation of ethical aspects. No advice offered. **1-2**	No evaluation of ethical aspects. Unethical, or no, advice offered. **0**
TOTAL	100	* **Note:** The number of available marks a llocated to each criterion will normally be as shown.					

DOMUSCO

Background

1 Domusco was formed 42 years ago, and became a listed company 30 years ago in its home country of Zee, a fictitious country in Southern Europe. Zee is not in the European Union (EU). The Domusco group structure comprises a number of wholly-owned subsidiary companies operating in different construction business segments. The three construction business segments that Domusco has are:

- major construction projects
- office building construction
- house building.

Domusco's group structure, together with its key personnel, are shown in Appendix 1.

2 Domusco's major construction project subsidiary company is structured around the type of project undertaken. The Domusco office building subsidiary company manages all office construction work from its Head Office based in Zee, for all office construction work in Zee, other areas of Europe and the Middle East. Domusco's house building subsidiary company is structured differently, as it has separate subsidiary companies for geographic areas. It has house building subsidiary companies based in Zee, and in another European country as well as a subsidiary in the USA, to enable management to be closer to the markets in which it operates.

3 The Domusco Group has been involved in residential house building since the company was formed. It entered the major construction projects segment over 30 years ago and then expanded into the office building construction segment 12 years ago. Domusco has established itself as a builder of high quality housing and apartments at the top and middle segment of the market. The Domusco group has been able to command premium prices, because of its good designs and quality specifications. Domusco has not been involved in any low cost or social housing projects to date.

4 Domusco has recently been awarded two contracts in a European country in which it has not previously operated. One is for the construction of a large office building. The other is for the construction of five blocks of high-rise apartments. Both projects commenced in early 2005 and are planned to last for three years. The latter project generated much international publicity, because of Domusco's innovative designs and high technology features that have been incorporated into each apartment.

The Board is hopeful that these latest contracts will lead to other contracts being awarded to Domusco.

Domusco personnel

The following directors are on the main Board of Domusco and their career histories and functional responsibilities follow:

5 *Tom Micol – Chairman*

Tom Micol, now 63, has been Chairman of Domusco for the past six years and previously was one of its non-executive directors. He is currently working part-time, following a recent spell of ill health. Tom Micol has worked in the construction industry all of his life and is proud of Domusco's recent expansion. He wants to see the company grow even stronger before he plans to retire in three years' time. Tom Micol is a close ally of Peter Kaye, and believes that Peter Kaye has brought in a huge amount of the new business since he joined.

6 *Will Umm – Chief Executive*

Will Umm, now 49, joined the company 14 years ago when the previous Chief Executive retired. Will Umm has seen the company's revenue grow at over 15% per annum for most of the last ten years. He has personally been the driving force behind many of the large construction projects that Domusco has been awarded over the last few years. He qualified as a civil engineer in Asia and has lived and worked in several countries.

Will Umm has good government connections and has always found time to deal with many personnel matters. He often visits sites and speaks to workers to hear what thoughts they have. He is considered to be fair in his business dealings and has been able to maintain Domusco's reputation as being scrupulously fair in its contract negotiations. He is very much in touch with his workforce and is well liked and respected by most of the Domusco Board as well. It is only the Finance Director, Martyn Lite, with whom he has not established a good rapport. This is primarily because Martyn Lite often argues that what Will Umm wants to do is not in the shareholders' interests. Martyn Lite often states that a project that appears to be profitable can be too risky, or that Domusco has taken on too much construction work and has insufficient management resources. On most occasions, Will Umm has overruled him and, although he respects Martyn Lite, he considers him to be too conservative.

7 *Martyn Lite – Finance Director*

Martyn Lite, now 52 years old, qualified as an accountant in his twenties while working for a major construction company in Europe. He moved to Zee and worked his way up in the finance department of a small construction company to become Finance Director. Within two years he transferred into a general management position, but decided that he missed the finance side of the role. He then reassessed his career and joined Domusco when its previous Finance Director retired in 1996.

He has now been with Domusco for over nine years and still has some challenging tasks ahead. He has been involved in much IT development and has tried to introduce the concept of shareholder value into Domusco. While the Domusco Board has accepted the principle, the ability to cascade down the identification of value on individual projects has been difficult. In the meantime, he has put more emphasis on growth in EPS and has had several boardroom clashes with the Chief Executive. He finds Will Umm too visionary with little understanding of financial matters. However, even Will Umm would admit that their joint skills have contributed towards the growth achieved over the last decade.

8 *Peter Kaye – Director of Major Construction Projects*

Peter Kaye, now 48, is an American citizen who joined Domusco five years ago when Domusco acquired a house building company in the USA, where he had held the role of Chief Executive. After successfully merging the US house building company into Domusco's group structure, he was appointed as Director of Major Construction Projects.

It is Peter Kaye's subsidiary company within the Domusco group that is responsible for contract negotiations for all of Domusco's major construction projects. These projects involve construction work that will be undertaken by the Major Construction Projects subsidiary company or by other subsidiary companies within the Domusco group. For example, if Domusco bids for a major construction project involving the construction of office buildings and motorway access, the relevant companies within the Domusco group are involved in costing and resource planning, but it is Peter Kaye's team which negotiates and signs contracts on behalf of Domusco. After contract signing, budgets will be allocated to the appropriate Domusco group companies and each company within the group will have operational authority for delivering to the agreed contract terms. Therefore, although Peter Kaye is bringing business into the company and negotiating delivery dates and pricing, it will be other areas of Domusco that will be responsible for delivery of the contracted construction work. There is much cross-company liaison and involvement in all major projects at an early stage, prior to signing of contracts.

Peter Kaye has worked for several international companies, but has only been involved in the construction industry for 16 years. He has helped Domusco to win several major construction projects in the last four years, some of which have been joint venture projects, and he has established a good reputation for bringing in business to Domusco. However, Peter Kaye has had many clashes with Martyn Lite. Martyn Lite finds Peter Kaye to be too outspoken, egotistic, and not very financially astute.

9 *Tan Lee – Director of Office Building Construction*

Tan Lee, now 54, joined Domusco over 20 years ago and has worked his way up in the company from structural surveyor. When the office building construction subsidiary company was formed 12 years ago, he was appointed as a main Board director responsible for this business segment that was new to Domusco. He is technically excellent and has good business and financial awareness. He usually supports Martyn Lite in any Board disagreements as he feels that the company has been expanding too fast in the last few years. He is a sound manager who has a proven track record of delivering the construction projects under his control on time and to budget. However, with the demands of international competition and the innovative features that Domusco now incorporates into its office buildings as standard, far exceeding legal requirements, margins have decreased from the levels achieved a decade ago.

10 *Marma Winge – Director of House Building*

Marma Winge, now aged 39, has progressed rapidly in his career with Domusco. He started as an architect and he has won awards for both innovative designs and the use of high technology to reduce energy consumption. His energy efficient house designs have been built extensively in Zee, as well as in many of the European countries into which Domusco has expanded. He was appointed as Director of House Building in 1997, and has overall responsibility for the three house building subsidiary companies (in Zee, other areas of Europe and the USA). He established a good working relationship with Peter Kaye during the acquisition of the USA-based house building company in 2000, and they have mutual respect for each other's abilities.

11 *Piers Moore – Director of Sales and Marketing*

Piers Moore, now aged 42, joined Domusco 12 years ago from a large international house building company where he had held the role of Sales Manager. He brought with him the mix of skills needed to complement Domusco's other directors' skills. He established a small corporate marketing department that supports the sales and marketing teams that are in place within each subsidiary company of Domusco.

In each of Domusco's subsidiary companies, the staff numbers in the sales and marketing departments vary greatly. Most of the construction work undertaken by the major construction projects and office building subsidiary companies is specifically commissioned and these Domusco Group companies have only a small sales and marketing support team.

Within the last five years, Domusco has been involved in the construction of many smaller office buildings which had not been specifically designed and built for a company prior to commencement of construction, but were instead sold during the construction period. The construction of these smaller edge-of-town office buildings has increased the working capital requirements of Domusco's office building construction subsidiary, but has improved the office building construction subsidiary's sales revenue and profitability.

Each of the house building subsidiary companies requires a large sales and marketing team to secure sales and ensure that all properties are sold before completion of construction work, or shortly after all work has been completed. Domusco has seen the type of house building change in the last decade, with a higher percentage of lower priced houses and apartments being built and fewer larger houses being constructed. House building companies also attempt to sell some of the planned properties 'off-plan' as soon as building plans have been approved. Off-plan purchase of houses or flats is defined as a customer committing to purchase the housing unit and paying a deposit prior to any construction work commencing on the housing unit. During the last decade, Domusco has seen a change in the timing of when customers purchase their houses or apartments, and they are making their decisions later in the construction process and the level of off-plan sales has fallen. All of these factors have adversely affected cash flows within Domusco's house building subsidiary, although profitability has increased year-on-year within the house building subsidiary.

12 *Jackie Paul – Human Resources Director*

Jackie Paul, now 46, has been involved in the construction industry all of her working life and her father managed a small construction company in the Far East where she grew up. She knows and understands the industry, which has helped her to reach her current position. She joined Domusco nine years ago as Human Resources Director, and has been involved in numerous changes, not least the doubling of the company's workforce, to make it less dependent on sub-contractors and due to growth in the volume of its construction work. She has been dominant in introducing performance-related pay for most levels of staff. She has also been heavily involved with some other Board members in the development, implementation and target setting for Domusco's corporate social responsibility reporting. She has been instrumental in establishing the Advisory Committee, which reports to the main Domusco Board.

An extract from Domusco's Corporate Social Report is shown in Appendix 2.

13 *Desmond Luna – Director of Health and Safety*

Desmond Luna, now 50, was injured in a construction accident when he was in his twenties and has worked very hard to reach his current role. He works tirelessly and often turns up on site unannounced to see for himself what is happening and the types of problems that are being experienced. Despite a good track record on safety in the last ten years, Domusco had two accidents involving the deaths of several construction workers, in Zee and in the Middle East, last year. Desmond Luna is working on improving site safety awareness and accident prevention, so that the events that led up to these accidents do not recur.

14 *Carlos Freer – Director of Business Planning*

Carlos Freer, now 47, joined Domusco eight years ago and has seen the company grow rapidly. He works closely with Martyn Lite, who he respects enormously, but finds the planning role frustrating at times due to the uncertain nature of the industry. It is difficult to plan when the company is usually only successful in being awarded contracts for around 25% of the projects that it has bid for. Furthermore, some major construction projects are awarded to the company with a very short time span between contract signing and start of the construction work. This makes manpower planning, as well as financial planning, difficult.

15 *Non-executive directors*

Domusco has three non-executive directors who are well experienced in industry and commerce.

Economic growth in Zee

16 The country has been a democracy for over 50 years and is experiencing a period of growth in consumer spending. Annual inflation has remained at a little over 4% per year for the last few years and the GNP is forecast to grow at 4% per year over the next few years. The country is a net importer, marginally, and its principal export market is the EU. The country's currency is the Zee dollar (Z$) and the exchange rate at 30 June 2005 is Z$3.25 to US$1 and Z$2.55 to €1.

Competitor analysis

17 In Domusco's home country of Zee, there are eight large construction companies, some of which only operate within Zee, whereas Domusco and three other companies are involved in construction work internationally. Domusco is one of three leading house builders in Zee and, during 2004, Domusco completed 6,924 housing units (one unit is equal to one house or one apartment) in Zee. On the basis of completed units, it constructed a little less than 12% of all new units during 2004 in Zee. Its operations in some European countries and in part of the USA are very small compared to other international companies and Domusco is likely to build less than 1% of all new housing units in these countries.

18 Domusco's international office building construction work is very small compared to many other international companies but Domusco has a substantial market share in the

office construction market in its home country of Zee. However, the volume of new office construction in Zee has fallen in the last five years, but Domusco has achieved around 20% of new office buildings in Zee during the last three years.

19 The major construction projects subsidiary companies of Domusco have been awarded more contracts within the last three years than they had undertaken in the decade prior to that. This has necessitated Domusco's major construction projects subsidiary company recruiting over 200 more employees in several countries, as well as using a high proportion of sub-contractors, to enable it to meet contract deadlines. Peter Kaye is the driving force for much of this new business and he is confident that he can grow this high margin business much further.

Domusco shareholding and share prices

20 Domusco has 441.6 million shares of Z$0.50 each in issue and has a total of 800 million authorised shares. Its share price at 30 June 2005 is Z$13.82, which is at an all-time high for the company, due partly to its good 2004 results. Institutional shareholders own over 80% of its shares, with no single large shareholder. Domusco's directors, staff and the general public own the rest of Domusco's shares.

Major construction projects currently under construction

21 The major construction projects subsidiary company within Domusco, headed up by Peter Kaye, had five main contracts under construction during 2004. These were:

- The construction of a sports stadium in the Middle East (in a country where it has undertaken many projects before), which is due for completion in February 2007. The total profitability on this project is forecast to be Z$78 million over four years.
- The construction of motorways and bridges in the neighbouring European country of Wye. More details on this project are shown later.
- The construction of a motorway in a different country in the Middle East, which is due for completion in September 2005. The overall updated forecast profitability on this project is Z$380 million over 2.4 years.
- Road and motorway construction and road improvements in Zee. The project spans two years and is due to be completed by mid-2005 and the forecast profitability is Z$220 million.

- Construction work on a new marina in Zee. Work commenced in August 2004 and is due for completion in November 2005. The total project profitability is forecast to be Z$270 million.

22 Domusco has not yet signed contracts for any other major construction projects. However, Domusco has bid for several other major construction projects. It is also currently negotiating a major construction project in the USA. If the USA contract were to be awarded to Domusco, it would be its first major construction project in the USA. Domusco currently has house building operations in the USA, but has no other construction work there to date.

Motorway construction project in Wye

23 Domusco has been involved in several motorway construction projects previously and it was selected from a shortlist of four international companies for a particularly difficult motorway construction project in a neighbouring country of Wye, because of its experience of building roads in difficult terrain. The motorway project commenced in Spring 2004 and was due for completion by the end of 2006. However, the project is currently behind schedule, on account of unforeseen extra construction work that will be required, because of the exceptionally heavy rainfall during late 2004 which caused some of the completed sections of the motorway and other foundation and bridgework to be partially washed away or damaged. Some areas of the motorway will require totally new, stronger foundations to be constructed.

24 Peter Kaye and one of his managers, Weng Zen, the Head of Motorway Construction in Domusco, are currently trying to renegotiate the budget for the project with the Wye Government. Peter Kaye has put forward the case to Wye's Government that the entire cost of 14 lost weeks and the additional construction costs should be met by the Wye's Government's road building budget, due to the exceptionally heavy rains, which were unforeseen. Wye's Government minister for transport has publicly stated that the agreed budget cannot be exceeded and that Domusco should have ensured that the quality of the foundations were stronger, to have withstood the heavy rainfall. However, in private it is understood that Wye's Government was surprised at the devastation caused in many areas of the country by the high rainfall. Peter Kaye has put forward the case to Wye's Government that all of the completed foundations had been fully inspected and approved by Wye's Government department, prior to the heavy rainfalls that damaged or destroyed them. He

therefore stated that the re-building costs should be borne entirely by the Wye Government road-building budget. The Wye Government has strongly disagreed with any claims and has refused to pay any compensation for the delays or any rebuilding work.

25 Peter Kaye reported to the May 2005 Domusco Board meeting that he did not want to harm the delicate relationship with the Wye Government at this early stage of this project, particularly with possible future major construction projects in Wye that Domusco is planning to bid for in the next few years. Peter Kaye advised the Domusco Board that the motorway project had a planned profitability of Z$105 million. However, it is now forecast to make an overall loss of Z$35 million, unless the Wye Government changes its mind on any compensation payments.

26 At the May 2005 Board meeting, Martyn Lite stated that Peter Kaye should not allow the possibility of future projects to adversely affect Domusco's negotiations with the Wye Government concerning payment for the delays and rebuilding costs. The Chief Executive, Will Umm, overruled Martyn Lite and stated that this was the first of many projects in Wye and that long-term profitability was more important than one single project. Martyn Lite disagreed and in a heated discussion stated that the Wye Government would assume the company's management is weak. Martyn Lite also stated that it would be more difficult to negotiate prices in the future if Domusco did not pursue compensation for the delays on this motorway construction project.

Office building construction

27 The sales revenue for Domusco's office building construction subsidiary company has risen from Z$732 million in 2003 to Z$768 million in 2004 and is forecast to be around Z$1,248 million in 2005, but profitability on some buildings has fallen.

28 Up until five years ago, all construction work of office buildings were bespoke projects commissioned by organisations. Recently, Domusco has constructed office buildings, both in Zee and in two European countries, where the office buildings have not been sold until part way through the construction process, or after completion of the building. Domusco has been involved in several office buildings construction projects in edge-of-town locations, where several construction companies have each constructed a range of buildings. These edge-of-town office

developments have proved profitable and have enabled Domusco to expand its range and size of office building designs.

29 Tan Lee was pleased to see the revenues generated from his company grow, although it is the smallest of Domusco's three main subsidiary companies, with sales revenue in 2004 only a little over 12% of the total Domusco Group sales. In 2004 profitability fell significantly for two reasons. Firstly, one office building that remained unsold for over one year after completion of construction was sold at a reduced price and resulted in an overall loss. Secondly, there have been some cost over-runs on two large office construction projects in Europe that were specifically commissioned by Domusco.

House building construction

30 Domusco's house building subsidiary company is split geographically, into three companies. One is responsible for all house building in Zee, another for house building in other European countries and the third for house building in the USA.

31 Domusco had acquired a small house building construction company based in the USA in 2000 for several reasons. Primarily it was to acquire its innovative designs and have access to its high profitability, which was due to its relatively low construction costs. It has managed to apply the principles learned from this acquisition and Domusco's house building subsidiary has used them in other countries to improve operating margins. Some cost savings have been due to a change in building techniques, which have removed some of the build stages in the construction process. This allows some construction processes to take place at the same time, resulting in labour savings and a reduction in the costs associated with late alterations. Peter Kaye, who is now Director of Major Construction Projects, joined Domusco from this USA-based house building company.

32 Traditionally in the construction industry, profitability and success has been measured by the company's return on capital employed (ROCE). However, Marma Winge found this measure misleading when comparing ROCE for the three subsidiaries. This is because the ROCE in one subsidiary has been depressed by the purchase of some state-of-the-art construction machinery. A summary of the

ROCE achieved by geographic region for Domusco's house building subsidiary companies for the past two years is as follows:

		Zee	Other European countries	USA	Total house building
Operating profit – 2004	Z$ million	193	165	91	449
Operating profit – 2003	Z$ million	183	150	82	415
ROCE – 2004		23.1%	25.0%	27.4%	24.0%
ROCE – 2003		21.0%	22.5%	26.1%	21.7%
Number of completed housing units					
2004		6,924	4,463	2,811	14,198
2003		6,700	4,607	2,695	14,002

33 There are also two other influences on the ROCE that is achieved. One is the size of the housing development. Generally, smaller developments achieve lower returns than a larger quantity of housing units that are constructed at the same site. Secondly, the type of housing influences returns achieved. Large apartment blocks generally achieve a higher ROCE than medium-priced houses. However, some of Domusco's new housing developments in Europe have been achieving exceptionally high returns, as Domusco had purchased the land plots at a low price a few years ago, compared to current land purchase prices, which have risen considerably.

Domusco's staffing levels and sub-contractors

34 Most companies operating in the construction industry use a mix of their own employees and sub-contractors. The mix varies by country and also by construction segment. In the house building segment, Domusco employs its own staff for site surveying and site management, as well as for a proportion of the house building construction work. Specialised sub-contractors undertake the rest of the house building construction work. Domusco also directly employs all of the sales and marketing teams and administrative support for Domusco's house building subsidiary companies. The majority of the sub-contractors that Domusco uses have worked closely with Domusco for several years.

35 In major construction projects, particularly motorway construction, specialised sub-contractors undertake the majority of the construction work. The location and the level of staffing required varies enormously with each major project and Domusco does not wish to employ

large numbers of staff that may be located in the wrong area or with unsuitable skills. The use of subcontractors gives Domusco flexibility.

36 Peter Kaye's operational management has experienced problems with the use of some subcontractors. Although Domusco has repeatedly used the same sub-contracting companies as on previous occasions, the make-up of the teams used on projects that undertake the work change far too often. Despite supervision by the sub-contractors' management and subsequent inspections by Domusco's project management, there are large numbers of unskilled workers who are not capable of completing certain stages of construction to the required standard, which causes delays while the extent of the faulty work is identified and rectified. In Zee and some other European countries, there is currently an increase in the amount of construction work being undertaken, and many sub-contractors are employing workers who have entered into this industry with little or no training and are both inexperienced and unskilled, which inevitably leads to quality issues. Additionally, as sub-contactors are paid a fixed fee for various stages of construction, they want to complete the job in the least possible time, so that their employees can move onto the next job. This leads to jobs being rushed and not thoroughly or professionally completed.

37 In the office building construction subsidiary of Domusco, Tan Lee has recruited a strong team of experienced staff and is less dependent on sub-contractors than are the other subsidiaries of Domusco. Domusco always uses its own staff for project management and surveys and inspections. One of the recent reports that Marma Winge's operational management is currently reviewing is whether Domusco's house building companies should increase their staffing levels, so that their dependence on sub-contractors would reduce. This would have a number of benefits including reducing costs, as sub-contractors cost more and, secondly, the quality of work is usually higher with their own staff. Domusco has had a number of incidents where sub-contractors have employed workers who were less skilled than usual which has resulted in delays and the need for rectification work. Marma Winge is particularly keen to increase the staffing levels that are employed in the house building subsidiary companies in Zee and other European countries and to reduce their dependence on some sub-contractors and so has presented a paper to the May 2005 Board with a proposal to increase staffing levels.

The development of the Hadsi area of Zee

38 For the last few years the government of Zee has been planning to sell for development a large amount of land in the area of Hadsi. There has been much speculation as to which construction company would buy the land and what type of development would be built on it. Media speculation in Zee feared that it would become another tourist area and this would not help local companies and local people with their housing needs. Despite expanding urbanisation of some cities in Zee, the large site in the Hadsi area of Zee, is still mainly empty and undeveloped. The Hadsi area is 40 kilometres east of the city of Prine. The Zee Government has launched an initiative to move people out of crowded cities to better housing. The Government also wants to attract companies in the IT industries to relocate to the Hadsi area. All office buildings are to be built with the latest high tech equipment to support 'intelligent buildings'. The Zee Government will be funding the transport infrastructure, which will mainly be the construction of all roads in the Hadsi area.

39 The Zee Government currently owns the land and wants to sell the entire area to one construction company. The Zee Government would prefer that the construction company that purchases the entire Hadsi area should then sell plots of land onto other construction companies. In this way, the development of Hadsi could be completed in a shorter period of time, possibly within four years, than if only one construction company were to be involved. Tom Micol and Will Umm had been invited to several meetings with Zee Government ministers regarding the future development of the Hadsi area and they reported back to the Domusco Board in Summer 2003 that it was likely that the Hadsi land would be usd for residential housing. In addition, a commercial centre is planned, as several international companies had expressed interest to the Zee Government and had indicated that they would establish offices in Hadsi. The Government ministers had also informed Tom Micol that the Zee Government planned to commission some community buildings, including schools, sports and recreational facilities. The media in Zee soon picked up this information, possibly leaked by the Zee Government, and the general reaction in Zee was positive, with much interest in this development project.

September 2003 Domusco Board meeting

40 The Chief Executive, Will Umm, reported back to the Board on the discussions held with the Zee Government about the proposed development of the Hadsi area. Will Umm surprised the Board when he reported in total confidence that his government connections had reliably informed him that the Zee Government had decided that its first choice of whom to sell the entire Hadsi land to was Domusco. The Zee Government envisages that over 23,000 housing units could be built on this land, together with schools and sports buildings and a large commercial centre. Will Umm stated that he felt strongly that Domusco should be involved in this major construction project in its home country and the other Board members agreed.

41 Will Umm advised the Board that the cost of the entire Hadsi land that the Zee Government was offering to sell would be around Z$900 million. Some of this cost would be recouped in a short period of time when plots of land were sold onto other construction companies. Will Umm completed his presentation to the Domusco Board by stating that this could be the single largest project the company had ever undertaken, and that his government contacts had confirmed that it was Domusco's to take, if it wanted it. After much heated discussion, the Domusco Board agreed by a majority vote that Domusco should seize this opportunity and acquire the Hadsi land if it were to be offered to it by the Zee Government. The Board requested Martyn Lite to arrange loan finance to cover this land purchase and Carlos Freer was requested to prepare financial forecasts for construction costs on the area of land that Domusco planned to develop itself. In deference to Martyn Lite's concerns about risk and Domusco stretching its financial and manpower resources too thinly, the Domusco Board agreed that Domusco would only undertake construction work on no more than 40% of the Hadsi land area. The other 60% of the Hadsi land would be sold off to other construction companies.

Acquisition of the Hadsi land

42 The Zee Government finalised the sale of the Hadsi land to Domusco during January 2004 at a final price of Z$830 million, a reduction of Z$70 million from the estimated price. The reduction had been negotiated by Peter Kaye, to enable Domusco to undertake the necessary land surveying and other environmental studies, prior to the start of development and the sale of plots of land to other con-

struction companies. Martyn Lite was also able to negotiate with the Zee Government that only one half of the price would be paid on signing contracts in January 2004, and the balance would be paid in December 2005.

43 As part of the contract for the purchase of the Hadsi land, the Zee Government also undertook to spend Z$20 million over two years on promotional and marketing costs to help support the marketing programme that Piers Moore felt would be necessary in order to generate public interest and sales of houses and commercial property in the Hadsi area. It was agreed with the Zee Government that any construction company involved with buildings in Hadsi would also market its own construction work to the general public, so that the early sales of offices and housing could reduce the amount of working capital required to finance this major development.

Domusco's construction plans in Hadsi

44 In January 2004, the Domusco Board requested Marma Winge to prepare outline plans for the housing development and to recommend what size plots of land Domusco should retain for its own planned construction work and not, therefore, sell to other developers.

45 In March 2004, the Domusco Board agreed to construct 12,000 housing units over three years, which will significantly increase the volume of its house building in Zee. This will result in significantly higher revenues and profits for Domusco's house building company over the next few years and will create many new jobs. In addition to housing construction, the Domusco Board agreed to construct a total of 50 commercial office buildings. The Domusco Board also agreed to bid for a contract to construct some roads and motorways connecting the Hadsi area to the nearby city of Prine, which are to be financed by the Zee Government. The Domusco Board had previously agreed in September 2003 that the total area of the Hadsi land that Domusco would use for construction work would not exceed 40% of the total area being developed, and the above planned construction work conforms to this.

Sale of some of the Hadsi land to other construction companies

46 The Zee Government sold the entire Hadsi plot of land to Domusco in January 2004 for Z$830 million and it envisages that the entire development of the area would be completed in about three to four years. The Zee

Government has given outline planning permission for Domusco's plans for the entire Hadsi area, but formal Zee Government approval will still be required prior to the start of any specific construction work by Domusco or any company to which Domusco may sell plots of land.

47 Representatives from Domusco held several meetings with other Zee-based and international construction companies about this specific high profile construction project in early 2004. These companies ranged from small and medium sized construction companies based in Zee to international construction companies who were keen take a part of this major development. Peter Kaye, Tan Lee and Marma Winge met with these companies and selected five companies to which Domusco contracted to sell plots of land on the Hadsi site. The five companies who have purchased land on the Hadsi site from Domusco will be involved with the construction of housing, public buildings, including schools and government-funded sports facilities and office buildings. The five companies will also be involved in bidding for road and transport infrastructure construction work.

48 Contract negotiations on the sale of land plots to these five companies continued throughout 2004 and the sale to all five companies occurred in early 2005. In the first half of 2005, Domusco received payments totalling Z$428 million for the sale of plots of land from the five other construction companies. The total volume of land sold was just over 51% over the total land. The Domusco Board has agreed that Domusco would retain a maximum of 40%, which still left 9% to be sold, which is located in the commercial area of Hadsi. However, by the end May 2005, Domusco had still not identified a construction company that was interested in acquiring some or all of this area of land for the construction of office buildings, until firm buyers for office space had been identified. Therefore this plot of land remained within Domusco's land bank and reported as inventory, together with other plots of land that Domusco owns worldwide.

Financing plans for the Hadsi development

49 At this early stage of the project, the forecast total construction costs for Domusco's planned construction work will be around Z$5,000 million in total over the four years ending 2007, as shown in the table below. The construction costs shown below do not include Domusco's share of the cost of the Hadsi land.

		2004	2005	2006	2007	Total
Housing units (completed)		0	3,000	4,000	5,000	12,000
Office buildings (completed)		0	12	16	22	50
Forecast construction costs:						
Housing	Z$ million	300	700	900	1,100	3,000
Office buildings	Z$ million	300	500	600	600	2,000
Total construction costs	Z$ million	600	1,200	1,500	1,700	5,000

50 Martyn Lite has negotiated loans with two international banks for the equivalent of Z$900 million. The loan finance is for a five-year period at 9% interest per annum, payable quarterly. The loan is forecast to cover working capital requirements for the start of the construction work.

51 The initial payment for the cost of the Hadsi land was paid from cash generated by the Domusco Group's operations. Subsequently, payments have been received from other construction companies for the sale of plots of land in the Hadsi area.

52 It is planned that the balance of the required payment to the Zee Government for the land, due in December 2005, would be financed by the sales of housing and offices that will be under construction. The amount of working capital cannot be forecast exactly as it is unknown what proportion of the housing will be sold 'off-plan' (sold in advance of construction commencing) but a conservative amount has been forecast. The two international banks, ALT and BRG, have confirmed that they are interested in providing Domusco with additional financing if required during the course of construction work.

53 Domusco's existing loans, to Zee-based banks, totaling Z$1,020 million are denominated in Zee dollars. The details of Domusco's new loans with ALT and BRG, denominated in US dollars and Euros, for the equivalent of approximately Z$900 million are shown below:

	Currency of loan	Loan value (million)	Exchange rate (as at loan date of 30 June 2004)	Z$ million
Bank ALT	US$	200	3.18	636
Bank BRG	Euros	105	2.51	264
Total new loans				900

Bad publicity for the Hadsi development

54 There has been a growing amount of adverse publicity concerning the Hadsi development, generated by lobbyists who are concerned that the Hadsi area will become another concrete area. The Hadsi area currently has a few endangered species of small wildlife animals, which are dependent on the existing habitat. While every effort has been made to preserve as many trees as possible, which enhances the appeal of the completed development, it was planned that there would be the need to clear a large area of forest where some of the housing and the commercial office buildings area would be constructed.

55 The adverse publicity about the removal of trees in parts of the wooded areas in Hadsi, and the changes to the local habitat that this has caused, has been growing. The management at Domusco has asked the Zee Government to support it, and the other construction companies, and to increase the amount of marketing it should undertake about the benefits of the completed Hadsi development, in order to counteract the level of adverse media publicity.

Sports stadium contract awarded to Domusco

56 At the Domusco Board meeting held in June 2005, Peter Kaye announced that, after negotiations lasting several years, Domusco had been awarded the contract for the construction of a large national sports stadium in a European country. He stated that he had understood that Domusco had been eliminated from the short list some months ago in favour of the leading construction company in that European country. It had come as a surprise when government officials from the European country had contacted him to confirm that Domusco had been awarded the contract. Contracts are due to be signed within the next month.

57 The sports stadium contract is for €180 million (approximately Z$459 million) and all payments to Domusco are to be made in Euros. The forecast profitability for this contract, which will span 18 months and must be completed by April 2007, is the equivalent of almost Z$83 million. However, if the contractual terms are not met, and the stadium is not completed on time, the final stage payment will be reduced by approximately Z$31 million.

58 Whilst Peter Kaye is pleased that Domusco has been awarded the contract, he is concerned at Domusco's available manpower and the very tight construction timetable, upon which the final stage payment would be made. Peter Kaye stated that he would not have accepted the same proportion of the Hadsi development proposal if he had believed that Domusco would have been awarded this contract. The contractual terms state that work has to be commenced no later than December 2005 and completed by end of April 2007. For a stadium of this size, the construction period could be as long as five years, and therefore the high price reflects the extra amount of manpower needed on this large project.

59 The Board discussed the problems of taking on this project, but agreed that it would not want to damage its reputation by not accepting it, which could put at risk its ability to win any future contracts of this type.

Note: Please also look at the questions for Appendices 3 and 4 below.

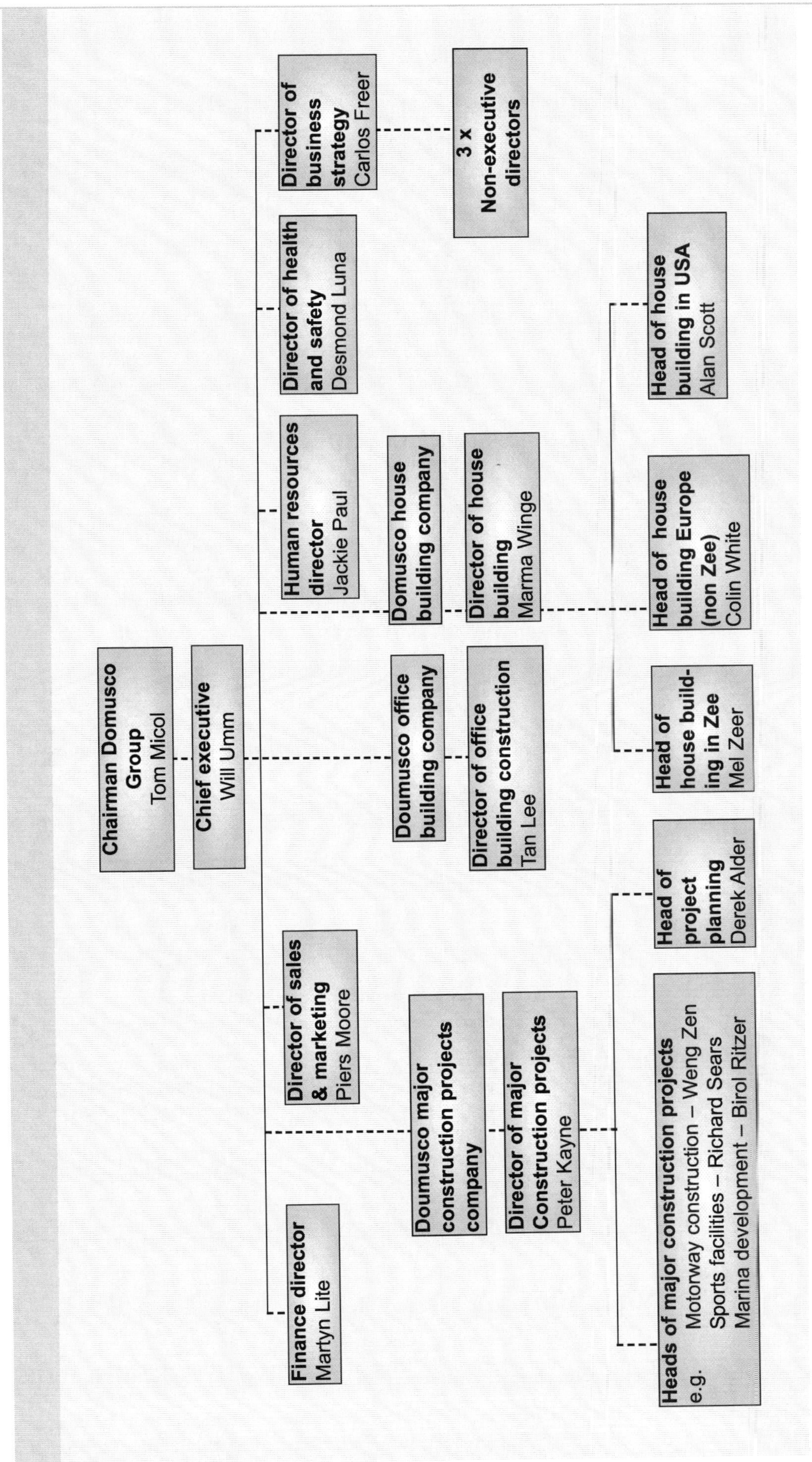

Chairman Domusco Group
Tom Micol
Chief executive
Will Umm
Finance director
Martyn Lite
Director of sales & marketing
Piers Moore
Human resources director
Jackie Paul
Director of health and safety
Desmond Luna
Director of business strategy
Carlos Freer
3 x Non-executive directors
Doumusco major construction projects company
Director of major Construction projects
Peter Kayne
Doumusco office building company
Director of office building construction
Tan Lee
Domusco house building company
Director of house building
Marma Winge
Heads of major construction projects
e.g. Motorway construction – Weng Zen
Sports facilities – Richard Sears
Marina development – Birol Ritzer
Head of project planning
Derek Alder
Head of house build-ing in Zee
Mel Zeer
Head of house building Europe (non Zee)
Colin White
Head of house building in USA
Alan Scott

Appendix 2

Extract from Domusco's Corporate Social report for 2004

	Key achievements in 2004	*Major targets for 2005 and beyond*
Social Responsibility	Established an Advisory Committee, which meets quarterly and reports to the Domusco main Board.	Clarify responsibility to shareholders, suppliers and customers. Improve supply chain.
	Improved internal controls and risk awareness.	Improve risk awareness among all managerial levels and train senior staff in risk management techniques.
Health & Safety (H&S) issues	100% of staff trained in H&S issues	Targets set for reduced number incidents.
	90% of our contractors inducted in H&S Procedures.	Tighter safety procedures in place to prevent the types of accidents that caused fatalities in 2004.
	Reduction of accident levels for both serious incidents and moderate incidents.	
Environment	Trained 90% of site management in environmental management.	Survey of suppliers' environmental policies. Increased use of technology to reduce energy waste during construction.
	Established a site specific environmental action plan.	Train 100% of site management in environmental management. Continue to train sub-contractors.
	Trained 60% of sub-contractors on environmental issues.	
	Improved the amount of site materials that are recycled.	Increased recycling targets set.
Employees	Results of third employee survey published and action plan to address issues drawn up.	A fourth employee survey, in an updated format, will be undertaken.
	Introduced new HR strategy, concerning working hours and performance-related pay.	Increased management training and support for staff to gain relevant qualifications.
	Increase of 18% in training hours per employee.	New training programme planned.

Appendix 3
Domusco Balance Sheet, Income Statement and Statement of Changes in Equity

***Note:** All data in this appendix are presented in international financial reporting format.*

Domusco Balance Sheet	As at 31 December 2004 Z$ million	Z$ million	As at 31 December 2003 Z$ million	Z$ million
Non-current assets (net)		124.8		120.3
Current assets				
Inventory (including land bank, work-in- progress and inventory of materials	5,339.6		4,470.5	
Trade receivables	841.2		727.1	
Cash and short-term investments	501.6		98.2	
		6,682.4		5,295.8
Total assets		6,807.2		5,416.1
Equity and liabilities				
Equity				
Paid in share capital	220.8		220.8	
Share premium reserve	327.6		327.6	
Retained earnings	2,880.8		2,469.6	
		3,429.2		3,018.0
Non-current liabilities				
9% Loan notes (redeemable in 2007)		324.0		324.0
10% Loan notes (redeemable in 2008)		696.0		696.0
9% Loan notes (redeemable in 2009)		900.0		-
Current liabilities				
Trade payables	747.4		728.0	
Tax	296.6		259.8	
Accruals	414.0		390.3	
		1,458.0		1,378.1
Total equity and liabilities		6,807.2		5,416.1

Note: Paid in share capital represents 441.6 million shares of Z$0.50 each.

Income statement	**Year ended *31 December 2004*** Z$ million	**Year ended *31December 2003*** Z$ million
Revenue	6,216.0	5,810.8
Total operating costs	5,104.8	4,861.5
Operating profit	1,111.2	949.3
Finance costs (net)	-128.4	-98.1
Tax expense	-296.6	-259.8
Profit for the period	686.2	591.4

Statement of changes in equity	Share capital Z$ million	Share premium Z$ million	Retained earnings Z$ million	Total Z$ million
Balance at 31 December 2003	220.8	327.6	2,469.6	3,018.0
Profit for the period	-	-	686.2	686.2
Dividends paid	-	-	-275.0	-275.0
Balance at 31 December 2004	220.8	327.6	2,880.8	3,429.2

Appendix 4: Extracts for the next five-years from Domusco's ten-year plan

	Actual	Plan				
	2004	*2005*	*2006*	*2007*	*2008*	*2009*
	Z$ million	Z$ million	Z$ million	Z$ million	Z$ million	Z$ million
Revenue						
Major projects	2,592.2	2,748	3,022	3,264	3,493	3,842
Office building	768.0	1,248	1,473	1,811	1,902	1,997
House building	2,855.8	3,541	3,896	4,246	4,671	5,231
Total revenue	6,216.0	7,537	8,391	9,321	10,066	11,070
Pre-tax operating profit						
Major projects	576.0	616	684	746	805	894
Office building	86.1	138	158	195	205	215
House building	449.1	561	629	691	774	883
Total pre-tax operating profit	1,111.2	1,315	1,471	1,632	1,784	1,992
Post tax profit for the period	686.2	783	876	999	1,121	1,274
Shareholder capital employed (Equity)	3,429.2	3,900	4,424	5,023	5,696	6,460
Loans (at end year)	1,920.0	2,420	2,420	2,096	1,900	1,900
Number of shares (million)	441.6	441.6	441.6	441.6	441.6	441.6
Earnings per share (EPS) Z$	1.55	1.77	1.98	2.26	2.54	2.88

Note: *Plan approved by Domusco Board in November 2004 and includes construction work forall contracts signed at that date (including Hadsi development).*

chapter

12

DOMUSCO: ANALYSIS OF THE PRE-SEEN MATERIAL

Contents

1 Industry awareness

1.1 Overview

Domusco operates in three different sectors of the construction industry:

- major construction projects
- office building construction
- house building.

While there are differences between these, as outlined below, they share the following key factors:

Political / Legal

- Construction is a hugely important industry in most countries – in the UK for example it accounts for approximately 8% of GDP.
- Government policies re transport, health and education will directly affect the demand for new roads, bridges, hospitals and schools – all major construction projects.
- Most governments have plans for regenerating areas of urban decline – this will create demand for new housing, office and other commercial developments.
- In many countries there is a shortage of (affordable) housing, so the government often sets targets for new houses – in the UK for example 60% of new houses are to be on brownfield sites (i.e. sites previously used for commercial uses).
- Obtaining planning permission for new developments is a key part of the construction process – in the UK 85% of house builders identified planning delays as a major constraint on their activities.
- Legislation on environmental issues is a key constraint in many European countries, e.g. concerning insulation, energy efficiency, fire safety, etc.
- There are wide differences between countries regarding what qualifications builders need to have – in Germany, for example, all builders need to be qualified whereas in the UK there are few such restrictions.

Economic

- As a whole, the construction industry has a high level of systematic risk and is very dependent on economic cycles.
- Demand for new roads and other major construction projects will be influenced by the government policy, which in turn will be linked to the state of the economy, predicted tax revenues, etc.
- Demand for factories is highly cyclical and depends on the health of manufacturing, wholesaling and retail sectors.
- Similarly the demand for offices is highly volatile with overcapacity being a problem in many major cities.
- The demand for new houses is dependent on consumer confidence – people are unlikely to commit to a larger mortgage if they are worried over job security and rising interest rates.
- In many countries there have been increases in employer liability insurance and higher professional indemnity premiums (increasing costs faced by construction companies).

Social

- In many countries an ageing population will increase demand for retirement flats, sheltered accommodation and nursing homes.
- Another trend is for there to be more single person households, resulting in an increase in the overall number of households – in the UK, for example, the number of households is forecast to increase by 14% from 2001 to 2021.
- Owning houses is still seen as an important status symbol in society.
- Increased activity from environmental pressure groups protesting against new roads, runways, etc results in higher costs and greater risk for construction companies.

Technological

- Prefabrication techniques make construction quicker and cheaper.
- New technology can be used to make buildings more energy efficient.
- Computer-based design packages allow greater customer focus in the office and housing sectors
- Advanced critical path analysis (CPA) software helps firms manage risks better.
- Internet marketing may mean quicker sales, reducing the length of the firm's operating cycle.

Competition

Competition in the industry is intense with thousands of smaller firms (usually involved in house building) as well as a large number of bigger domestic and international operators. The larger UK firms, for example, operate across Europe and the Middle East. Even the largest firms, however, may enter into joint ventures with local companies for larger projects.

Larger firms should have advantages over smaller competitors with regard to the following factors:

- greater bargaining power when purchasing prime development sites
- dealing with major customers
- economies of scale (e.g. in using prefabrication building techniques)
- pursuing planning applications
- better able to offset risk
- better able to use sophisticated techniques such as CPA needed for larger developments
- more able to offer part-exchange deals to house buyers.

However, this must not be taken for granted:

- The individuality of each construction project limits economies of scale – especially when it comes to materials usage.
- High distribution costs tend to force firms to use local materials where possible.
- It may be difficult for firms to differentiate their product – particularly if tendering to make what the client's architect has already designed.
- Even small firms can benefit from learning effects e.g. house building.

1.2 Major construction projects

Most major construction projects are commissioned by a client – often a local government department.

Key factors often include the following:

- Having a strong sales team to pitch for tenders.
- Building good relationships with government planning departments.
- Having a good record on social responsibility and the environment may be important to get government contracts.

- Getting repeat business is an important part of risk management. It is very difficult to perform long-term planning when you are dependent on a relatively low number of large projects, particularly when the chances of winning a tender may be fairly low, given the amount of competition in the industry.
- This is an area where cost and time overruns can be legendary (e.g. the Millennium Dome, the Channel tunnel, etc), so accurate budgeting and good project management are vital. (Note that in many cases cost overruns can be recovered from the client.)
- The complex nature of the projects often necessitates the use of techniques such as CPA to identify likely problems and to help planning decisions, e.g. use of penalty clauses to prevent delays, whether extra money should be spent to reduce the time for certain activities.
- Such projects often involve the use of sub-contractors so controlling quality, cost and time would be critical success factors.
- The operating cycle may stretch into years so cash management may be critical.
- Some countries, such as the UK, have schemes such as the Public Finance Initiative (PFI) schemes where a construction company might build a hospital, say, and then lease it back to the state (NHS).

1.3 Office building construction

There are three approaches here:

(1) Offices may be built to order.

(2) Purchase land, build offices and then try to sell them.

(3) Purchase land, build offices and then try to let them.

Approach 1 is the least risky with critical success factors being those mentioned above relating to tendering, accurate budgeting, good project management and control.

Approaches 2 and 3 are more risky as there may be difficulties getting planning permission and problems finding customers, both resulting in capital tied up for long periods of time and / or losses. When successful, however, these approaches can yield higher profits.

Critical success factors here also include identifying potential locations, acquiring the land at the right price, gaining planning permission and marketing the properties to gain customers. Some offices may be sold or let 'off plan', i.e. before the building has been started. Attempts are then made to sell remaining offices while the property is being built. This will reduce risk but prices are usually discounted to attract customers. Building commercial property without a buyer arranged is seen to be particularly risky.

1.4 House building

The normal approach to house building is to purchase land without planning permission, gain planning permission, build the houses and then sell them. Some firms may prefer to buy land that has already gained outline-planning approval, as this is a less risky option. Unfortunately such land is more expensive.

Critical success factors thus relate to the following:

- Managing a 'land bank', i.e. buying land at the right price in the right place at the right time.
- Gaining planning permission – typically in the UK firms will have planning permission for half the plots held at any time.
- Project management.
- Understanding what types of properties are required, e.g. the increase in demand for single-person dwellings in the UK outlined above.
- Marketing to sell properties off-plan or quickly after completion to release funds.

As stated above the health of the housing market is driven by the health of the economy and consumer confidence. A slow market could result in depressed profits and properties taking much longer to sell.

In the UK, for example, house prices are at record highs due to over a decade of low interest rates and low unemployment. Some analysts, such as Capital Economics and the Joseph Rowntree Foundation, feel that prices are too high with the average house price to average earnings multiple (HPE) being over 5. The last time this happened was in 1988, just before a crash in the UK housing market.

Note that high house prices do not necessarily mean higher profits for building firms, as land prices will also rise. The key factor is to be able to sell properties quickly in a buoyant market.

1.5 Finance

Land held for development is usually regarded as a self-liquidating asset and is therefore classified as work-in-progress, which typically accounts for around 80% of the total assets of construction companies.

Usually this is financed by medium- and short-term loans, often from banks, with such borrowings amounting to between 50% and 70% of total assets.

1.6 Real-world firms to explore

A useful summary of the major players in the UK and their records on corporate responsibility can be found here:

(http://www.corporatewatch.org)

The main players in the UK market are:

- Amec plc (www.amec.com) – one of the world's largest construction companies
- Balfour Beatty (www.balfourbeatty.com) – UK's biggest construction company as well as a major European player
- Bovis (www.bovishomes.co.uk)
- McAlpine (www.alfredmcalpineplc.com)
- Mowlem (www.mowlem.com) – an international construction firm
- Redrow (www.redrow.co.uk)
- Tarmac plc – a member of the Anglo American plc group (www.tarmac.co.uk)
- Wimpey (www.georgewimpeyplc.co.uk) – one of the world's largest house builders, especially in the UK and the USA.

The top ten European players are as follows (note that all of the websites listed have English versions):

- Bauholding Strabag AG (www.strabag.at) – Austrian – operates mainly in Austria, Germany, and Hungary and in other countries in Central and Eastern Europe
- Bouygues Construction SA (www.bouygues-construction.com/en) – French – a world leader with operations on five continents
- Eiffage SA (www.eiffage.fr)
- Grupo Dragados – part of the ACS group (http://www.grupoacs.com) – a global player.

- Grupo Ferrovial (http://www.ferrovial.com) – Spanish – a multinational group with a stable presence in a dozen countries in Europe (UK, Poland, Portugal, Ireland and Italy), North America (the USA and Canada), Australia and Latin America – mainly, Chile
- Hochtief AG (http://www.hochtief.com) – German – a global firm
- NCC AB (http://www.ncc.se) – Swedish – mainly operating in Scandinavia and Germany
- Skanska AB (http://www.skanska.com) – Swedish – home markets are Sweden, USA, UK, Denmark, Finland, Norway, Poland, the Czech Republic and Argentina
- Vinci Group SA (www.vinci.com) – French – one of the world's largest construction companies.

Note: Jargon – you may come across the abbreviation 'ACE' when searching websites – this stands for the architectural, construction and engineering service industry.

Another useful site: http://www.constructiontimes.co.uk

1.7 Other country specific data

Growth areas

Euroconstruct is a pan-European construction forecasting group. They have given the following forecasts (www.euroconstruct.org).

Construction output is expected to increase robustly in Eastern Europe between 2005 and 2007. Poland will see the largest rise (23%), closely followed by Hungary (19%) and the Czech Republic (17%). With the exception of Sweden, rates of growth will be significantly higher in Eastern European countries than in Western Europe.

Over the entire Euroconstruct region, output is forecast to increase by 2.2% in 2005, 1.5% in 2006 and 1.7% in 2007.

Turkey (some students suspect that the fictitious country Zee is based on Turkey)

Experts estimate that Turkey requires an additional 1.5 million housing units in the next five years, due to population growth and continued urbanisation. With the addition of the effect of the existing housing deficit and the rebuilding of single and multi-family residential units in the earthquake stricken region of western Turkey, this requires that more than 500,000 new housing units must be constructed each year.

Additionally, with a growing economy and rapid urban expansion, there is a need for the construction of more commercial/office/professional buildings. Likewise shopping malls and retail establishments need to be built as consumer spending is increased. Tourism development continues to generate new construction projects.

When possible, foreign firms should consider joint ventures with Turkish firms to take advantage of low Turkish labour costs and local familiarity with bureaucracy.

2 Precis the case – Domusco

2.1 Background

Domusco is a listed construction company based in Zee, a fictitious country in Southern Europe but outside the EU. Domusco operates in three different construction business segments:

- major construction projects
- office building construction
- house building.

Domusco seeks to be competitive by offering good designs, quality specifications, innovation and the use of high technology. These result in being able to command premium prices.

2.2 Group structure

Each of the main business segments is represented by a subsidiary company.

Domusco's house building subsidiary company also has separate subsidiary companies for different geographic areas (Zee, USA and rest of Europe).

In addition to having directors in charge of business units, Domusco has a matrix feel with directors in charge of functional aspects such as setting business strategy, sales and marketing, finance, HR and health and safety.

Another feature to note is that Peter Kaye, Director of Major Construction Projects, will often be involved in negotiating large contracts even when this involves other subsidiaries, such as office building.

2.3 Board of Directors

The Board shows great experience and breadth of skills. The main concerns are as follows:

- Tom Micol, the Chairman, plans to retire in three years' time.
- The mix of the Board is such that more visionary directors often outvote the more conservative members. Some directors fear that this exposes Domusco to excessive risk in the pursuit of growth and profit.

2.4 Major construction projects

It is particularly difficult to plan in the major construction projects division as projects are by definition large and Domusco wins only 25% of tenders. Furthermore there is often a very short time span between contract signing and start of work, making manpower planning difficult.

There were five main contracts under way in 2004, three of which are due for completion in 2005.

Domusco has had particular problems with a motorway contract in the neighboring country of Wye. The project is behind schedule and adverse weather conditions have caused cost overruns. The Board hopes to get the Wye Government to pay some of the extra costs. If it refuses, Domusco will see a predicted profit of Z$105 million on the contract turn into a loss of Z$35 million.

2.5 Office building construction

Domusco has a 20% share of the Zee office building market, a declining market, but is a small player outside Zee. Growth of 63% is forecast for 2005.

Domusco has recently won two large contracts in one European country. One has generated much international publicity, because of Domusco's innovative designs and high technology features.

There have been three main problems:

- International competition and, some would argue excessive innovation, has seen margins decrease from the levels achieved a decade ago.
- An office building remained unsold for over one year and resulted in an overall loss.
- There have been cost over-runs on two large office construction projects in Europe that were specifically commissioned by Domusco.

2.6 House building construction

Domusco has established itself as a builder of high quality housing and apartments at the top and middle segments of the market but has not been involved in any low cost or social housing projects to date.

Domusco acquired a small house building construction company based in the USA in 2000 to acquire its innovative designs and expertise regarding low cost construction.

The type of houses demanded has changed in the last decade, with a higher percentage of lower priced houses and apartments being built and fewer larger houses being constructed. House building companies also attempt to sell some of the planned properties 'off-plan' as soon as building plans have been approved.

All of these factors have adversely affected cash flows within Domusco's house building subsidiary, although profitability has increased year-on-year.

2.7 The Hadsi project

In January 2004 Domusco bought a large plot of land in Hadsi, Zee, from the Zee Government for Z$830 million, with half of the price paid on signing contracts in January 2004 and the balance paid in December 2005.

The Zee Government envisages that over 23,000 housing units could be built on this land, together with schools and sports buildings and a large commercial centre. Domusco would only undertake construction work on no more than 40% of the Hadsi land area, building 12,000 housing units over three years.

In the first half of 2005, Domusco received Z$428 million for the sale of just over 51% plots of the total volume of land to five other construction companies. To date 9% of the land remains unsold.

The key risks are:

- people may not wish to move to Hadsi when it is 40km from the nearest large center, Prine
- bad publicity and concerns over the environment
- problems resourcing such a large contract.

The project has been financed to date by:

- existing funds
- two loans, equivalent to Z$900 million, one in US$ and one in Euros
- sale of land to other developers

To continue funding the project it is vital that properties are sold when built.

Sports stadium contract awarded to Domusco

At the Board meeting held in June 2005, Peter Kaye announced Domusco had been awarded the contract for the construction of a large national sports stadium in a European country. Contracts are due to be signed within the next month.

The contract is for €180 million (approximately Z$459 million) and all payments to Domusco are to be made in Euros. The forecast profitability for this contract, which will span 18 months and must be completed by April 2007, is the equivalent of almost Z$83 million. However, if the stadium is not completed on time, the final stage payment will be reduced by approximately Z$31 million.

The Board is concerned about the resource implications of doing both this project and the Hadsi development but did not want to damage the company's reputation by not accepting it, which could put at risk its ability to win any future contracts of this type.

2.8 Staffing issues

Despite a good track record on safety in the last ten years, Domusco had two accidents involving the deaths of several construction workers, in Zee and in the Middle East, last year.

Like most companies operating in the construction industry, Domusco uses a mix of its own employees and sub-contractors. The majority of the sub-contractors that Domusco uses have worked closely with Domusco for several years but problems still have occured:

- the make-up of the teams used on projects change far too often
- inadequate skills resulting in poor quality and delays
- jobs being rushed.

As a result of this there are plans to consider increasing the number of employed staff.

2.9 Financial performance

Domusco has 441.6 million shares each in issue with a share price at 30 June 2005 of Z$13.82, which is at an all-time high for the company.

Institutional shareholders own over 80% of its shares, with no single large shareholder. Domusco's directors, staff and the general public own the rest of Domusco's shares.

The financial statements show good growth, strong profitability and a healthy balance sheet. Five-year plans show this growth continuing into the foreseeable future.

3 Analysis: business strategy perspective

3.1 Consolidate your understanding of the strategic position of Domusco using a SWOT analysis

Strength	*Weaknesses*
• Established competitive strategy of differentiation based on good designs and quality specifications allowing • Domusco to command premium prices • International reputation • Innovative • Listed company, so it is easier to raise finance • Share price at a high, perhaps reflecting industry confidence • Strong balance sheet, profitable • Directors have a great deal of relevant expertise and experience • Government connections • Spread of shareholdings suggests that Domusco is unlikely to be under short-termist pressure and can focus on long-term goals • Performance-related pay, together with many staff owning shares, should result in more motivated employees	• Lack of diversification – all business areas are very risky being dependent on the state of the economy. This also results in planning difficulties· • Falling margins on office contracts • Small player outside Zee so may lack the economies of scale of larger rivals in those countries. Even in Zee Domusco is much smaller than other house builders • Lack of balance in the Board of Directors – at present it appears that the more visionary directors are out-voting the more conservative ones, thus exposing the company to higher risk • There may be conflicts if operating companies feel that Peter has negotiated a price/timetable/other terms that they are unable to deliver • May be trying to grow too quickly – in particular Domusco may not have the resources to complete both the Hadsi project and the new stadium contract • Poor performance management – use of ROCE for example • Recent accidents could indicate inadequate control systems to safeguard staff welfare • Contracts do not seem to include clauses dealing with recovering costs if they exceed budget· • Possible succession issues when Tom retires in three years' time

Opportunities	Threats
• Greater demand for cheaper housing • Greater demand for apartments • Hadsi project may win the contracts to build motorways and other transport infrastructure • More contracts in Wye if the current issues over the motorway contract are handled properly • At some stage Zee may seek to join the EU • More overseas expansion • It is likely that there will be more legislation towards buildings becoming more energy efficient, using more recycled materials and having less impact on the environment	• Hadsi is a major development. If people are not tempted to move to the area then huge losses could follow • Domusco may not be able to deliver the new stadium contract on time and to the required level of quality • Possible loss on the Wye contract • Reputation could become damaged making it much harder to win government contracts • Increasing international competition • The office market in Zee seems to be declining • Customers may be unwilling to pay the extra for Domusco's advanced features, undermining the basis of their competitive advantage • Reduced demand for larger houses • Customers delaying making purchasing decisions so harder to sell off-plan • Foreign exchange risk • Larger international firms may seek to tender for more contracts in Zee • Further cost overruns • Quality problems if Hadsi relies too heavily on subcontractors

In summary, the key issues for Doumsco are as follows:

- Highly competitive, risky industry.
- Domusco tries to succeed through a competitive strategy of differentiation based on innovative designs and new technology. The extent to which the firm can maintain its competitive advantage is likely to be key to the case.

- The key threats to Domusco's competitive strategy are larger international competitors, damage to its reputation and quality problems due to using sub-contractors.
- The key opportunities are towards low cost affordable housing and looking to more markets outside Zee.
- The other main risks relate to the Hadsi development and the new stadium contract.

3.2 Assess the construction industry using Porter's five forces analysis

Competitive rivalry – very high

- Large number of domestic and international firms.
- It is difficult to differentiate your product.
- Firms typically have high fixed costs.

Threat of entry – higher in housing, lower in construction and offices

- It is relatively easy for a firm in one country to tender for projects in another.
- For new firms entering the industry the main barriers are as follows:
  - economies of scale
  - need initial finance to acquire land
  - large working capital requirements in the large construction projects sector
  - need good relationships with planning offices if building without being commissioned by a client in advance
  - may need good contacts with government departments to win contracts
  - capital requirements are low – construction is labour intensive, most equipment can be hired if necessary
  - the extent of legal barriers depends on the country concerned.
- Overall these barriers are likely to be higher in the large construction sector (giving a lower threat of entry) but lower in the housing sector (giving a higher threat of entry).

APLAN PUBLISHING

210

Threat of substitutes – high

- Main threat is the availability of second-hand property for rent or purchase.
- This will depend on the country concerned – some countries have housing and office shortages (e.g.Turkey) whereas others have booming housing and commercial property markets.

Power of suppliers – low for materials, higher for land and planning permission

- Material suppliers have low power – numerous suppliers, undifferentiated products.
- Suppliers of prime land sites are in a strong position and can command high prices.
- Local planning office has very high power.

Power of customers – high in commercial sector, lower in the housing sector

- In the housing sector customers have more choice but individually have low buying power.
- Governments and other clients putting larger jobs out to tender have much higher power to push for lower prices and better specifications.

Summary: A very competitive and hence very risky industry, stressing the need for a clear competitive strategy.

3.3 What evidence is there to suggest that Domusco may be in danger of trying to grow too quickly? In particular is Domusco in danger of overtrading?

Arguments that Domusco is growing too quickly

- The more adventurous members of the board have outvoted the more conservative members on a number of occasions.
- The Hadsi plan involves building 12,000 housing units over three years, equating to 4,000 per annum on average. Compared to Domusco's existing figures of 6,924 units in Zee in 2004 this would be a 58% increase in domestic volume, raising fears that the project is too big for Domusco.
- May be difficult to resource both the Hadsi project and the new stadium contract, especially as the stadium contract involves doing five years work in 18 months!
- Falling margins in some areas – especially office work. Have maybe prices been cut to boost growth?
- 62.5% growth predicted in office building in 2005.
- Switch in strategy away for only building in response to client requests towards building and selling off plan results in greater working capital requirements.

Arguments that the growth should not be a problem

- Extra labour resources can always be obtained by the use of sub-contractors, plant and machinery can be hired and there should be no a problem obtaining materials. The only issue here is whether further use of sub-contractors would cause control and quality problems.
- In the major construction projects division three out of its five main projects finish in 2005, releasing resources.
- The company could easily raise more long-term finance if required.

Overtrading

Overtrading is a serious problem that rapidly expanding businesses can easily fall into. Signs of overtrading are:

- A rapid increase in stock levels, matched by a large increase in trade creditors or bank overdraft.
- A deteriorating current ratio (ratio of current assets to current liabilities) and quick ratio (ratio of current assets excluding stocks to current liabilities).
- A significant slow-down in the average time for paying trade creditors.
- Sometimes, a large increase in debtors, with debtors also taking longer to pay. (Rapidly growing businesses might sell on easy credit terms to win new customers).
- Overtrading firms usually see a sharp increase in the asset turnover ratio as output increases are often obtained by more intensive utilisation of existing fixed assets, and growth tends to be financed by more intensive use of working capital.

Applying this checklist to Domusco we see the following:

A rapid increase in stock levels	**Questionable** – inventory up 19%
A large increase in trade creditors	**No** – trade payables only up 2.7%
A large increase in bank overdraft	No – cash in hand
A deteriorating current ratio	**No** – has improved from 3.84 to 4.58
A deteriorating quick ratio	**No** - has improved form 3.84 to 4.58
A significant increase in creditor days	**No** – down from 55 to 53 days
A large increase in debtors	**No** – debtors only up
Debtors also taking longer to pay	**Yes** – up from 55 to 60 days
A sharp increase in the asset turnover ratio	**No** – down from 1.07 to 0.91

In summary, Domusco does not exhibit the classic signs of overtrading.

3.4 Using Ansoff's matrix, outline possible directions for growth for Domusco

Ansoff's matrix – product / market mix

	Existing products	**New products**
Existing markets	*Market penetration* • Could cut prices to win more tenders • Maybe spend more on advertising • Small improvements to products - e.g. building more energy efficient buildings • Maybe buy rivals? Little information given about them	*Product development* • Could move into the building of low cost affordable housing • Could develop more sophisticated building techniques to offer high quality housing that can be built very quickly • Could develop technology to enble building to withstand earthquakes better
New markets	*Market development* • Could try new customer segments - specialise in single occupancy dwellings and retirement flats to respond to the demographic changes occurring across Europe • Could try penetrating new foreign markets, perhaps via joint ventures	*Diversification* Related diversification e.g. • buy a supplier company that makes high quality windows (backwards vertical integration) • buy companies that make and install kitchens, bathrooms, etc • expand into the installation of power lines, sewerage pipes and other infrastructure to offer a complete solution

3.5 Domusco is involved in three areas of construction – discuss the extent to which there are crossover synergies between these business segments

The main crossover synergies are as follows:

- Better utilisation of equipment such as cranes, bulldozers, lorries, etc.
- Presumably much of the labour force can switch skills to build houses rather than offices. The scope for switching labour may be less between major construction projects and houses and offices.
- Designers and architects may be able to design houses, offices and stadiums. Again the synergy may be less pronounced between major construction projects and the other two.
- Economies of scale when purchasing materials that are used in common e.g. sand, hire of plant, etc.
- Domusco is able to offer a more complete solution to major clients, as seen with the Hadsi project.
- There may be limited scope for a reputation gained in one area to be transferred to another – e.g. a government department aware of Domusco's expertise in house building may be more willing to give them a contract to build offices.

The extent to which Domusco benefits from these synergies will be limited by its essentially divisional structure.

3.6 Outline the key HR issues Domusco is facing

The main HR issues facing Domusco are as follows:

- Recruitment – the extent to which staff should be employed rather than using sub-contractors – this is discussed in detail in the commentary on the 'preseen' earlier in this book.
- Staff turnover – high staff turnover is a common feature of the industry and can result in quality problems if training is not controlled adequately.
- Training – should staff be multi-skilled to facilitate switching between business segments to improve efficiency?
- Safety – it is imperative that recent accidents are not repeated. This may mean further training.
- Motivation – Domusco wants to ensure that quality is not sacrificed to get work finished quicker.
- Location – should Domusco use Zee citizens and arrange for them to complete projects in other countries or employ local citizens? The former approach should lead to better quality and better utilisation; the latter would be cheaper and would keep local governments happier.

4 Analysis: Financial strategy persective

4.1 Analyse the financing statements of Domusco using ratio analysis

	Working	*2004*	*Working*	*2003*
Profitability				
ROCE	1,111.2/6,807.2	16.3%	949.3/5,416.1	17.5%
Return on equity	1,111.2/3,429.2	32.4%	949.3/3,018.0	31.5%
Operating profit margin	1,111.2/6,216.0	17.9%	949.3/5,810.8	16.3%
Asset turnover	6,216.0/6,807.2	0.91x	5,810.8/5,416.1	1.07x
Liquidity				
Current ratio	6,682.4/1,458.0	4.58	5,295.8/1,378.1	3.84
Quick ratio	(841.2+501.6)/1,458.0	0.92	(727.1+98.2)/1,378.1	0.60
Total inventory days	5,339.6/5,104.8 x 365	382 days	4,470.5/4,861.5 x 365	336
Trade receivables days	841.2/5,104.8 x 365	60 days	727.1/ 4,861.5 x365	55 days
Trade payables days	747.4/5,104.8 x 365	53 days	728.0/ 4,861.5 x 365	55 days
Length of operating cycle	382+60-53	389 days	336+55-55	336 days
Gearing				
Debt/Equity – book values	(324+696+900)/ 3,429.2	0.56	(324+696)/3,018.0	0.34
Debt/Equity – market values	(324+696+900)/ 6,102.9	0.31	Insufficient data	
Interest cover	1,111.2/128.4	8.7	949.3/98.1	9.7
Dividend cover	Dividend yet to be announced?	-	591.4/275.00	2.15

Comments

Profitability

- Revenue and operating profit have both increased (revenue by 7% and operating profit by 17%).
- ROCE has fallen, presumably because of the large increase in capital employed due to the Hadsi project.
- Return on equity has improved slightly.
- Operating margins have increased, partly due to the increase in volume.
- Asset turnover has weakened suggesting that negotiated prices may be lower than before.
- Overall a healthy set of results.

Liquidity

- Current and quick ratios have both improved – the current ratio because of extra land from the Hadsi project and the quick ratio because of cash raised by a new loan.
- Stock and debtor days have both worsened, resulting in a lengthening operating cycle.
- This indicates that the firm may have problems with working capital – in particular coping with the growth.

Gearing

- Gearing has increased due to the new loan but the resulting gearing level would not be considered to be excessive.
- Interest cover has fallen but is still high enough not to be a cause for concern.
- Overall the balance sheet looks healthy.

4.2 Produce a cash flow statement for Domusco for 2004 and comment

	Z$m
Operating profit	1,111.2
Less: increase in inventory (5,339.6 – 4,470.5)	(869.1)
Less: increase in trade receivables (841.2 – 727.1)	(114.1)
Plus: increase in trade payables and accruals (747.4 + 414.0 – 728.0 – 390.3)	43.1
Net cash inflow from operating activities	**171.1**
Dividends paid	(275.0)
Tax paid – 2003 bill	(259.8)
Finance costs – 2004 figure	(128.4)
Increase in non-current assets (124.8 – 120.3)	(4.5)
Net cash outflow before new financing is considered	**(496.6)**
New finance raised – 2009 loan notes	900.0
Increase in cash and short-term investments (501.6 – 98.2)	**403.4**

- Operating activities generated a cash flow in 2004, despite the Hadsi project involving a payment of Z$415 million in January 2004 for the land and Z$600 million construction costs.
- The new finance of Z$900 million was needed to preserve liquidity.

If the Hadsi project cash flows are taken out, then the rest of the group would have generated a net cash inflow of –496.6 + 415 + 600 = +Z$518.4 million without the need for the loan. This would indicate that firstly the group has a healthy cash flow, and secondly that the Hadsi project is big enough to cause Domusco problems.

4.3 Assess the ten-year plan given in Appendix 4

1 Forecast growth rates

	Actual 2004	2005	2006	2007	2008	2009
Revenue						
Major projects		6%	10%	8%	7%	10%
Office building		62.5%	18%	22.9%	5%	5%
House building	1.4%	24%	10%	9%	10%	12%
Total revenue	7%	21%	11%	11%	8%	10%

Comments

Major projects

- As major projects last over several accounting periods, it is important to know Domusco's policy on revenue recognition – is the revenue only recognised when the project is finished or does it recognise revenue and profit each year based on % completion? The latter is more likely.
- Given that three out of five major projects in existence in 2004 finish in 2005 it is difficult to see how there is major growth in 2006 onwards. The Hadsi project might generate some contracts to build motorways but nothing has been awarded yet.
- Note that the new stadium contract was announced in the June 2005 Board meeting and the plan in Appendix 4 included all contracts signed by November 2004, so it is unlikely that this has been included in the figures.
- Has the potential loss on the motorway contract in Wye been included?
- Overall the major construction forecasts seem over optimistic as stated but would look more reasonable were the news stadium contract included.

Offices

- We are not given a breakdown of the 2003 or 2004 office developments so it is difficult to assess the growth in 2005 of 62.5%. We do know that the Hadsi project is expected to have 12 new office buildings completed in 2005. If we assume that this represents the 62.5%, then in 2004 Domusco must have completed 19 buildings. The 16 Hadsi buildings in 2006 would then give growth on 2005 of approximately 4/31 = 13% going some way to explain the 18% figure in the plan for 2006. A similar argument can be applied to 2007. When the Hadsi project is finished growth drops to 5%, a more reasonable figure.

- Overall growth looks reasonable as long as the Hadsi project estimates can be achieved.

House building

- In 2004 Domusco completed 14,198 housing units (see paragraph 32 of the pre-seen material). The Hadsi project would involve completing 3,000 units in 2005 giving growth of 21% so the rest of the company is only expected to see growth in 2005 of around 3%.
- In 2006 the Hadsi project would provide 4,000 units, a further 1,000 over 2005 or growth of 6% – again this suggests that the rest of the housing division will achieve growth of around 4%.
- The story in 2007 is similar but it is difficult to see where the growth of 10% in 2008 and 12% in 2009 will come from as the Hadsi project will be finished by then.
- Overall the house building forecasts seem reasonable as long as the Hadsi estimates can be achieved.

Overall

- Apart from the growth figures for large construction projects, the plan seems reasonable provided the Hadsi project can be delivered according to budget as it gives most of the growth.

2 Forecast operating margins

	Actual					
	2004	*2005*	*2006*	*2007*	*2008*	*2009*
Major projects	22.2%	22.4%	22.6%	22.9%	23.0%	23.3%
Office building	11.2%	11.1%	10.7%	10.8%	10.8%	10.8%
House building	15.7%	15.8%	16.1%	16.3%	16.6%	16.9%
Overall	17.9%	17.4%	17.5%	17.5%	17.7%	18.0%

Comments

- Overall margins seem steady with slight increases in major contracts and house building.
- The increase in margins for office buildings could be explained by more out-of-town developments (see paragraph 28 of the pre-seen material) or further projects to complete buildings and then try to sell them. However increasing international competition and less demand for Domusco's innovative features (see paragraph 9 of the pre-seen material) would suggest that a fall in margins would be a more realistic assumption.
- The increase in margins for house building could be due to improved methods of construction but one would expect margins to fall, as part of the Hadsi development would have to be for smaller lower margin properties. It is unrealistic to assume that 40% of the development could be made up of larger more expensive properties.
- Overall, therefore, the estimated margins seem a little optimistic but not excessively so.

Summary

In summary the plan has some concerns but seems reasonable at least until 2007, provided the Hadsi project estimates can be achieved.

4.4 Analyse the financing arrangements used by Domusco to date and comment on the options available for raising finance in the future

Ratios

As discussed in the analysis of the financial statements above, the balance sheet looks healthy:

	Working	2004	Working	2003
Gearing				
Debt/Equity – book values	(324+ 696+ 900)/	0.56	(324 + 696)/ 3,018.0	0.34
Debt/Equity – market values	(324+696+900)/ 6,102.9	0.31	Insufficient data	
Interest cover	1,111.2/128.4	8.7	949.3/98.1	9.7
Dividend cover	Dividend yet to be announced?	–	591.4/275.00	2.15

- Gearing has increased due to the new loan but the resulting gearing level would not be considered to be excessive.
- Interest cover has fallen but is still high enough not to be a cause for concern.

Debt finance

The main source of debt finance has been short- or medium-term loan notes issued to banks. This is normal for the industry – in the UK, for example, many construction companies use short-term bank loans to acquire land, especially when building houses.

The normal payment profile for loan notes would be to pay interest only until the last payment, when the full capital would also be repaid. This should give a good fit with project cash flows as the consideration is received on completion (unless progress payments are involved). The main problem it generates is if properties cannot be sold and Domusco is left to find large lump sums to redeem the loan notes.

We are not told what security arrangements have been made with the banks. The value of non-current assets is unlikely to be sufficient unless the balance sheet seriously undervalues them. The loans must therefore be secured on the land and buildings in inventory. Certainly there are enough of them – Z$5,339.6 million inventory versus Z$1,920 million loans.

One of the interesting issues concerning the debt is why Domusco took out the new Z$900 million loans in US$ and Euros when financing a Zee development. Normally one would seek to match the finance currency with the currency of the investment to hedge foreign exchange risk. Also, given the stated inflation of Zee (4%) being higher than that of the USA (2%) and the Euro zone (2%), one would expect the Z$ to weaken so Domusco would have to find more Z$ to meet repayments.

The only sensible conclusion is that Domusco wanted to develop a relationship with international banks. Such banks are more likely to want to lend in major currencies such as US$ and Euros rather than Z$. The question is then why would Domusco want to borrow from international banks rather than from Zee banks with whom it has a good history already? It may be that Zee banks were unwilling to lend more (unlikely given the low gearing) or that the international banks were cheaper (possible due to economies of scale) or that Domusco is planning more international expansion in the future.

Further debt should be readily available due to the following:

- low gearing levels
- the company is profitable and growing
- the company is quoted
- there appears to be ample security available
- ROCE has been improving.

Equity

Share issues do not seem to feature in Domusco's financing plans for the foreseeable future. Being listed, however, Domusco should be able to raise the sums it needs via rights issues and public issues if necessary. Given the spread of shareholdings, there are unlikely to be any control dilution problems if new shares are issued.

The main source of equity finance seems to be in retained earnings. In 2003 a dividend of Z$275 million was declared out of profits of Z$591.4 million – a payout of 46%.

Other

There has been no mention of government grants – one would have expected this to be a promising source of funding for new developments, especially the Hadsi project.

4.5 To perform further detailed calculations for Domusco, such as NPV or SVA, we will need a suitable discount rate. Calculate the WACC of Domusco

Cost of debt (K_d)

We are not given a valuation for the loan notes, so must make some assumptions in order to calculate a cost of debt.

One approach is to assume that they are valued at par and will be redeemed at par.

Kd = Coupon rate x (1 – tax rate)

The tax rate can be estimated from the income statements in Appendix 3:

	2004	**2003**
Operating profit	1,111.2	949.3
Finance costs	(128.4)	(98.1)
Net profit before tax	982.8	851.2
Tax	(296.6)	(259.8)
Effective rate of tax	30.2%	30.5%

These would suggest a rate of 30%.

9% loan notes K_d = 9 x (1 – 0.30) = 6.3%

10% loan notes K_d = 10 x (1 – 0.30) = 7.0%

Note: An alternative approach would be to suggest that the most recent loan notes give the best estimate of the current cost of debt. Thus the cost would be 6.3% for all of the loan notes. This may appear simpler, but we would have to revalue the 10% loan notes to 90% of their par value to give the correct cost: MV = 90% x 696 = Z$626.4 million. The two approaches do give the same answer so you may find the first easier to use.

Cost of equity (K_e)

Estimating the cost of equity is made easier by the fact that Domusco is a listed company.

We are told that the share price at 30 June 2005 is Z$13.82, giving a total market capitalisation of 441.6m x 13.82 = Z$6,102.9 million.

The easiest way to calculate a cost of equity is to use the dividend valuation model:

Ke = {D1 / MV} + g

To use this we need to estimate next year's dividend and determine a future dividend growth rate.

A dividend of Z$275 million is given in Appendix 3. This could be the 2004 dividend but it is more likely to be the 2003 dividend:

- It states that the dividend has been paid – the 2004 dividend would usually be announced after the accounts have been audited and then paid in 2005.
- This is more consistent with IFRS approach to dividends.

Two years' growth will have to be included to get the dividend in one year's time from June 2005 – most likely the 2005 dividend being paid.

Calculating a growth figure is more difficult as we do not have a dividend history to work with. A common assumption is to take growth in earnings as a proxy for dividend growth.

From the information given there are two approaches we can use to get earnings, and hence dividend growth:

1 Look at historic figures in Appendix 3:

   Profit grew from Z$591.4 million in 2003 to Z$686.2 million in 2004, giving a growth rate of 16%.

2 Look at the business plan in Appendix 4:

   EPS is forecast to grow from Z$1.55 to Z$2.88 in five years giving an average growth rate g such that 1.55 x $(1+g)^5$ = 2.88 or g = 13%.

The problem with either of these figures is that they are unlikely to be sustainable in the long run as they clearly exceed overall industry growth. The formula is based on growth into perpetuity! An industry growth rate could be used but that would underplay the high growth expected in Domusco for at least the short-term future.

For illustrative purposes we shall use the 13% here.

$K_e = \{D_1 / MV\} + g = \{275 \times (1.13)^2 / 6{,}102.9\} + 0.13 = 0.1875$ or 18.75%

WACC

Weighting according to market values:

Finance	Cost(%)	MV(Z$m)	WACC(%)
Equity	18.75	6,102.9	14.26
9% loan notes 2007	6.30	324.0	0.25
10% loan notes 2008	7.00	696.0	0.61
9% loan notes 2009	6.30	900.0	0.71
Total		8,022.9	**15.83**

For discounting purposes a figure of approximately 16% can be used.

4.6 Martyn Lite would like to see a greater emphasis on shareholder value. Apply the Shareholder Value Analysis (SVA) methodology to the forecasts in Appendix 4 to value the company

We can use the WACC of 16% calculated in Q2 above.

Getting appropriate cash flows is more difficult. The 'obvious' starting point would be the post-tax profits in Appendix 4 but the figures given would have to be adjusted for the following:

1 The figures probably do not include the new stadium contract.

2 We may want to adjust for the potential loss on the disputed motorway contract (the unseen information may shed more light on the situation here).

3 We really want 'free' cash flows, i.e. excluding financing flows – so it would be better to start with future pre-tax operating profits and remove the appropriate tax (i.e. not deducting finance costs).

4 We may want to delay the tax flows.

5 The figures will not show the second payment to be made in December 2005 to the Zee Government for the Hadsi land. On the other hand the cost of the land is probably recognised in the plan as a cost when properties are sold.

6 Profits on large construction projects may have been apportioned in the plan based on % completion. These would need to be replaced by progress payments and any final payment.

7 We would want to reverse out depreciation and other non-tax flows from the profit.

8 We need figures for working capital and fixed capital investment. Replacement fixed capital investment is often equated with depreciation but the growth would necessitate incremental fixed capital investment.

9 We may want to adjust for the timings of cash flows, e.g. construction costs occurring before revenues.

With all of the above, the key question is how complicated do you want to make it? For illustrative purposes items 1 to 3 will be adjusted with the others left unless the unseen information gives further detail.

Before we can start, however, there are two other problems:

- When do we set time t = 0? The normal assumption is that cash flows occur at the end of the period concerned (December year ends here) but 'now' is July 2005 making the year ends

  t = ½, 1½, 2½, etc. This makes the discounting more complex than it needs to be. One solution is to set t = 0 at 1 January 2006. The other is to use t = 0 as 30 June 2005 but assume cash flows occur halfway through the accounting period.
- What to do with the cash flows beyond 2009? We could assume growth of 13% into perpetuity or use an industry average (not given) or have a level perpetuity. In the calculations here we shall use the last approach for simplicity.

Z$ million	**31/12/05** t=0	**2006** t=1	**2007** t = 2	**2008** t = 3	**2009** t = 4	**t = 6** to ∞
Pre-tax operating profits per Appendix 4	1,315	1,471	1,632	1,784	1,992	1,992
Stadium contract		(376)	459			
Extra costs on motorway contract (105 + 35)		(140)				
Net cash flow	1,315	955	2,091	1,784	1,992	1,992
Tax at 30%	(395)	(287)	(627)	(535)	(598)	(598)
Free cash flows	920	668	1,464	1,249	1,394	1,394
Discount factors @ 16%	1	0.862	0.743	0.641	0.552	0.552 x 1/0.16
PV	920	576	1,088	801	769	4,809

	Z$ million
Total PV of free cash flows	8,963
Less: value of debt	(1,920)
Value of equity	7,043

This is much higher than the current market value, suggesting that the market does not know about or perhaps does not believe the growth rates anticipated in the plan.

4.7 Discuss how the market value of Domusco could be estimated using earnings, assets and dividend approaches

1 *Earnings approach*

Given that Domusco is quoted, we can determine its P/E ratio:

P/E ratio = share price / earnings per share = 13.82 / 1.55 = 8.92

Obviously if we just apply this figure to the stated earnings of Domusco, then we arrive back at the quoted value of Z$13.82. However, this P/E ratio could be used to value potential acquisitions or to see the impact of different scenarios on Domusco.

For example, suppose the decision to use fewer sub-contactors and recruit more staff resulted in an overall cost saving of Z$100,000 per annum. This should result in Domusco increasing in value by 8.92 x 100,000 = Z$892,000.

If we were given the industry average P/E ratio, then we could see Domusco has a higher valuation than average or lower.

For example, suppose the industry average P/E were 8. Domusco has a higher P/E indicating that its earnings are perceived by the market to be higher quality – usually a mixture of higher growth and / or lower risk. Domusco has higher growth than the industry average but probably higher risk as well.

This would be the main problem if we used an industry P/E to value Domusco – it may have higher risk and growth than the average industry player, so the P/E ratio given would be less useful.

If one were considering a possible takeover, then synergies would need to be factored into the earnings figure.

2 *Net assets approach*

Book value of equity = Z$3429.2 million.

This is substantially lower than the market value of Z$6,102.9 million.

One would normally expect an asset valuation to be more useful for a construction company as it would hold significant levels of land, buildings, vehicles and materials. The large difference between book value and market value is probably due to the following:

(a) The balance sheet does not show goodwill.

(b) Land and WIP are shown at cost rather than NRV.

It should be feasible to calculate a more accurate NRV figure using the services of surveyors / professional valuers. The main problem would be in valuing part-completed buildings – especially if constructed without being commissioned.

3 *Dividend valuation model (DVM) approach*

To use the DVM we need to know a Ke and dividend growth. We have calculated Domusco's Ke in the answer to Q2 above and have already discussed the problems of getting a suitable growth rate.

As with the discussion of the earnings approach, the Ke and growth estimated are only useful if valuing potential acquisitions or valuing Domusco using changed figures.

Again, if given an industry Ke, we could use this to value Domusco and compare the answer to the share price as given by the market.

The DVM is only really useful if valuing a minority stake, in which case it would be easier to use the market share price.

4.8 Domusco uses ROCE for performance measurement. What alternative approaches could be used to assess potential investments?

To link in more with the stated objective of maximising shareholder wealth, Domusco could use any of the following:

- Net present value – the classic approach to investment appraisal
- Cash flow return on investment (CFROI)
- Economic profit

- Economic value added (EVA)
- Market value added (MVA).

If the unseen information details a foreign investment, then the following NPV approach is probably best:

Suppose the investment is in the USA:

Calculate cash flows for US project, taking into account US tax.

↓

Forecast the exchange rates over the life of the project using either purchasing power parity or interest rate parity.

↓

Convert the US$ cash flows into Z$ cash flows, taking into account any remittance restrictions.

↓

Compute any Zee tax liability, taking into account double tax relief and royalty payments.

↓

Discount the post tax Z$ net cash flows using a Z$ discount rate.

5 Analysis: Risk and control perspective

5.1 Assess the risks facing Domusco under the following headings and summarise

Risk area	Domusco
Business risks	
	• Very competitive industry
	• High threat of entry from other inter national firms
	• Very difficult to plan over the longer term, especially for major construction projects
	• Penalties if stadium contract not completed on time
	• Problems resourcing both the stadium and Hadsi contracts – if more sub-contractors are used, then there could be quality problems
	• Cost overruns, e.g. the motorway contract in Wye
	• Need to forecast accurately what type of property is required, e.g. growth in single-person dwellings
	• Switching to building more property without being commissioned by clients in advance exposes Domusco to more risk but the possibility of higher margins
Financial risks	
	• Low gearing risk
	• Low credit risk
	• Working capital management is key due to the long operating cycles involved
	• Some exposure to currency risk for the Hadsi contract where loans are in US$ and Euros but costs in Z$

Political and legal risks

- Many large contracts are awarded by government departments – government policies will thus have a huge impact on the industry
- Domusco is based in Zee – outside the EU – so will face trade barriers. EU enlargement will enable some of Domusco's competitors in countries like Poland easier access to other EU markets
- Middle East countries in which Domusco is involved could be unstable politically (e.g. Lebanon) or a possible target for US action (e.g. Syria)
- New legislation regarding health and safety, labour rights and building regulations
- Unlikely to face litigation except for safety issues

Technology risk

- Domusco is keen to utilse new technologies in its builds. While this can give competitive advantage there is also the risk that, over time, problems are found with these new techniques and materials

Economic risk

- High systematic risk with the indus try being closely linked to the state of the economy
- This includes government spending plans, consumer confidence and whether people have the money to afford luxury housing
- The level of interest rates will have a major bearing on the housing market, as the majority of customers will need mortgages

- For EU contracts Domusco is likely to use local materials and staff, limiting exchange risk but the final profit will be exposed to exchange rate movements between the Euro and the Z$

Reputation risk

- Domusco's reputation is key to winning contracts so anything that could damage that reputation should be viewed as a serious risk
- Key areas relate to damaging the environment, sustainability, health and safety, employment rights and ethics. All of these are covered in more detail in question 3 below

Overall the key risks are business risks.

5.2 Suggest some KPIs that could be used to monitor operations, using the balanced score card as a framework

Financial perspective

- ROCE and RI – overall and by SBU
- Margins – overall and by product / customer / country
- Different costs as a percentage of sales e.g. labour costs / sales, sub-contractor costs / sales
- Sales growth
- Cash flow targets
- Market share

Customer perspective

- Percentage of scheduled targets met – especially whether contracts are finished on time. Percentage of repeated business
- Number of complaints received
- Targets for new customers won
- Percentage of apartments sold off-plan for such developments

Internal business perspective

- Percentage of tenders won
- Percentage of utilisation of fixed assets – vehicles, plant and machinery
- Percentage of contracts with cost overruns
- Cost overrun as percentage of budgeted cost· Targets for employee productivity
- For staffing, environmental and health and safety measures see Q3 below.

Innovation and learning perspective

- Number of patents established for new methods / technologies
- Percentage of new materials used compared to total materials
- Percentage of total revenue coming from new buildings using new structural innovations in their design

5.3 Discuss the importance of social responsibility to Domusco. On what areas should Domusco focus to enhance its reputation? Suggest some KPIs Domusco could use

The construction industry will be closely scrutinised by environmental groups so firms who fail to meet standards are likely to receive a great deal of negative publicity. There are two main implications of such adverse publicity:

(1) The firm may struggle to win contracts, particularly with governments.

(2) Activist groups may target the firm's activities, causing disruption, delays, control problems and extra costs.

It is essential that Domusco has clear policies and targets to protect its reputation. These could cover the following areas:

- protecting the environment
- health and safety
- employment rights
- ethics

Protecting the environment

Domusco should actively manage the environmental impact of its sites and projects. A term often used by contractors in the UK is 'sustainable development'. Typical areas of interest can be:

- conserving natural habitats
- integrating structures into their surroundings
- managing resources
- waste recycling.

Suitable metrics could include:

- number of environmental prosecutions
- number of environmental enforcement actions
- number of 'notifiable' incidents (local legislation will define what is 'notifiable' and what is not)
- number of non-notifiable incidents
- percentage of employees working within an ISO 14001 compliant Environmental Management System
- Domusco's rating in independent benchmarking such as the Business in the Environment Index
- percentage of waste recycled rather than dumped.

Health and safety

The nature of the industry is that accidents are likely to occur, so the firm must put in place clear policies and targets to protect staff, and must create a strong health and safety culture.

Suitable metrics could include:

- number of fatalities
- number of permanently disabling injuries
- number of enforcement actions
- Accident Frequency Rate (AFR) i.e. the number of reportable (major and over three-day sick leave) accidents per 100,000 hours worked
- Lost Time Incident Frequency Rate (LTIFR)
- sickness absence rate
- health and safety training rate (days/employee)
- percentage of employees working within an ISO 18001 compliant Health and Safety Management System.

Employment rights

As well as protecting staff health, Domusco will want to be seen to be a 'good' employer who offers equal opportunities, training and promotion prospects.

Suitable metrics could include:

- workforce gender composition – generally, amongst senior managers, etc
- employee instigated turnover
- other employee turnover
- new hires
- employees taking their first job with Domusco
- new trainees
- promotion rate
- internal hire rate
- employment cost
- training spend ratio to employment cost.

Ethics

There is a great deal of scope in the construction industry for practices that some may deem unethical such as:

- bribing government officials to win contracts
- poor terms of employment and working conditions for staff in countries where it is not illegal to do so
- pollution and poor waste management in countries where it is not illegal to do so
- cutting costs in ways that expose staff to higher risks
- using sub-standard materials in buildings to cut costs but increasing the risk that the building may collapse in an earthquake, for example.

In all these areas Domusco would be wise to adopt the best practice from all of the countries it deals with.

Some of the metrics mentioned already relate to ethical issues such as the environment and health and safety. Domusco should also set up a helpline for staff to call if they have concerns. It could then measure calls to the helpline and any disciplinary actions that resulted.

5.4 Concerns have been raised over the use of sub-contractors. How could contractors be controlled to ensure that they do at least as good a job as employed staff?

Selecting contractors

- Where possible, Domusco should only use contractors who it has used before and who have clearly demonstrated that they are able to deliver work to the required timescale and quality.
- Where this is not possible, Domusco could insist on only using firms with appropriate quality accreditation, such as ISO 9000 series.
- Review environmental group websites to see if a contractor has a bad reputation, whether they have faced litigation over work carried out, etc.

Training contractors

- Domusco should insist that all contractors' foremen and engineers attend training days detailing how to use Domusco's methods and technology and demonstrating the quality required.

Controlling contractors

- Domusco should ensure that they have their own engineers on site throughout the duration of the project, inspecting the work carried out and ensuring that any quality issues are rectified immediately.
- Domusco could insist on seeing evidence that all contractors' staff have a minimum of two years' experience, say, or have appropriate qualifications.
- Contractors should be set detailed targets on what exactly must be done by what date.
- Contractors should be made subject to penalty clauses covering the following:
  - staff continuity
  - time deadlines
  - quality issues.
- Rather than a fixed fee, contracts could include bonuses relating to completion of work on time and to the required quality as an alternative to penalty clauses. (Note that a penalty clause is a common feature of the industry.)

chapter

13

DOMUSCO: SEPTEMBER 2005 – UNSEEN MATERIAL

Contents

1 Question requirement

"You are the consultant appointed by the Domusco Board.

Prepare a report that prioritises and advises on the main issues facing Domusco and makes appropriate recommendations."

2 Rest of the unseen material

Success of Hadsi development to date

Domusco is planning to construct a total of 12,000 housing units in the Hadsi area over a three-year period. When Domusco's housing plans were launched during 2004 for the first phase of 3,000 housing units, the public interest was good. By the end of August 2005 Domusco had cumulative sales in the Hadsi area of over 78% of the first phase of 3,000 housing units. This comprised a higher level of pre-sales (defined as sales made prior to the start of construction work) as well as a high level of sales made after the start of construction. Interest in Domusco's housing remains strong and Domusco is confident that all 3,000 housing units in the first phase will be sold before the completion of construction work. Domusco decided to bring forward the launch of the second phase of housing units in Hadsi and in August 2005 has presales of over 18% of the phase two housing units, some six months before construction is even due to commence. Domusco's sales of housing in other areas of Zee were also strong, as well as in other areas of Europe and the USA. Domusco forecasts that its total completed housing units in 2005 might be as high as 18,800 units, including the sale of the first phase of 3,000 housing units in the Hadsi area.

The Domusco house building subsidiary company's cash balance had quickly changed from a deficit to a surplus of Z$1,200 million at the end of August 2005.

The development of the Hadsi region of Zee has been acclaimed as a success by the media and many companies were planning to move into the region. Many companies chose to move to Hadsi as the technology incorporated in the new office buildings used ecological and energy-saving solutions for air conditioning and heating. The Zee government was very pleased with the success of the Hadsi area and also announced the relocation of one of its government agencies to Hadsi. The Zee government chose to purchase one of the larger office buildings that Domusco was in the process of constructing and contracts for the purchase were signed at the end of August 2005.

In August 2005, Domusco announced that it intended to relocate its offices to one of the most prestigious of all of the new office blocks in the Hadsi region, as it has outgrown its present Head Office building in Zee. The new offices are forecast to meet the requirements of Domusco's Zee-based staff for the next eight years, assuming the company expands in accordance with its ten-year plan. In addition to the Hadsi office building that Domusco plans to move to, Domusco had signed contracts with a total of seven other companies for office buildings in Hadsi by the end of August 2005.

Construction of sport stadium in Europe

In August 2005 Domusco signed contracts for the construction of a large national sports stadium in a European country. The contract value was €180 million (approximately Z$459 million). Peter Kaye is very concerned at the lack of available experienced manpower within the company that can be allocated to this major construction project. He has been requested by the Domusco Board to consider whether part of the work could be sub-contracted to a large international company (which the contract terms allow) or whether to recruit staff locally in the European country on short-term contracts. Peter Kaye is also concerned about the tight deadlines and the final stage payment of €12 million (approximately Z$31 million) that will only be paid if the stadium is built to the agreed deadline of April 2007.

Construction work in Wye

Domusco has been unable to renegotiate the motorway construction budget for the large project that Domusco is currently constructing in Wye. This project is now forecast to make a loss of Z$44 million but Domusco is contractually bound to complete the motorway construction.

At the August 2005 Domusco Board meeting, it was decided that Domusco would no longer undertake any further construction work in Wye that is funded by the Wye Government. This will result in Domusco declining to bid for a number of major construction projects for the Wye Government, which are in Domusco's current plan. Domusco will continue to build a small amount of housing in Wye, which it sells to private buyers. Therefore Domusco's current plan is overstated. The effect on the Domusco Group's post-tax cash flows for the next five years due to the removal of Wye Government-funded projects is as follows:

	2005	2006	2007	2008	2009
	Z$ million	Z$ million	Z$ million	Z$ million	Z$ million
Reduction in Domusco Group cash flows due to removal of Wye Government-funded projects	80	110	110	120	140

Updated cash flow forecast as a result of recent events

The high sales of housing and offices in Zee, including the Hadsi development, and the high housing sales in other countries, as well as the newly awarded contract for the sports stadium (that was not in the current plan), has been incorporated in an updated cash flow forecast for the Domusco Group. However, the updated forecast cash flows, shown below, have not yet been adjusted for the removal of government-funded projects in Wye.

By the end of August 2005 the Domusco Group had a cash balance of Z$1,000 million. The current cash balance and forecast end year cash balances for the next five years, after tax, loan repayments and planned dividend payments, are now forecast to be as follows:

	End August 2005	End December 2005	End December 2006	End December 2007	End December 2008	End December 2009
	Z$ million	Z$ million	Z$ million	Z$ million	Z$ million	Z$ million
Forecast cash balance	1,000	1,300	1,800	1,700	1,600	1,400

The above cash forecast assumes that Domusco does not increase its loans during 2005, as included in the current plan (Appendix 4 to the pre-seen material).

Development in Metsa

The Zee Government has announced that the area of Metsa, west of the Hadsi region, is the next area of the country that could be developed. It is further along the coast from Hadsi, in rugged terrain and is much smaller than the area of the Hadsi land. The Zee Government is pleased with the way that Domusco has managed the Hadsi development. The Zee Government has now offered the entire plot of land in Metsa to Domusco at a cost of Z$500 million.

Peter Kaye is proposing that Domusco retains the entire plot and undertakes the entire development of the Metsa land. However, Peter Kaye's team cannot forecast the construction costs with any accuracy until further survey work is undertaken and construction work is commenced. As the terrain in this area is more difficult, initial land preparation would be more difficult and more expensive. However, Peter Kaye's team have prepared two levels of cash flows depending on what problems they encounter during construction, together with estimated probabilities.

These cash outflows (before tax), which exclude the cost of the land of Z$500 million, are shown below:

Cash outflows for Mesta construction project	**Probability**	**2006**	**2007**	**2008**	**2009**	**Total**
		Z$ million	Z$ million	Z$ million	Z$ million	Z$ million
High cost scenario cash outflows	75%	250	340	480	580	1,650
Normal cost scenario cash outflows	25%	130	160	340	380	1,010

The proposed revenues mainly from housing, with some office buildings, for the Metsa development, are forecast to be as follows:

	2006	**2007**	**2008**	**2009**	**Total**
	Z$ million	Z$ million	Z$ million	Z$ million	Z$ million
Metsa forecast revenues	0	600	850	1,000	2,450

The revenues and cash outflows given above are before tax, and tax should be assumed to be 30%. Martyn Lite stated that a suitable risk-adjusted discount rate for evaluating this construction project is 12% post-tax.

Marma Winge stated at the August 2005 Domusco Board meeting that he considered that the housing market in Zee was growing too fast and the level of growth in the sales of new housing could not be expected to continue. He also reminded the Domusco Board that the company had a land bank of around Z$1,900 million of land in Zee for future development. He did not have confidence, despite the success of the Hadsi project so far, that Metsa would be as successful. He was also concerned that Domusco should not undertake the entire development of Metsa on its own. He stated that there was a risk that the housing in Metsa would not sell as well as in the Hadsi area.

Will Umm is concerned about the development in the Metsa area due to concerns from environmental groups. Domusco managed to overcome the environmental issues in its development in Hadsi, by making some compromises and allowing a small forest to remain intact and reducing the size of the commercial area in Hadsi. However, the world's media has already supported the local opposition groups who do not want to see the Metsa area developed, as it has a number of sites of archaeological interest. However, the Zee Government has publicly stated that the development of the Metsa area is required to help Zee to sustain its economic growth.

Proposed joint venture with Olan

The government in a European country is funding the construction of a large sports stadium. Olan is a leading construction company in this European country, but it has not constructed a sports stadium of the size specified for construction. The government has indicated to Olan that it considers that the stadium could be built to budget and on time if an experienced company were to be involved in a joint venture with Olan. Olan has approached Domusco with a proposal for a joint venture. Bids for this stadium are due to be submitted in January 2006 and the decision to award the contract will be announced in March 2006.

Peter Kaye is concerned that most of his employees are already committed on other projects, including the recently awarded contract to construct a sports stadium in another European country. He recognises that Domusco would need to recruit additional staff as he considered that a project of this size, even taken on as a joint venture, could not rely on Domusco's current high level of sub-contract staff. Peter Kaye's department has estimated that this proposed joint venture with Olan, if awarded, would need an additional 1,200 man-years, over the three-year project timescale. This would result in the recruitment of an additional 400 employees.

If Domusco were awarded the joint venture contract with Olan, it would be Domusco's largest ever contract for a single building, at the equivalent of Z$2,400 million total revenue (which would be shared with Olan in the agreed joint venture split, which has not yet been agreed). If Domusco agreed to be a 50/50 joint venture partner, its share of the contract would be Z$1,200 million and its share of the profits for the contract over three years, would be over Z$300 million.

Peter Kaye has estimated that, if Domusco did bid for this contract, in a joint venture with Olan, then it could have an 80% probability of being awarded the contract. Martyn Lite is concerned that working capital requirements would be high for this contract, as the European government has stated that stage payments would only be paid after the completion of different stages of construction. Within the first 12 months, the total working capital for the entire project would be the equivalent of around Z$850 million.

Will Umm is not entirely confident about the proposed joint venture with Olan. Olan has suffered from bad press coverage on several occasions. There was a reported incident when Olan had been accused of bribery to win government contracts in its home country, but this was never proven. Additionally, Olan has a bad track record with the way in which it treats its subcontractors and its employees. Its safety record, which is public knowledge, is poor. Olan is keen to work with Domusco. However, Domusco's non-executive directors are unsure about the proposed joint venture.

Employee survey

Domusco has undertaken its fourth employee survey and the management is now considering the findings. The points raised by employees include the following.

(a) **Issues concerning sub-contractors**

Domusco employees continue to complain about the quality of the work undertaken by sub-contractors. The employees are also aware that some sub-contractors are paid a larger daily fee than their own salaries, and feel that they are under-valued.

Domusco employees report that there are a greater number of sub-contractors who are employing workers with insufficient training or inadequate experience. Zee is experiencing a construction boom at present, and a variety of inexperienced people have sought work in the construction industry. Some of Domusco's sub-contractors have employed inexperienced staff, which has led to some workers ignoring safety issues and demonstrating a lack of awareness for the importance of safety. Some Domusco employees have refused to work at one site where there have been a number of accidents caused by sub-contractors.

(b) **Employee sickness**

Domusco has a number of employees absent on long-term sickness leave. The main reason for long-term sickness is not for work-related injuries, but is due to stress.

(c) **Shortage of managers**

Some of Domusco's managers have reported that they feel under pressure to complete their jobs in unrealistic timescales. They also state that they have insufficient junior managers to support them and they are under pressure to meet budgets and deadlines.

August 2005 Domusco Board meeting

When the Board met in August 2005, it was agreed that Domusco was experiencing its most successful phase in its building history, despite the forecast loss on the Wye motorway contract. Domusco's share price had risen slightly to Z$13.95.

Carlos Freer announced that the unsold land in the Hadsi area, that Domusco owned, would be sold to either of two office construction companies that were both very interested in it. Both companies were keen to purchase the land following the recent high profile sales of office space in Hadsi and each construction company was trying to finalise its bid price. Domusco is hoping to be able to receive over Z$200 million within the next three months for the land that it has in the group balance sheet as inventory for Z$102 million.

Martyn Lite was pleased to announce that the Domusco Group had a very strong positive cash flow at present, and a cash balance of Z$1,000 million at the end of August 2005. The Board discussed a number of ways in which it could expand its business, given its current strong cash position.

In addition to the Metsa and Olan proposals detailed above, some further uses of the cash balance discussed were:

- Martyn Lite is keen to repay loans. The company has a Z$324 million loan which is due to be repaid in 2007, but could be paid back early. Additionally the company took out two loans to finance the start of the construction work on the Hadsi development, which could be repaid early if the Board decided to.
- Marma Winge wants to expand the USA house building operations by organic growth, but needs sufficient working capital to do this. He plans to set up a further subsidiary company that would need around Z$200 million funding to open offices, acquire land, construct some houses and market them in this new geographic area within the USA. He considers that there is huge potential for new business and that the USA market is growing rapidly. This expansion in the USA is in the company's ten-year plan, but not until 2007. Marma Winge would like to bring this project forward.

- Will Umm stated that Domusco is permitted to buy back its shares on the stock market in Zee, but asked for advice as to whether the company should use some, or all, of its surplus cash to buy back shares.

Investigations into cash shortages

It had been brought to the attention of Jaz Grue, who is one the senior finance managers based in Domusco's Head Office in Zee, that one of the cash reconciliations could not be reconciled. Jaz Grue was inquisitive and pursued the reconciliation problem, which concerned reconciling deposits paid by customers for their houses in Zee to cheques banked. Jaz Grue works in Domusco's subsidiary for house building in Zee and has a dotted line responsibility to Martyn Lite, but his direct manager is Marma Winge.

With the large volume of sales of houses in Zee, the bank reconciliation between the value of cheques banked and sales receipts issued showed a shortfall of around Z$1.6 million. After his investigations, Jaz Grue discovered that a number of house sales, both in the Hadsi area and elsewhere in Zee, have not had deposits accounted for as paid. Instead he has uncovered what could be a major fraud involving a group of eight of Domusco's employees in the house building subsidiary based in Zee. The missing cheques from Domusco customers had not been identified as the customers are not due to pay a further instalment, or the final payment for their new houses for many months. Initially, the difference was considered to be due to timing differences.

Jaz Grue was unsure of what to do or whom to approach. On Friday 2 September 2005, he decided to speak to Jackie Paul, Human Resources Director. On hearing the extent of the fraud, Jackie Paul decided to instantly dismiss Jaz Grue, as she considered that he had been negligent in allowing the fraud to occur and for not identifying the cash shortfall before it had reached such a large sum. Jackie Paul has now advised Marma Winge and Martyn Lite of her action of dismissing Jaz Grue.

Appointment of consultant

The Domusco Group has been through a very busy phase with the high growth of sales in Zee and elsewhere and Tom Micol is undecided on where the company should use its resources.

The Board has decided that it would like to have the advice from an experienced consultant. It has appointed a leading global consultancy company.

chapter

14

DOMUSCO: SEPTEMBER 2005 SAMPLE SOLUTION

Contents

1 Introduction

What follows is a possible answer for the Domusco September 2005 exam. It is more complete (though still not perfect by any means!) than some of the other answers in this text book and gives a better idea of the potential scope of a solution rather that what could realistically be completed in the time available.

Given that, it is still just one possible solution and, as always, alternative interpretations may be valid.

2 Sample script

REPORT (CONFIDENTIAL)

To: The Board of directors, Domusco

From: A Consultant

Date: Today

Domusco: Current issues and future strategies

Contents

Appendices

1 Introduction

Domusco is currently witnessing a period of unparalleled growth and profitability and has a cash balance of Z$1,000 million available at 31 August 2005. The Hadsi contract in particular appears to be a major success.

Future growth is forecast to be even higher with major new contracts being considered in Metsa and a joint venture with Olan.

The key challenge facing the firm is how to use its current cash surplus – which projects should be undertaken and whether and how funds should be returned to shareholders.

2 Terms of reference

This report has been prepared at the request of the Board of Directors of Domusco, to examine and advise on the future strategies for Domusco, looking in particular at how best to spend the cash available.

Each of the major strategic options currently being considered by the Board is discussed in detail and recommendations are made.

3 Prioritisation of key issues

A detailed SWOT analysis of Domusco is shown in Appendix 1. Out of these the key points are as follows.

3.1 Top priority: How to use the existing cash balance of Z$1,000 million

Domusco has a cash surplus of Z$1,000 million at the end of August 2005 and must consider how best to use the money. This issue is prioritised as first due to its size and because the Board of Domusco has specifically asked us to examine it.

This issue is discussed in more detail in section 4.1 of this report.

3.2 Second priority: The proposed joint venture with Olan

Olan, a large European construction company, has proposed a joint venture with Domusco to construct a new stadium. The Board thus needs to make a decision whether to accept the proposal.

This issue is seen as key due to its size – it would be the largest single building contract ever attempted by Domusco – and urgency – as bids for this stadium are due to be submitted in January 2006.

This issue is discussed in more detail in section 4.2 of this report.

3.3 Third priority: The proposed development in Metsa

Given the success to date of the Hadsi contract, the Zee Government is keen for Domusco to undertake a similar contract in Metsa. The Board thus needs to decide whether to accept this proposal.

This issue is seen as key due to its size – it would involve an investment of Z$500 million – and its strategic significance as a refusal could damage ongoing relationships with the Zee Government.

This issue is discussed in more detail in section 4.3 of this report.

3.4 Fourth priority: The use of sub-contractors on the new stadium contract

Domusco is under pressure to finish the stadium contract by April 2007. If this is not achieved then Z$31 million will be lost. The Board thus needs to evaluate different options to finish on time, notably the use of sub-contractors.

The issue is considered key due to its urgency and the size of the potential loss.

This issue is discussed in more detail in section 4.4 of this report.

3.5 Fifth priority: Construction work in Wye

Given the recent losses on the motorway contract in Wye and the Zee Government's refusal to contribute towards the cost overruns, the Board has decided to withdraw from further contracts with the Wye Government. This issue is considered significant due to the scale of the potential cash flow implications of this decision.

This issue is discussed in more detail in section 4.5 of this report.

3.6 Other issues

While not considered major at this stage, the Board should also consider the following:

US house building

We agree with plans to expand the US house building operations in 2007 for the following reasons:

- The US housing market is experiencing high growth at present.
- Recent hurricanes have resulted in a surge in demand for both affordable and luxury housing in the southern States.
- The weak US dollar could make financing easier if Domusco decides to use existing funds. However, it is more likely that US$ loans would be used to finance US expansion to hedge currency risk.

Non-commissioned office building

We recommend that you cease from undertaking non-commissioned office work for the following reasons:

- Such developments are more risky and have resulted in Domusco only being able to sell some finished building at a loss.
- Clients may not want the features Domusco has designed into the building. Domusco's strength lies in responding to customer needs, rather than anticipating them.

Human resources problems

Staff are currently stressed, resent sub-contractors and are struggling with deadlines. Furthermore there is a lack of junior managers. All of these issues can be addressed by a policy of further recruitment and career development. There will also be a need for sub-contractors but we recommend that their importance be reduced and greater emphasis placed on employed staff.

4 How to use the existing cash balance of Z$1,000 million

Key principles

The main principle to consider when deciding how to use surplus cash is that attractive projects are undertaken to generate shareholder value. This usually means using surplus cash for investment before considering repaying capital. There is little point reducing capital employed in one part of the business while raising finance elsewhere. The key question is thus which projects to undertake.

Obviously there are other factors to consider – for example, Domusco could use US$ loans to finance US expansion to hedge currency risk while using Z$ to repurchase shares in Zee.

Once attractive projects have been exhausted, Domusco needs to consider how much cash it needs to have. Then any surplus can be used to reduce capital employed.

Share buy-backs

The main reasons for share repurchases are as follows:

- to return surplus cash to shareholders
- to increase the share price
- to increase eps as comparable earnings are shared over fewer shares.

The main problems for Domusco are:

- a one-off larger dividend would be simpler and cheaper
- the move will increase Domusco's gearing level.

Reducing gearing

The main issue when considering repaying debt is the level of gearing wanted. Domusco has been increasing its gearing levels for the last few years and a reduction in gearing may be welcomed by city investors. On the other hand, less gearing also means a reduced tax shield and the benefits of cheap debt finance.

A reduction in debt would also give management more freedom in the use of cash as interest commitments are reduced.

Possible scenarios

Assuming that Domusco continues to withdraw from future Wye Government contracts, its future cash flows will be as follows:

Z$ millions	**2005***	**2006**	**2007**	**2008**	**2009**
Current cash flow forecast	300	500	(100)	(100)	(200)
Excluding Wye Government contracts	(80)	(110)	(110)	(120)	(140)
Net CF	220	390	1,610	1,400	1,180
Bal b/f	1,000	1,220	1,610	1,400	1,180
Bal c/f at 31 December	1,220	1,610	1,400	1,180	840

* The 2005 period is for the four months to 31 December 2005.

The different investment opportunities would require the following investments in 2005:

- Metsa contract Z$500 million
- Oman contract Z$425 million (assuming a 50% stake)
- US expansion Z$200 million

The following scenarios are thus possible:

- All three of these could be financed from existing funds but would leave little working capital.
- A better option would be to use a US$ loan to finance US expansion, use existing cash to finance both the Metsa and Olan contracts and still have Z$295 million cash for running the business.
- Use a US$ loan for the US expansion, reject the Olan deal, finance the Metsa deal, repay Z$500 million of finance and have Z$220 million cash left.
- Use a US$ loan for the US expansion, reject the Metsa deal, finance the Olan deal, repay Z$500 million of finance and have Z$295 million cash left.

As stated above, the key is to decide which projects to undertake first. Detailed discussion of each of the possible projects is carried out below.

5 Proposed joint venture with Olan

The proposed joint venture with Olan to build a new stadium in a country where Domusco does not yet have a presence is an example of market development, according to Ansoff's matrix.

The main arguments for and against the proposal are as follows:

Arguments for a joint venture

- The project is planned to make Z$600 million over three years. If Domusco gets a 50% share of this then it would gain an average of Z$100 million pa, increasing shareholder value and EPS.
- Olan has local expertise, contacts and resources.
- A joint venture may be the only way of Domusco winning the contract.
- Domusco has some experience of building stadia.
- Risks are shared with Olan.

Arguments against a joint venture

- Olan has a poor reputation regarding alleged bribery and poor treatment of sub-contractors. The risk is that Domusco's reputation would be similarly tarnished if problems arise on the contract. The public may not be able to distinguish between the different parties when apportioning blame. What control could Domusco exercise to alleviate this?
- Olan has limited experience in building large stadia.
- Domusco's resources are already stretched and this project would require Domesco to recruit and train a further 400 employees.

- Even with only a 50% share, the project would be larger than the Hadsi investment and would constitute a significant risk exposure.
- There is a danger of Olan gaining expertise from Domusco that could later be used against the company.

Summary

This is a substantial project with massive upside potential. The main problem lies with the choice of partner i.e. Olan. On balance Olan needs Domusco more than Domusco needs Olan. The main options are that an alternative partner be sought or, failing that, Domusco can try to get more than 50% control of the stadium contract to safeguard its interests.

6 The proposed development in Metsa

The Government proposal for Domusco to manage a major construction project in Metsa is a market penetration strategy, according to Ansoff's matrix.

The main arguments for and against acceptance are as follows:

Arguments for Metsa

- Based on probabilities, the expected NPV of the investment is positive Z$49.5 million, indicating that the investment will increase shareholder value (Appendix 2).
- The Zee Government is very keen for the development to proceed. Supporting the Metsa project could result in further contracts.
- Domusco now has more experience of running such a project, given the apparent success of the Hadsi development. The Metsa project could be a good way to capitalise on good publicity generated by the Hadsi development.
- The Metsa project is smaller than Hadsi so could be considered less risky.

Arguments against Metsa

- While on average the project will generate a positive NPV, there is a 75% chance of reducing shareholder value (Appendix 1).
- Metsa is in a more remote location and will probably be more costly to develop. The remoteness, especially from major centres such as Prine also puts a question mark over whether anyone will want to move there. Most people who want to relocate from cities may already have done so to Hadsi.
- The terrain in Metsa is more difficult than in Hadsi. Domusco's experience of difficult terrain in Wye should provide a warning to the risks inherent here.

- There are a number of environmental and archaeological concerns over the site. This could result in bad publicity for Domusco and will be more difficult to solve than with the Hadsi development.
- If the feared market slowdown happens, Domusco may not be able to sell the houses as quickly as needed.
- Domusco's resources are still stretched by the Hadsi project.

On balance the key issue is risk. One option would be to delay making a decision until more detailed surveying can be done.

7 The use of sub-contractors on the existing stadium contract

If the current stadium project is not finished by April 2006, then Domusco stands to lose a final progress payment of Z$31 million. To ensure completion Domusco could consider the following:

- further use of sub-contractors – this is considered in more detail below
- switching existing resources from other projects – this is discounted on the grounds that no spare resources exist and this option would only create new problems in different parts of the company.

In general, the main arguments for and against using sub-contractors are as follows.

Arguments for using sub-contractors

- Provides resources allowing Doumsco to undertake projects that would otherwise not be feasible.
- Flexibility e.g. Domusco may wish to use a new contractor that can offer a cheaper / better service.
- Lower fixed costs and operating gearing – this is a particular concern given the volatile nature of the industry.
- Sub-contractors may be specialists and would do a better job than Domusco staff.
- Employed staff are not always in the right area or have the correct skills. It may not be cost-effective to recruit and train staff for projects, knowing that they will be made redundant when the project finishes.

Arguments against using sub-contractors

- Reduced control over quality e.g. ensuring that all staff are suitably trained, better continuity of staff, jobs less likely to be rushed.
- Employing staff may work out cheaper, especially as this would avoid paying sub-contactors' profit margins.

- Existing staff feel undervalued when they see sub-contractors paid more then they are.
- Existing staff have expressed concerns at the level of accidents incurred by sub-contractors.
- Can become over-dependent on sub-contractors, especially with major construction projects where contractors may have to be hired at short notice.
- Communication can be more difficult – especially getting advance notice of potential problems.
- Conflicting objectives – sub-contractors may be more interested in finishing a job quickly because of other commitments rather than achieving the desired quality standards.

Summary

The two main areas where sub-contractors are used extensively are in the major construction contracts company and house building construction.

This type of work should be relatively simple in which case it would be harder for Domusco to perform it better or cheaper than an outside specialist, explaining why sub-contractors have been used here.

For Domusco a key concern is quality – the basis of its competitive advantage lies in offering a better product to clients. This should be the basis upon which decisions are made – where quality is compromised by sub-contractors, then hire staff; where quality is not an issue, then the benefits of flexibility should take preference.

In the case of the existing stadium contract the key issue is whether or not it will be finished on time. The use of sub-contractors could be justified here to avoid penalties and because the sub-contractor is a large and presumably experienced firm.

8 Withdrawal from government contracts in Wye

The Board has recently decided to withdraw from further Wye Government contracts because of recent problems with existing contracts. In this section the arguments concerning this decision are reviewed.

The withdrawal from government contracts in Wye can be justified on the following grounds:

- The Wye Government refused to co-operate when cost overruns arose on existing projects and may be equally unsympathetic if problems arise on other contracts.

- The Wye Government may not view Domusco as favourably in future tenders because of problems with this contract.

However, such a withdrawal may be premature as:

- There may be scope for putting more detailed clauses covering various scenarios in future contracts and still have a chance of winning profitable contracts.
- Domusco is now more experienced in the possible problems in Wye and can incorporate this into negotiations.
- Continuing to tender could be seen as a sign of good faith by the Wye Government.
- Further Wye contracts were forecast to contribute cash inflows totalling Z$560 million over the next five years.

9 Ethical considerations

The main ethical issues facing Domusco are as follows.

The dismissal of Jaz Grue

The dismissal of Jaz Grue for 'whistle blowing' was ethically wrong for the following reasons:

- Jaz Grue had done nothing wrong to warrant dismissal so has been unfairly treated.
- Good practice procedures have not been followed, such as giving a written warning prior to any further action being taken.
- It encourages a culture of secrecy.

Jaz Grue should be reinstated immediately and the cash shortages investigated further before apportioning blame.

The Metsa contract

Any large construction project will generate stakeholder conflicts between developers and environmentalists.

There are a number of environmental concerns over the Metsa site, so being involved in the contract could result in bad publicity for Domusco. It is essential that a detailed environmental review be undertaken prior to any work being commenced and further concessions made if necessary.

Joint venture with Olan

Olan has a poor reputation regarding alleged bribery and poor treatment of sub-contractors. A joint venture could result in Domusco's reputation being compromised as well. If Domusco decide to continue, then it should insist on greater controls and improved work practices in these areas.

10 Recommendations

Using the existing cash surplus

We recommend that surplus cash be used to finance attractive projects first and then used to reduce gearing levels. Reducing debt is preferred to repurchasing shares or paying a high one-off dividend because of the recent history of increasing gearing. Specific project recommendations are given below.

Olan joint venture

The stadium project does look attractive. However, we recommend that you see if another more reputable firm is willing to tender for the project with you. Should you decide that the Olan offer is worth taking further, then we recommend that you clarify the following with regards to the nature of the joint venture:

- the precise formula for splitting costs and revenues
- sharing out risks and returns between the different parties
- how possible conflicts over operating decisions – e.g. dividends – will be resolved
- how quality can be guaranteed
- what level of support will be required from each party
- whether the stadium contract will contain penalty clauses and how such penalties would be shared between the two parties.

In particular you should try to get more than 50% of the control. This should be clarified prior to acceptance.

Metsa contract

We recommend that you try to get the Zee Government to give Domusco first refusal on the Metsa project so surveys can be done to see whether the costs will be normal or high before committing to the project. Alternatively see if the Government would be willing to insert a bail-out clause if Domusco subsequently discovers that the project is not viable.

If you do decide to continue, then run the project like the Hadsi development to get other firms involved to share risks and reduce resourcing requirements.

Existing stadium contract

The option of sub-contracting to a major international firm to complete the existing stadium contract is recommended as they are presumably experienced and the Z$31 million penalty saved will more than cover any extra cost. This could also free up some resources for other projects. In the longer term Domusco should seek to be less reliant on sub-contractors.

Wye Government contracts

Rather than pulling out of Wye completely, we recommend reconsidering each proposed contract in detail to assess the risks involved to see if any are still worth considering.

We also recommend investigating whether the Wye Government would consider suitable clauses in contracts before withdrawing completely from such business.

Other

All of the plans currently being considered are examples of further market penetration and market development with little emphasis on either product development or diversification. We recommend that alternative directions for growth, such as product development, be considered as well.

11 Conclusion

Domusco's competitive advantage is based on excellent designs, innovation and the use of high-technology features. This has resulted in high growth and a large cash surplus.

The key to future development and spending plans is to continue the high growth without exposing the firm to excessive risks and resourcing problems. This will involve careful choice of partners and focusing on key strengths.

Appendix 1: Position analysis using SWOT framework

Strengths

- Established competitive strategy of differentiation based on good designs and quality specifications
- Good financials – cash rich, strong balance sheet, profitable
- International reputation
- Innovative
- Listed company, so it is easier to raise finance
- Share price at a high, perhaps reflecting industry confidence

Weaknesses

- Lack of diversification – all business areas are very risky as dependent on the state of the economy. This also results in planning difficulties
- Falling margins on office contracts
- Small player outside Zee so may lack the economies of scale of larger rivals in those countries. Even in Zee Domusco is much smaller than other house builders
- May be trying to grow too quickly – in particular Domusco may not have the resources to complete both the Hadsi project and the new stadium contract

Opportunities

- Metsa development
- Joint venture with Olan
- More overseas expansion, especially in the USA
- Greater demand for cheaper housing
- Greater demand for apartments
- Hadsi project may win the contracts to build motorways and other transport infrastructure

Threats

- Domusco may not be able to deliver the new stadium contract on time to the required level of quality
- Reputation could have become damaged due to refusing to do more contracts in Wye, making it much harder to win government contracts
- Increasing international competition
- The office market in Zee seems to be declining
- Reduced demand for larger houses

Appendix 2: Evaluation of the proposed investment in Metsa

1 High cost scenario

Z$ millions	**2005**	**2006**	**2007**	**2008**	**2009**
	t = 0	t = 1	t = 2	t = 3	t = 4
Revenues			600	850	1,000
Costs (high)		(250)	(340)	(480)	(580)
Net		(250)	260	370	420
Tax @30% (Note 1)		75	(78)	(111)	(126)
Land	(500)				
Tax re land (Note 2)			37	52	61
Net CF	(500)	(175)	219	311	355
DF at 12%	1	0.893	0.797	0.712	0.636
PV	(500)	(156)	175	221	226
NPV	**(34)**				

2 Normal cost scenario

Z$ millions	**2005**	**2006**	**2007**	**2008**	**2009**
	t = 0	t = 1	t = 2	t = 3	t = 4
Revenues			600	850	1,000
Costs (normal)		(130)	(160)	(340)	(380)
Net		(130)	440	510	620
Tax @30% (Note 1)		39	(132)	(153)	(186)
Land	(500)				
Tax re land (Note 2)			37	52	61
Net CF	(500)	(91)	345	409	495
DF at 12%	1	0.893	0.797	0.712	0.636
PV	(500)	(81)	275	291	315
NPV	**+ 300**				

3 Expected NPV = 0.75 x –34 + 0.25 x 300 = +49.5 m

Note 1: Timing of tax flows: an assumption needs to be made regarding when tax is paid. The easiest assumption is to have cash flows occurring at the end of the accounting period concerned.

Note 2: Tax treatment of land: land is treated as inventory on the balance sheet so, rather than making an assumption regarding capital allowances, the cost of the land has been apportioned to match revenues for tax purposes.

Z$ millions	**2005**	**2006**	**2007**	**2008**	**2009**
	t = 0	t = 1	t = 2	t = 3	t = 4
Apportioned land cost			(122)	(173)	(205)
Tax @30%			37	52	61

Possible alternatives include assuming 100% FYAs on land purchases, straight line WDAs, etc.

Appendix 3: Ansoff's matrix analysis

	Existing products	**New products**
Existing markets	*Market penetration* • Metsa contract • US expansion	*Product development* • No plans suggested • Could move into the building of low cost affordable housing • Could develop more sophisticated building techniques to offer high quality housing that can be built very quickly
New markets	*Market development* • Joint venture with Olan	*Diversification* • No plans suggested • Could consider buying a supplier company that makes high quality windows (backwards vertical integration) • Could expand into the installation of power lines, sewerage pipes and other infrastructure to offer a complete solution

Summary

All of the plans currently being considered are examples of further market penetration and market development with little emphasis on either product development or diversification.

3 Commentary

The unseen information did not crystallise any particular issues identified in the pre-seen material, but added to them. Add in the usual general question requirement and you are left with the problem of how to structure your report, which issues to address and so on.

This gives rise to two opposing traps:

1 You try to cover everything in detail and end up either running out of time or lacking depth in key parts of your report.

2 You only address specific matters mentioned in the unseen material (Metsa, Olan, US expansion, how to spend the money, etc) but your report ends up without a clear structure and issues are discussed without a context.

The first trap is more dangerous – failure to reach conclusions and make recommendations will result in you failing the paper.

The above answer follows the leading of the unseen material to 'play it safe'.

Note: In some respects a more logical structure would have been to look primarily at the different SBUs of the firm with a co-ordinating theme of looking at risk in particular. It could then pull everything together by looking at the cash flow implications.

As for calculations, the above answer looks at the more obvious areas of assessing the Metsa plan using NPV and examining how much cash Domusco has and how it could be spent. Other calculations could have included sensitivity analysis to discuss risks, quantifying the impact of various options on EPS, etc.

Within the NPV calculations you had to make assumptions regarding some of the tax flows, trying to achieve a sensible balance between what is easy and what is more typical. The key here is to state your assumptions.

The main areas where the answer could have been improved are:

- more reference to real world market conditions and the activities of real-life firms
- alternative strategies could have been discussed further
- more could have been done using ratio analysis.

chapter

15

REUSER: PRE-SEEN MATERIAL

Scenario – Pre-seen material

This case study was the TOPCIMA case for the May 2005 examination paper. When analysing this material and answering the examination question, you should assume that 'now' is early 2005.

May 2005 - Assessment Matrix for TOPCIMA (Recycling - ReuseR and NOW)

Criterion	Marks*	Clear pass	Pass	Marginal pass	Marginal Fail	Fail	Clear fail
Technical	10	Thorough display of relevant technical knowledge. **9-10**	Good display of relevant knowledge. **6-8**	Some display of relevant technical knowledge. **5**	Identification of some relevant knowledge, but lacking in depth. **3-4**	Little knowledge displayed, or some misconceptions. **1-2**	No evidence of knowledge displayed, or fundamental misconceptions. **0**
Application	10	Knowledge clearly applied in an analytical and practical manner. **9-10**	Knowledge applied to the context of the case. **6-8**	Identification of some relevant knowledge, but not well applied. **5**	Knowledge occasionally displayed without clear application. **3-4**	Little attempt to apply knowledge to the context. **1-2**	No application of knowledge displayed. **0**
Diversity	10	Most knowledge areas identified, covering a wide range of views. **9-10**	Some knowledge areas identified, covering a range of views. **6-8**	A few knowledge areas identified, expressing a fairly limited scope. **5**	Several important knowledge aspects omitted. **3-4**	Many important knowledge aspects omitted. **1-2**	Very few knowledge aspects considered. **0**
Focus	10	Clearly distinguishes between relevant and irrelevant information. **9-10**	Information used is mostly relevant. **6-8**	Some relevant information ignored, or some less relevant information used. **5**	Information used is sometimes irrelevant. **3-4**	Little ability to distinguish between relevant and irrelevant information. **1-2**	No ability to distinguish between relevant and irrelevant information. **0**
Prioritisation	10	Issues clearly prioritised in a logical order and based on a clear rationale. **9-10**	Issues prioritised with justification. **6-8**	Evidence of issues being listed in order of importance, but rationale unclear. **5**	Issues apparently in priority order, but without a logical justification or rationale. **3-4**	Little attempt at prioritisation or justification or rationale. **1-2**	No attempt at prioritisation or justification. **0**
Judgement	10	Clearly recognises alternative solutions. Judgement exercised professionally. **9-10**	Alternative solutions or options considered. Some judgement exercised. **6-8**	A slightly limited range of solutions considered. Judgement occasionally weak. **5**	A limited range of solutions considered. Judgement sometimes weak. **3-4**	Few alternative solutions considered. Judgement often weak. **1-2**	No alternative solutions considered. Judgement weak or absent. **0**
Integration	10	Diverse areas of knowledge and skills integrated effectively. **9-10**	Diverse areas of knowledge and skills integrated. **6-8**	Knowledge areas and skills occasionally not integrated. **5**	Knowledge areas and skills sometimes not integrated. **3-4**	Knowledge areas and skills often not integrated. **1-2**	Knowledge areas and skills not integrated. **0**
Logic	20	Communication effective, recommendations realistic, concise and logical. **16-20**	Communication mainly clear and logical. Recommendations occasionally weak. **11-15**	Communication occasionally unclear, and/ or recommendations occasionally illogical. **10**	Communication sometimes weak. Some recommendations slightly unrealistic. **5-9**	Communication weak. Some unclear or illogical recommendations, or few recommendations. **1-4**	Very poor communication, and/or no recommendations offered. **0**
Ethics	10	Excellent evaluation of ethical aspects. Clear and appropriate advice offered. **9-10**	Good evaluation of ethical aspects. Some appropriate advice offered. **6-8**	Some evaluation of ethical aspects. Advice offered. **5**	Weak evaluation of ethical aspects. Little advice offered. **3-4**	Poor evaluation of ethical aspects. No advice offered. **1-2**	No evaluation of ethical aspects. Unethical, or no, advice offered. **0**
TOTAL	100	*Note The number of available marks allocated to each criterion will normally be as shown.					

1 Case and commentary

Recycling - ReuseR and NOW: Background

The marketplace

1 Recycling has two significant impacts on the global environment. First, the use of recycled materials reduces the consumption of the world's natural resources. Second, recycling waste avoids the over-use of landfill refuse sites, which in turn reduces the level of potential pollution or contamination. Additionally, manufacturing costs can be reduced, as energy savings of around 5% can be achieved when, for example, new cans are manufactured using recycled aluminium. Also, recycled aluminium cans may end up being manufactured into sheet metal for car or aeroplane bodies.

2 Glass recycling is very efficient because a glass container is 100% recyclable and can be recycled over and over again with no loss in quality or purity. The use of recycled glass is also not restricted to making new glass, as it can also be recycled into construction aggregate and abrasive material for blasting and also into garden paving slabs. Another significant area of recycling is paper. In Western Europeans' household waste, around 40% of it is paper waste, and paper is currently one of the fastest growing recycled products. Aside from waste reduction, paper recycling makes ecological sense as recycling around 17 pounds (which is less than 8 kg) of paper can save one tree. Paper is usually recycled into new paper products, such as tissues, printing paper and chipboard.

3 More and more businesses are also seeing the sense in selling off their waste paper and many new companies are entering into, or expanding their own, recycling business. Additionally, in today's business world, a company's image is one of its most important assets. A company that has a positive environmental profile will attract quality customers, employees and suppliers. It can also command a share price premium, as corporate investors are increasingly aware of the demand for 'green' investments. There is also increasing external pressure to demonstrate effective environmental practices and to recycle waste. It is likely that within the next decade there will be a statutory requirement for businesses within the European Union (EU) to adopt processes such as waste recycling. To assist companies to reduce and recycle their waste, a large number of service companies have entered this growing market.

4 Over ten years ago, recycling companies were small and operated only within their home country but, with the freedom to operate across boundaries within the EU, many of the larger recycling companies have made acquisitions to strengthen their position and to expand into new markets. Additionally, many large multi-national organisations have become more aware of waste and 'green' issues and have established their own recycling departments, which recycle waste materials from other parts of the company.

5 Most European governments have established a variety of ways in which both domestic and industrial waste can be minimised and materials recycled. To support the various government initiatives, a wide range of specialist companies has been able to increase the volumes of materials recycled. There are many companies of all sizes in the recycling industry, which is still in its early stages, and the recycled materials market is expanding rapidly.

Details follow on two recycling companies

6 This material gives details on two fictitious companies operating in the recycling industry, mainly in Europe. The two companies are Reuse Refuse (ReuseR) and No Waste (NOW). Details on both companies and their operational and financial data are shown below.

Reuse Refuse (ReuseR)

7 Reuse Refuse (which trades as ReuseR) is a quoted company operating in a northern European country, with subsidiary companies across Europe. The company collects waste and recycles a wide range of products, but its single largest recycled product, which is also one of its most profitable, is recycled glass. It currently supplies recycled glass to 12 customers spread over 8 countries in Europe. It sources its recycled glass supplies from hundreds of sources, including its many contracts for the collection and recycling of domestic waste. ReuseR also recycles a range of other waste products, including wood, paper, metal, tyres and a number of other materials.

8 ReuseR has expanded its operations across Europe by the acquisition of many smaller recycling companies. Since 2000, with the pressure on governments and the general population to recycle waste materials, it has introduced several innovative ways in which various types of waste are collected for recycling and sold to a range of manufacturing companies.

9 Entrepreneur Kurt Finehart, who is the Chairman and Chief Executive, had acquired the company in the 1980s when it

was small and operating only in one country. Kurt Finehart always had ambitious plans for the company and was ahead of his time, with his vision of recycling waste. In the late 1980s the company became listed and the current directors and employees collectively own over 53% of the shares. The rest of the shares are spread over a wide range of investors with no large shareholdings.

The key senior management team in ReuseR is as follows.

10 *Kurt Finehart - Chairman and Chief Executive*

Kurt Finehart is a very flamboyant 48 year old, who has strong government connections in his home country. He is from a wealthy family, which helped him to acquire the company initially. He has proved himself to be a serious businessman, with close links with several of his key customers. He is a non-executive director of two other companies, one of which is a glass manufacturing and printing company, to which ReuseR sells some of its recycled glass and paper. Kurt Finehart is also actively involved in many global environmental groups and is highly respected in the recycling industry. His catch phrase, which the press repeats often, is 're-use, not refuse'.

11 *Jean-Paul Gamell - Finance Director*

Jean-Paul Gamell joined ReuseR over ten years ago and has improved the company's financial strength and its ability to manage its increasingly complex business covering eight EU countries. He has a small, strong head office team and has established finance teams in each country where ReuseR operates. In each country in which ReuseR operates, a separate subsidiary company manages its operations and acts as an autonomous business unit. Communication between some of the finance teams in the subsidiaries and head office needs to be improved and it is a problem area that Jean-Paul Gamell is aware of and on which he has planned to concentrate, but he has continually been under pressure with the many recent acquisitions that ReuseR has made.

12 *Clement Weiss - Business Development Director*

Clement Weiss joined ReuseR five years ago and has been the driving force behind many of the company's recent acquisitions. The recycling industry is very fragmented and many small, privately owned, local companies operate successfully and profitably. Clement Weiss believes that economies of scale can be achieved by building upon ReuseR's existing collection and distribution network that it operates in eight EU countries. Some of the small companies that ReuseR has acquired in the last two years handle a range of recycled products that ReuseR had not dealt with previously. ReuseR is currently recycling these additional materials, including electronic waste, old vehicles and plastics and is considering which of these recycled materials should be continued with a view to future expansion of its recycling business.

13 *Allain Chambers - Operations Director*

Allain Chambers, now 53 years old, had worked in the transportation business for over 20 years before joining ReuseR in 1994. He had previously managed his own small fleet of lorries but, when a large European logistics company had acquired his company, he felt that he wanted to stay in the industry, and personally felt strongly about recycling. The opportunity to manage the European operations and logistics at ReuseR was a challenge, but he felt he had a lot of experience to help ReuseR achieve its goals of cost reduction and improved operational safety and performance. He has been key in the selection and implementation of a €12 million IT project using satellite navigation technology that enables the company to track and monitor its large fleet of specialised vehicles.

During the early 1990s the company had experienced a few minor safety incidents, prior to Allain joining the company. The safety problems arose where employees had been involved with hazardous materials, which had resulted in personal injury claims. Allain Chambers feels strongly that the assets of the company are its staff, who should always be looked after as its first priority, and that a 100% safety record should be aimed for, despite the company's complex, and sometimes difficult, business.

14 *Ellouise Matin - Human Resource Director*

Ellouise Matin had joined ReuseR eight years ago after the unfortunate health and safety problems had occurred. She agreed with Allain Chambers that the staff should be better managed and safety procedures improved. These two directors have both put pressure on the Board to improve pay and conditions and to reduce working hours. In the past some staff had worked excessively long hours with large payments for overtime. Ellouise Matin considered that staff could not work effectively for long hours on a regular basis. She had initiated a recruitment drive to replace overtime with full and part-time employees. She is well respected by the ReuseR workforce for many of the Human Resources (HR) changes that have occurred.

The company has experienced problems with recruiting, and also retaining, employees, despite providing training, good rates of pay and allocation of free shares for staff after two years of employment. The company is still experiencing a high staff turnover in some countries and in certain sectors of the business. HR and operational management are looking at ways in which team building and more flexible working could improve staff retention and commitment to the company.

Cost control and international logistics in ReuseR

15 The ReuseR Board has asked Jean-Paul Gamell to investigate why the increased volumes and increased turnover have not resulted in corresponding increases in margins. At the December 2004 Board meeting Jean-Paul Gamell tabled an analysis of costs. This demonstrated that the current level of spend on improved IT facilities was one of the contributing causes of the lower than expected margins, together with training and recruitment costs of new staff, which he explained was an ongoing high cost as the company was continuing to expand.

16 The Board approved a new IT project in December 2004, which has been outsourced, following on from the successful implementation of the satellite navigation tracking system in 2003. This minor additional software solution will improve the reporting of waste materials, collected and the location and status of recycled materials. The system will additionally incorporate the automatic production of legal paperwork for cross-border deliveries. This IT project is forecast to cost a total of €1.5 million and to be operational before the end of 2005. The project is justified financially on the basis that it will eliminate delays due to incorrect or missing paperwork, and it will also speed up deliveries of recycled waste to ReuseR's customers.

17 Two of ReuseR's main costs are staff costs, in respect of the collection of waste and distribution costs associated with recycled materials. As the volume of waste collected has increased, the collection costs have reduced as a proportion of the volume of waste collected, due to economies of scale. However, ReuseR has identified that its distribution costs of recycled materials have increased significantly more than changes in volumes of materials handled would justify in recent years. Allain Chambers has led a project team to identify what costs are currently incurred and to benchmark the costs against other European recycling companies, as well as other European distribution companies.

18 It is planned that the investigation and report will be completed in March 2005 and that a report recommending changes will go to the ReuseR Board in April. Early findings are that transportation costs have increased significantly, while waste sorting and handling costs have fallen, mainly due to the introduction of new recycling plants in some countries. Allain Chambers has stated that the bulk of some types of recycled products, some of which have a low resale value, has contributed to the reduced margins that ReuseR has experienced in the last few years. He wants his team to identify which materials are not cost effective to transport and recycle, so that the company can take a strategic decision not to handle these products.

19 However, Clement Weiss has pointed out that ReuseR has won a number of long-term waste collection and recycling contracts (many with local government departments for the recycling of domestic waste) on the basis that over 80% of all materials collected will be recycled. He therefore argues that the company cannot renege on its contracts, some of which are 10- and 15-year contract periods, and that the company cannot change its strategy by selecting which materials it will, or will not, handle.

20 Allain Chambers is therefore under pressure to identify which costs within the distribution and waste handling operations could be reduced. In some of the countries in which the company has only been operating recycling plants for a short period of time, ReuseR has not yet reached a critical mass, which would enable it to enjoy economies of scale. One additional factor is that recycled glass is currently sold to only 12 customers in Europe, whereas only three years before ReuseR sold glass to over 30 companies. The company changed its customer profile to generate higher revenues. However, it now has higher transportation costs to move this bulky product to fewer customers over greater distances. Allain Chambers pointed out that ReuseR was able to secure longer-term contracts for the supply of recycled glass to its 12 main customers and that the contracts secured higher prices per tonne. However, the contracts stated that ReuseR would bear the transportation costs to customers' factories. Allain Chambers agreed to provide a detailed analysis of margins by recycled product for the next Board meeting.

ReuseR shareholdings, share price and earnings per share (EPS)

21 At the end of November 2004 there were 200 million authorised shares, with a nominal value of €0.20 per share, and 90 million shares were issued and fully paid up.

The main shareholdings were as follows:

	Number of shares (000) at 30 November 2004	% shareholding
Kurt Finehart	20,500	22.8%
Jean-Paul Gamell	7,300	8.1%
Clement Weiss	5,900	6.6%
Allain Chambers	4,100	4.6%
Ellouise Matin	1,000	1.1%
Institutional and other investors	41,800	46.4%
Employee shares*	9,400	10.4%
	------	-------
Total number of shares issued	90,000	100.0%
	------	-------

***Note:** Employee shares are purchased by ReuseR and issued to employees free of charge.

22 The share price of ReuseR had risen slowly during the 1980s and 1990s, and during 2004 ranged from €1.91 to €2.61. ReuseR has a current P/E ratio of 10. The industry average P/E ratio is 9. The company achieved EPS of €0.24 in 2004. The company plans to increase its EPS, in accordance with its five-year plan, to €0.39 per share by 2009.

Appendix 2 shows an extract from the accounts for ReuseR.

Establishment of ReuseR's first recycling operations in the Middle East

23 ReuseR opened a recycling plant in October 2004 in a country in the Middle East. The move is to a stable country in the region, which has a very high record of recycling. This country is keen to establish itself as an example of high recycling levels to the rest of the world. ReuseR had wanted to establish a base in this country before the market for waste became too competitive and this would enable ReuseR to establish its name as a leading waste recycling company. However, it is forecast that this will result in operational losses for the first two years. The company has had many meetings with the large companies

operating in this country and to date has signed two contracts for the recycling of waste.

Potential acquisitions by ReuseR

24 ReuseR has expanded its operations in the past mainly by acquisition, both by expanding into recycling different products and also into other countries. ReuseR is planning to make a number of further acquisitions to grow the business and also to give it access to new markets in other EU countries, and elsewhere, in which the company does not currently operate. The management of ReuseR believes that it has the business skills to recycle a range of materials, and that the company has existing customers who want these recycled materials. However, if recycled materials are transported back to existing customers in the EU, it is forecast that transportation costs could increase in the short term. However, within two years of ReuseR expanding its operations into a new country, it is forecast that ReuseR will have located new customers to which it could sell the recycled materials produced within that country.

25 The ReuseR Board has set the following criteria as a guideline for possible acquisitions:

- Gross margins (defined as sales less all direct costs, variable and fixed) must be similar or higher than those achieved by ReuseR (ReuseR gross margin is over 50%).
- Sales revenue of between €10 - €30 million per annum;
- Must be a stand alone company, rather than a recycling division of a larger company. ReuseR has historically found it quite difficult to manage the merger of operations post acquisition, when it has acquired only the recycling division of a larger company.
- Must be willing to be acquired (for cash or share exchange), as ReuseR's management does not want to pursue a hostile takeover.

26 The business development department of ReuseR, headed by Clement Weiss, had identified a list of 30 possible targets for acquisition, of which most are operating in EU countries. However, some potential acquisitions are operating in countries in which ReuseR does not currently operate, as well as some countries outside Europe. From this initial list, Clement Weiss has eliminated 15 companies as unsuitable for acquisition and he has selected 3 companies that he considers would be particularly suitable for ReuseR to acquire.

27 Clement Weiss has requested his managers in the business development department to prepare further detailed reports on a few of the other potential acquisitions from the

original 30 that had been identified, and to continue to identify new companies that are emerging in this growing marketplace. Depending on the size of the company and the price required, and whether shares or cash are used, ReuseR, is planning to acquire as many as 8 companies over the next 18 months.

28 Jean-Paul Gamell has been in negotiations with a leading European bank to secure loan financing of €40 million in order to fund ReuseR's aggressive acquisition plans. **Appendix 1** shows an extract of the news report about the announcement of ReuseR's new financing plans agreed with this European bank.

ReuseR Board meeting in February 2005

29 Following on from strategic planning meetings attended by ReuseR senior managers during January 2005, a proposal was put to the Board meeting in February 2005 to agree to three proposed acquisitions. All three companies are privately owned companies.

30 Jean-Paul Gamell announced to the Board that financing plans had been finalised for the loan of €40 million over eight years, at a variable interest rate of 2.15% above European lending rate, repayable in 2013. ReuseR will now have loans totalling €60 million.

31 The Board agreed in principle to the three acquisitions, of RED, KLL and MER. Details of these companies are shown in **Appendix 4**. The basis for ReuseR's proposed acquisitions is as follows:

32 (1) Acquisition of RED on the basis that ReuseR does not have any recycling operations in this Eastern European country (now in the EU) and wishes to expand its geographical coverage. All investigations have shown that RED's operations are efficient and the company is operating profitably. However, it has not invested in advanced recycling plants and much capital expenditure on equipment, plant and vehicles will be necessary post acquisition.

33 (2) Acquisition of KLL on the basis that this will help consolidate operations in a northern European country where ReuseR already has established recycling operations and has a growing customer base. This will enable it to acquire a larger customer base and better utilise the new recycling facilities that it has opened in two regions of this country to achieve operating synergies.

34 (3) Acquisition of MER, which was one of the first recycling companies operating in the same Middle East country in which ReuseR set up a recycling plant in October 2004. The country has seen recycling rates increase rapidly and the ReuseR Board agreed that there is huge potential in this country. Additionally, ReuseR considers that this privately owned company would benefit from ReuseR's experience and expertise.

No Waste Recycling Services Ltd (NOW)

35 No Waste Recycling Services Ltd (which trades as NOW) recycles a range of products and has established long-term relationships with a number of its larger customers from whom it collects waste materials. Some of these customers are local government departments and divisions of multi-national companies. NOW is highly regarded as a leader in waste management and it provides its customers a high level of customer service.

36 NOW is a privately owned company whose shares were originally owned by two families, who ran a transportation company. However, after over 20 years in the transportation business, and increasing wage costs and competition, the company changed its trading name to NOW in 1996 and decided to enter the growing business of recycling waste. NOW handles a number of recycled products, but its two dominant business areas, which together account for almost 50% of its sales revenue are the recycling of waste paper and wooden pallets. The next most profitable sector of its recycling business is recycled glass, which accounts for almost 20% of the company's sales revenue.

37 When NOW first started in the recycling industry, it was able to establish very good links with a number of companies, and commenced with recycling these companies' waste paper. It soon established a high reputation as a recycling company and it has been able to forge strong links with several European-wide manufacturers to whom it sells recycled products.

38 The shareholders and management team of NOW at the end of 2004 are detailed below.

39 *Imran Patel - Chairman*

When his parents, who started the family's transportation business, retired, Imran Patel took over as Chairman, in 1996. As a shrewd businessman, Imran Patel, then 38 years old, saw the gap in the market for companies requiring recycled products and for their need for a specialised waste disposal and recycling service. He had worked in the transportation business all of his career and understood logistics and the need to provide customers with a quality service. Imran Patel strongly believed that the company could rapidly gain a good reputation in the growing recycling industry by exceeding customers' expectations, both in service quality and price. He is a perfectionist and very hard working, which has helped NOW maintain a high growth in turnover.

40 *Ernst Heist - Chief Executive*

Ernst Heist, now aged 48, had identified a gap in the market for recycling domestic waste and he had established quite a reputation for himself and the media dubbed him the 'the man who made gold out of rubbish'. Fifteen years ago he had worked as an adviser to government departments and had close political links with central government in his home country in northern Europe. Then he founded his own recycling company and was its Managing Director, until NOW acquired it in 1999. This acquisition enabled NOW to expand geographically in Europe and also to almost double its turnover. For the past five years Ernst Heist has held the role of Chief Executive of NOW.

41 NOW's acquisition of Ernst Heist's previous company had given NOW the opportunity to expand its operations into neighbouring countries, which are all operating profitably. By 2001 the company decided to expand its recycling facilities and to commence handling certain waste materials from local industries. With the help of a government grant and bank loans the recycling facilities were quickly operating at almost maximum capacity.

42 *Peri Patel - Operations Director*

Peri Patel, who is Imran Patel's younger brother by three years, had not previously worked in the family's transportation company. He was the first member of the family who had graduated from university (with a degree in marketing management), and he then joined an international shipping company. Later he moved to an electrical manufacturing company. When his brother took over the family business in 1996, Peri agreed to join the company and to head up marketing and operations. Since the company has grown, a new marketing director has been recruited and Peri Patel has concentrated on operations. Peri Patel has sound management knowledge and experience and he has been the driving force behind the professionalism that NOW has established within the company. Together with his brother's demand for high quality service, they make a formidable team.

43 *Val Rines - Sales and Marketing Director*

Val Rines, then 33 years old, joined NOW in 2000 as Sales and Marketing Director. Initially she had no equity interest, but has since invested €0.9 million (financed by a personal loan secured on her family property) in the company. Val Rines had previously worked in a local government department responsible for refuse and recycling and then as the sales director for a small competitor in the recycling industry. She has much knowledge of recycling and had graduated with a degree in environmental studies.

44 *Rik Mal - Finance Director*

Rik Mal, then 45, joined NOW in 1997 shortly after the company started in the recycling business and he bought shares in NOW during 2001. He is a steady, reserved character and has a close bond with the Patel brothers who respect his conservative attitude to business. They fully appreciate that Rik Mal has managed to keep the company's finances under control, given the company's rapid expansion over the last nine years.

NOW shareholdings

45 NOW has 20 million authorised shares, at a nominal value of €0.50 each, of which 10,620,000 shares have been issued and are fully paid up. The main shareholdings are as follows:

	Number of shares (000) at	
	31 December 2004	**% shareholding**
Imran Patel	4,000	37.7%
Ernst Heist	2,500	23.5%
Peri Patel	1,700	16.0%
Val Rines	320	3.0%
Rik Mal	300	2.8%
Employee shares*	1,800	17.0%
Total number of shares issued	10,620	100.0%

***Note:** The employee shares have been given to employees free of charge.

Appendix 3 shows an extract from the accounts for NOW.

[You may wish to turn to Appendix 3 to assess the firm's financial statements before continuing here.]

Growth of NOW since 1996

46 NOW had grown the recycling business rapidly since 1996 and has expanded its operations into six European countries. The business has always been a strong cash generator and the company has reinvested much of the cash generated from operations into expansion. It has also invested in a number of recycling plants, many of them small plants, which are located close to the main cities in which it operates waste collection services. This gives the company flexibility and reduces transportation costs.

47 The company has also embraced the use of IT in the business, which enables its customers from whom it collects waste, to monitor volumes collected as well as collection dates and times. Its IT systems also enable customers who purchase recycled materials to place their orders and get immediate confirmation of delivery dates and volumes.

48 During early 2004, one of Ernst Heist's innovative plans came to fruition with the introduction of new recycling containers at over 800 large shopping centres in several countries. Previously most of the domestic waste that was recycled relied on the continued social pressure to recycle goods and the increased publicity of environmental problems caused by landfill sites. Ernst Heist's new plan was to pay cash to the members of the public for each and every item recycled. The new recycling containers that NOW had designed paid cash for each item of waste that was recycled, based on weight or type of waste, for example per glass bottle. Therefore, the public could now recycle paper, clothes, glass, batteries and certain other items and the new recycling containers weighed or measured the input and reimbursed coins. These newly designed recycling containers had the added advantage that waste collected was also pre-sorted, thus reducing labour costs at recycling depots.

49 Following a month's trial at 30 sites during 2003, the level of recycled goods had increased dramatically. The financial justification of these new 'recycle for cash' containers was that, if the level of recycled goods increased by more than 70%, then this would cover the increased costs, primarily the cash payments, and the higher costs for logistics for emptying the recycling containers and filling up the cash payment machines. At one site during the trial, one of the containers filled up within one day and the cash payment

machine was empty, whereas the old containers were usually less than half full when they were emptied weekly. Therefore daily emptying of the 30 trial sites proved necessary to maintain public confidence in the scheme.

50 At the end of the one-month trial, the overall level of recycling had increased much more than the required 70%, with some sites achieving 300+% higher recycling rates. This proved that cash payments do appeal to the public. NOW decided to invest in these new 'recycle for cash' recycling containers for over 800 sites. This involved an investment of over €3 million. However, it was decided that the company would move the existing old style recycling containers (which had no payment mechanism) from these sites, when the new 'recycle for cash' containers were installed, to other sites.

51 After monitoring the ongoing volumes of recycled goods, which generate increased turnover for NOW, most sites showed a substantial increase over previously experienced recycling levels. Overall the level of recycled goods at 'recycle for cash' sites was increased by over 180% (that is, the recycled goods volume had almost trebled).

52 However, it has since been established that collection of domestic waste (by NOW's regular weekly collection that NOW operates on behalf of local government departments) has seen a decline in volumes recycled. Therefore NOW's management has reached the conclusion that some of the waste that it used to collect as part of the local government contract for domestic waste recycling, is now being collected via the 'recycle for cash' containers, and is having to pay for. Therefore the increased volume is not entirely due to customers recycling more goods, or even new customers recycling goods for the first time, but is due to astute customers who are now recycling their waste using a different method and getting paid for recycling it.

53 During 2003 and the start of 2004, the company consolidated its position after a period of three years during which several acquisitions had been made. Peri Patel, the Operations Director, ensured that all of the sites that had been acquired were rationalised, and some waste storage sites were closed. Additionally, in some of the businesses that NOW had acquired, it was decided to cease handling some waste materials. NOW had no plans to be involved with liquid waste treatment and this had formed a small part of one of its recent acquisitions. NOW has been able to sell some areas of recycled waste that it did not wish to be involved with to other waste recycling companies. NOW decided that it wanted to concentrate on its core strengths,

which are the collection and processing of paper waste and reselling of the pulp to manufacturers of paper products; the recycling of wood products and glass recycling.

NOW's secure collection and pulping of waste paper for recycling

54 Another new development during 2003 was that NOW opened three new waste paper pulping plants which handle all of the waste paper collections in two of the Northern European countries in which it operates. By supplying paper pulp to several newspaper printers, rather than the waste paper itself, the transportation costs were reduced as the bulk being transported was reduced. Additionally, the revenue rate per tonne of pulped recycled paper was significantly more than the price achieved for waste paper that needed treatment and pulping. The company considered that this new change to the way in which it handled the paper side of its business could generate an additional 12% gross margin, on top of the 40% gross margin currently achieved in this recycled product sector, even after taking into account the direct incremental fixed costs of treatment and pulping.

55 NOW has also been innovative in the collection of waste paper and has been building up the number of companies to which it supplies a secure collection and destruction of waste paper service. It operates a fleet of purpose-designed vehicles that collect confidential waste paper and then pulps the paper on customers' premises. NOW then removes the pulped paper from customers' premises and sells it onto its customers who require recycled paper pulp. This service gives many companies the reassurance that all confidential material is being securely disposed of.

56 By the end of 2004, NOW had contracts with eight large international companies to dispose of their office waste paper securely on their premises, as well as a number of smaller customers. NOW has a contracted schedule to collect and pulp customers' waste paper. Generally it has met the agreed schedule. However, it has experienced a high staff turnover in this area of the business. To maintain the company standards, new recruits have undergone on-site training, which has slowed up the collection and pulping service even more. Recently there have been repeated instances where customers have been left without a collection. Customers are disappointed but so far have only complained. No contracts have been cancelled as NOW has been able to reassure customers and it is putting in place plans to ensure that agreed customer collections are met.

57 During January 2005, NOW secured two major new contracts; the first was from a local government department in a northern European country. This will generate turnover of €1.5 million per year and is for six years. Also, NOW is hopeful that securing this contract could lead to other contracts within that country. The other major contract was from a large international IT company to collect, pulp and recycle, in a secure manner, all of its waste paper. The IT company has appointed NOW for a trial period of two years in two European countries. If it is satisfied that NOW can meet its collection requirements within the contract terms, it may lead to a European-wide contract for waste paper collection and pulping, which could generate an additional turnover for NOW of over €5 million per year. NOW currently operates waste recycling plants in all of the European countries in which the IT company has offices, but it does not operate the specialised waste paper pulping vehicles in all countries. However, these could be purchased if NOW were to be awarded the European-wide contract in two years' time.

NOW Board meeting to discuss future strategy

58 In January 2005, the quarterly NOW Board meeting had an item on its agenda concerning future growth strategies. During 2003 and part of 2004, NOW had not acquired any other smaller recycling companies, and Imran Patel considered that the time was right for further expansion, following a small acquisition in December 2004. He also felt that the company had a strong balance sheet and was generating cash from operations and that NOW should speed up its acquisition and expansion plans, so that economies of scale and synergies can be achieved. NOW had recently announced that it would be paying a final dividend of €0.245 per share to its shareholders.

59 Imran Patel stated at the meeting that NOW could not just sit back and continue to see cash being generated, as the company cannot control its destiny. In order to survive and grow it will have to continually balance its performance with its suppliers, customers, competitors and the community in which it operates. He stated that this would not be an easy task as NOW is operating in several European countries.

60 As NOW has grown it has reviewed and changed its business structure. Only five years ago, each country operated as a stand-alone strategic business unit. Following a review of operating activities and a reassessment of the European market, the company changed its organisation structure to enable it to deliver better customer solutions. This also involved outsourcing of some activities, those for

which Ernst Heist felt the company did not have the correct skill mix to retain within the company. The treasury function was outsourced to its bankers and IT development and implementation work to a global IT company. The company now has one centralised finance department in its Europe-wide HQ building with small teams operating in a few offices around Europe. IT operations were also centralised in the HQ building following the review. NOW has established business units by type of recycled product, such as paper, wood or glass. This enabled line managers within each business to better serve its European customers.

61 After much discussion on alternative expansion plans, some of which are included in NOW's current five-year plan, Imran Patel has requested Ernst Heist and Rik Mal to prepare an updated plan of future expansion for the next Board meeting in April 2005.

Pricing

62 NOW used to set its prices for recycled products based on the customers' ability to pay. However, with the increasing number of companies and governments involved in collecting and recycling a wide range of products, NOW has identified, in the last two years, a decline in the prices it can command for some recycled products, particularly with some of its major customers who buy large quantities of recycled paper, wood, glass and metal.

63 Ernst Heist has requested that Val Rines should review prices and customer mix, and consider whether NOW should change its customer mix. He considers that, if the company were to sell a lower quantity of recycled products to its few large customers, and more to smaller companies, it could achieve at least 15% more in sales revenue. Val Rines stated that NOW's larger customers had continued demand for its recycled materials and NOW should not put at risk its customers' loyalty to achieve higher margins in the short term. Val Rines wants to set up long-term supply contracts so that NOW's long-term waste collection contracts can be matched by region and by product type. Val Rines does not feel that the company should be looking to make short-term profits by selecting higher revenue generating customers at the expense of long-term customer stability.

Appendix 1

European News

25 February 2005

Finehart secures loans of €40 million today with a leading European bankEntrepreneur, Kurt Finehart, Chairman and Chief Executive of leading recycling company, ReuseR, today announced that loan financing had been secured to fund further European acquisitions of recycling companies, as well as expansion into the rapidly growing recycling industry in some of the Middle East countries.

Finance Director, Jean-Paul Gamell stated, 'this loan will enable ReuseR to expand its operations to other European Union countries which will enable the company to benefit from further economies of scale. I am confident that ReuseR's planned growth strategy will have a long-term positive effect on the company's share price.'

Finehart stated, 'the financing package agreed is good for the company, good for the EU and good for the environment'. He added, 'With ReuseR handling higher volumes of waste for recycling throughout Europe, this will result in more materials being recycled and less waste and pollution.'

The news was received positively in the market and ReuseR's share price rose 5.8% to €2.68 per share at the close of trading today. It is believed that negotiations with possible companies that ReuseR is planning to acquire are well underway. The market expects that bid announcements will be made over the next few weeks.

Appendix 2

Note: All data in the appendices are presented in International Financial Reporting format.

ReuseR

	As at 30 November 2004		As at 30 November 2003	
Balance sheet	€ million	€ million	€ million	€ million
Non-current assets (net)		**131.9**		**123.3**
Current assets				
Inventory	20.8		19.9	
Trade receivables	46.5		39.1	
Cash and short-term investments	6.4		4.1	
		73.7		**63.1**
Total assets		**205.6**		**186.4**
Equity and liabilities				
Equity				
Paid in share capital	18.0		18.0	
Share premium reserve	21.6		21.6	
Profit and loss reserve	109.8		95.1	
		149.4		**134.7**
Non-current liabilities				
7% Loan notes (redeemable in 2011)		**20.0**		**20.0**
Current liabilities				
Trade payables	22.5		19.6	
Tax	6.1		5.9	
Accruals	7.6		6.2	
		36.2		**31.7**
Total equity and liabilities		**205.6**		**186.4**

Note: Paid in share capital represents 90 million shares at €0.20 each.

Income statement	**Year ended 30 November 2004** € million	**Year ended 30 November 2003** € million
Revenue	214.2	184.0
Total operating costs	185.0	155.9
Operating profit	29.2	28.1
Finance costs	-1.4	-1.4
Tax expense (effective tax rate at 22% after allowances)	-6.1	-5.9
Profit for the period	**21.7**	**20.8**

Statement of changes in equity year ended 30 November 2004

	Share capital € million	**Share premium** € million	**Retained earnings** € million	**Total** € million
Balance at 30 November 2003	18.0	21.6	95.1	134.7
Profit for the period	-	-	21.7	21.7
Dividends paid	-	-	-7.0	-7.0
Balance at 30 November 2004	**18.0**	**21.6**	**109.8**	**149.4**

Appendix 3

Note: All data in the appendices are presented in International Financial Reporting format.

NOW

	As at 30 November 2004		As at 30 November 2003	
Balance sheet	€ million	€ million	€ million	€ million
Non-current assets (net)		**53.8**		**44.8**
Current assets				
Inventory	5.9		7.1	
Trade receivables	12.9		12.1	
Cash and short-term investments	2.3		0.4	
		21.1		**19.6**
Total assets		**74.9**		**64.4**
Equity and liabilities				
Equity				
Paid in share capital	5.3		5.2	
Share premium reserve	4.0		3.6	
Profit and loss reserve	44.4		34.7	
		53.7		**43.5**
Non-current liabilities				
Bank loan (repayable in 2005) at 10% interest per year		**0.0**		**2.5**
Bank loan (repayable in 2009) at 10% interest per year		**11.9**		**11.9**
Current liabilities				
Bank loan (repayable in 2005)	2.5		0.0	
Trade payables	3.3		3.2	
Tax	2.9		2.2	
Accruals	0.6		1.1	
		9.3		**6.5**
Total equity and liabilities		**74.9**		**64.4**

Note: Paid in share capital represents 10.62 million shares at €0.50 each.

Income statement	**Year ended 30 November 2004** € million	**Year ended 30 November 2003** € million
Revenue	55.8	48.3
Total operating costs	39.2	35.1
Operating profit	16.6	13.2
Finance costs	-1.4	-1.4
Tax expense (effective tax rate at 19% after allowances)	-2.9	-2.2
Profit for the period	**12.3**	**9.6**

Statement of changes in equity year ended 30 November 2004

	Share capital € million	**Share premium** € million	**Retained earnings** € million	**Total** € million
Balance at 30 December 2003	5.2	3.6	34.7	43.5
Shares issued during the period (to employees)	0.1	0.4	-	0.5
Profit for the period	-	-	12.3	12.3
Dividends paid	-	-	-2.6	-2.6
Balance at 30 November 2004	**5.3**	**4.0**	**44.4**	**53.7**

Appendix 4

Data on ReuseR proposed acquisitions

All figures have been restated in € million for latest financial year	RED	KLL	MER
Geographic location	*Eastern European EU*	*Northern European*	*Middle East*
Turnover	12.0	18.0	28.0
Gross margin	6.1	10.1	18.2
Net profit (after tax)	1.0	2.0	7.6
Gross margin %	51%	56%	65%
Net margin %	8%	11%	27%
No of shares	10,000	6,000	38,800
Company status	Privately owned	One operating division of a privately owned company	Privately owned
Form of acquisition: cash or shares	Cash	Cash or ReuseR shares	Cash or ReuseR shares
No of employees	96	220	292
Recycled products	Glass, tyres, industrial waste	Domestic recycled waste only	Glass, chemicals, paper and some other industrial waste
Other relevant data:	Local press reports state that company is struggling with a cash shortage and that it has been unable to secure further loans.	This is a small competitor of ReuseR that has secured a number of government domestic waste recycling contracts by under-cutting ReuseR on price. ReuseR would like to eliminate this competitor before it grows larger and becomes more of a threat. It would also help ReuseR to achieve greater economies of scale in this country.	This would be ReuseR's first acquisition of a company operating outside of Europe. MER is operating in the same Middle East country in which ReuseR opened a recycling plant in October. ReuseR's five-year plan had identified a number of regions globally that have an increasing recycling industry. The Middle East is achieving high levels of recycling and this company could provide ReuseR with a customer base in this country from which to increase trade.

chapter

16

REUSER: ANALYSIS OF THE PRE-SEEN MATERIAL

Contents

1 Industry awareness

Note: All figures are for the UK unless otherwise stated.

1.1 Introduction/overview

What is waste?

Anything we throw away because we do not need it.

Why is it an issue?

There are two main consequences of throwing away rubbish:

- lost resources
- damage to the environment.

Together these give a problem of sustainability, a key political issue giving rise to increasing legislation.

Main sources of waste

The main sources of waste are as follows:

Household/municipal	8%
Office and commercial	19%
Construction and demolition	24%
Mining	21%
Agricultural	20%
Sewage sludge	<1%
Dredged spoils	8%

This case study is mainly concerned with the first two categories. However, do not dismiss the others, as they could be opportunities for expansion.

Household/municipal waste

Household/municipal waste is mainly made up of the following:

Garden waste	21%
Paper and board	18%
Kitchen waste	17%
Glass	7%

In the case study, ReuseR's main product is recycled glass whilst NOW's main areas of business are waste paper, wooden pallets and glass. For both, treatment of garden waste could be an opportunity.

Office and commercial waste

Office and commercial waste is mainly made up of the following:

Food	21%
White paper	20%
Cardboard	14%
Newspapers and magazines	13%
Other paper	13%

In the case study, NOW appears to have a bigger emphasis on commercial/office waste, particularly collecting and destroying office paper. Given that nearly 80% of office waste is paper-related, this appears to be a good fit with the industry.

What happens to the waste?

The waste management hierarchy (with the most desirable option at the top) is as follows:

- Reduce it (prevention and minimisation)
- Reuse it e.g. second-hand furniture schemes
- Recover it (includes recycling, composting and energy recovery)
- Disposal
  - Landfill
  - Incineration
  - New waste treatment technologies including anaerobic digestion and mechanical biological treatment (MBT).

In the UK, for example, municipal waste in 2002/3 was managed as follows (source DEFRA):

Landfilled	75%
Recycled/composted	16%
Incinerated	9%

This compares with a target, set in Waste Strategy 2000, to recycle/compost 25% of household waste by 2005/6.

The recycling sector has seen huge growth - for example, in the UK:

	Kilograms per person per year				
	1983/4	*1991/2*	*2000/1*	*2001/2*	*2002/3*
Waste not recycled	394	417	453	453	446
Waste recycled/ composted	3	11	57	65	76
Total waste	397	428	510	517	521

Local authorities have been set targets to increase recycling to 10 – 33% over the next few years.

Through these and additional measures, the hope is to increase the recycling of household waste to the targets set by the Government and the Welsh Assembly, which are:

- to recycle/compost at least 25% of household waste by 2005
- to recycle/compost at least 30% of household waste by 2010
- to recycle/compost at least 33% of household waste by 2015.

Recovery targets for municipal waste are:

- to recover value from 40% of municipal waste by 2005
- to recover value from 45% of municipal waste by 2010
- to recover value from 67% of municipal waste by 2015.

In the rest of the EU, the figures vary. Greece, Ireland, the United Kingdom and Italy dispose of three-quarters or more of their municipal waste to landfill, whilst Denmark, Netherlands, Sweden and Germany dispose of a quarter or less of their municipal waste in that way.

In Denmark and Luxembourg, incineration is the single main method of disposal and over half of their municipal waste is treated in that way. Austria recycles/composts over 60% of its municipal waste, and Belgium and the Netherlands recycle/compost almost half of theirs.

The relevance to the case study is that some countries provide more opportunities for further recycling than others - particularly the UK!

1.2 Further detail on legislation

Most UK legislation impacting on waste management is now implemented as a result of European Directives. The European Union's waste legislation comprises three main elements:

- **horizontal legislation**, establishing the overall framework for the management of wastes, including definitions and principles
- **legislation on treatment operations**, such as landfill or incineration, which may set technical standards for the operation of waste facilities
- **legislation on specific waste streams**, such as waste oil or batteries, which may include, for example, measures to increase recycling or to reduce hazardousness.

There are a significant number of directives affecting waste management, including some which may not immediately appear relevant such as the Directive on Groundwater or the Habitats Directive.

The key horizontal directive is the Directive on Waste (75/442/EEC, as amended). Known as the Waste Framework Directive, the Directive establishes a framework for the management of waste across the European Union. It also defines certain terms, such as waste, recovery and disposal, to ensure that a uniform approach is taken across the EU.

The directive requires member states to:

- give priority to waste prevention and encourage reuse and recovery of waste
- ensure that waste is recovered or disposed of without endangering human health and without using processes which could harm the environment
- prohibit the uncontrolled disposal of waste
- ensure that waste management activities are permitted (unless specifically exempt)
- establish an integrated and adequate network of disposal installations
- prepare waste management plans
- ensure that the cost of disposal is borne by the waste holder in accordance with the polluter pays principle
- ensure that waste carriers are registered.

Related UK legislation

The Waste Framework Directive has been implemented in the UK through the following national legislation:

- the Environmental Protection Act 1990
- the Control of Pollution (Amendment) Act 1989
- the Waste Management Licensing Regulations 1994 (as amended)
- the Controlled Waste (Registration of Carriers and Seizure of Vehicles) Regulations 1991.

Duty of Care

The Duty of Care is a law which requires every business in the UK to take all reasonable steps to keep their wastes safe. It was introduced through Section 34 of the Environmental Protection Act 1990 and covers any businesses that produce, import, carry, keep, treat, dispose or broker-controlled waste.

EU Landfill Directive

Given the high level of waste disposed of into landfill sites, the EU Landfill Directive is also particularly relevant in the UK. Under this directive, over the next 20 years, the UK must dramatically reduce the amount of biodegradable municipal waste sent to landfill.

To facilitate this, one Government policy is that waste going to landfill is now taxed. This is gradually reducing the perceived cost benefit of landfilling waste, and is providing funding for alternative waste management. In April 2004 the landfill tax rate for active waste increased by £1 to £15 per tonne. The Chancellor's Pre-Budget Report 2002 announced that the landfill tax for active waste would be increasing by a minimum of £3 per tonne from 2005-06, until it reaches a rate of £35 per tonne in the medium to long term – a rate which will bring the UK in line with other European countries.

In the case study, this signals further potential opportunities for ReuseR and NOW.

1.3 Further detail on waste management methods and processes

Landfill

Landfill is more than just placing waste in a hole in the ground and covering it with soil. Today, landfill is a complex process, typically involving lining and capping individual 'cells' into which waste is compacted and covered to prevent the escape of polluting liquid or gases. Systems are installed to capture and remove the gases and liquids produced by the rotting rubbish.

The biodegradable component of municipal waste that will break down is known as 'BMW' and includes kitchen and garden waste, paper, card and more. The diversion of biodegradable municipal waste (BMW) from landfill is a key objective under the Landfill Directive. Within the Landfill Directive, only 75% of the 1995 quantities of BMW are allowed to be landfilled by 2010, 50% of 1995 quantities by 2013, and 35% of 1995 quantities by 2020.

Consequently, composting and other technologies to deal with this waste stream are growing in importance. The Landfill Regulations and the Waste & Emissions Trading Act 2003 have transposed these targets into English law.

Household waste recycling

Recyclate from recycling collections are frequently sent to a materials recycling facility (MRF).

At the MRF, the materials typically travel along a conveyor belt and the specific fractions are gradually removed: metals may be extracted using magnets, paper taken off by weight, and other screening devices used. Following separation, the constituent materials are baled prior to sending to reprocessors.

The activities at these plants are specific to the material being processed – pulping and shredding of paper, granulation of plastics, and melting of metals and glass to name but a few.

Note: These are part of what both ReuseR and NOW do.

Composting

Composting allows BMW to break down, and results in the formation of compost that can be used as fertiliser. Although compost can be made at home, councils are increasingly developing centralised composting schemes for residents' garden waste to tackle this large and problematic part of the waste stream.

Incineration

Incineration is the burning of waste. Incineration may be carried out with or without energy recovery. The energy released from burning the rubbish is often used to generate electricity.

New technologies

Anaerobic digestion is the process in which biodegradable waste is decomposed in the absence of oxygen to produce methane, which can be collected and burnt as a fuel to produce electricity.

Mechanical biological treatment occurs when residual mixed waste (usually post MRF) is mechanically sorted into recyclable materials, refuse-derived fuel (RDF) and an organic fraction. The organic fraction is treated and used as soil conditioner, and the RDF goes for further treatment and is then used for energy from waste (EfW). Some material is rejected and landfilled.

Biological mechanical treatment. The residual, mixed, unsorted waste is homogenised and treated by part composting and drying. Sorting and treatment follows, using mechanical processes so that recyclate, RDF and soil conditioner streams, as well as the rejected fraction of residual waste, are produced.

Refuse-derived fuel (RDF) is created from fractions of the waste stream with a high energy content – typically paper, plastics, and wood, etc.

Mixed waste is separated using screens and mechanical processes, to remove glass and metals for recycling, the biodegradable content and RDF.

1.4 Further detail on glass recycling – key to both ReuseR and NOW

The two main types of glass recycled are:

- Container glass – largely bottles and jars, and representing around 80% of the recycled glass market.
- Flat glass – the second largest sector of glass manufacture. As opposed to container glass, flat glass tends to be used in long-term applications. This longevity lessens the environmental impact of waste glass, but waste flat glass is arising as windows and car windscreens are replaced and cars are scrapped.

Glass can be recycled indefinitely as part of a simple but hugely beneficial process, as its structure does not deteriorate when reprocessed. In the case of bottles and jars, up to 80% of the total mixture can be made from reclaimed scrap glass, called 'cullet'. Cullet from a factory has a known composition and is recognised as domestic cullet. From bottle banks it is known as foreign, and its actual properties will not be known. One of the main problems is the mix of colours present.

The UK has a current municipal recycling rate of 34% for container glass. This is poor, considering that Switzerland and Finland recycle more than 90% of their container waste and recycling figures of more than 50% are the norm.

Glass can also be recovered from businesses, such as pubs and restaurants, and from companies, schools or organisations that are able to have a bottle bank on site.

Glass is classified as a packaging material so, by 2006, the UK will be obliged by European law to recycle at least 70% of glass in the packaging waste stream.

To ensure that firms meet their obligations, the waste is monitored using PRNs and PRENs:

- PRNs are Packaging (Waste) Recovery Notes. Each tonne represents a tonne of UK packaging waste reprocessed in the UK.
- PERNs are Packaging (Waste) Export Recovery Notes. Each tonne represents a tonne of UK packaging waste reprocessed abroad.

PRNs and PERNs are numbered documents – similar to cheques – issued by an accredited reprocessor as evidence of the amount of packaging waste recycled. You can use PRNs or PERNs, or a mixture of both, to fulfil your obligation.

1.5 Further detail on paper recycling – key to both ReuseR and NOW

There are different sources of waste fibre used as a source material for manufacturing recycled paper:

- **Mill Broke** is 'waste' paper that has never been used - either printers' off-cuts or rolls damaged during production. When mixed with water, the fibres are freed into pulp.
- **Post-consumer waste** is paper that has been printed on and used. Recycling is more problematic (e.g. de-inking), but is still worthwhile.

Paper cannot be recycled indefinitely as some virgin pulp must be introduced into the process to maintain the strength and quality of the fibre.

At present there are no laws directly targeting paper recycling. Paper, as a biodegradable material, is covered by the EU Landfill Directive, so there are targets for municipal waste as a whole, of which paper is a part.

The Household Waste Recycling Act 2003 states that every household (unless uneconomic, or alternatives are already in place) must have a kerbside collection of at least two materials by 2010. As paper is a relatively easy material to collect/recycle it is likely that any new kerbside schemes introduced will include paper as one of the materials.

1.6 Some real-world firms in the industry

Reuse Glass UK

Reuse Glass UK operates one of Europe's most modern cullet treatment plants in Knottingley (West Yorkshire), which currently supplies its full capacity of 200,000 tonnes on a long-term contract to the UK's largest glass packaging manufacturer, Rockware Glass.

Berryman, a subsidiary, is the largest glass recycling company in the UK.

Berryman concentrates solely on recycling glass and is located near Pontefract in the heartland of the British glass container manufacturing industry. Berryman collects from over 100 local authorities directly, and treats bottle containers from another 100.

Berryman also collects flat/plate glass from smaller glaziers up to the largest glass processors on the mainland. Situated throughout the UK in West Yorkshire, West Midlands, Essex and Scotland, Berryman aims to work in partnership with all parties who have influence on the waste stream and its management away from landfill. Perhaps, most importantly, Berryman is working closely and flexibly with local authorities on an individual basis and nationally. Glass is collected from bottle banks, kerbside and commercial services by some 40 specialist vehicles with lifting arms and segregated compartments which retain the colour separation of the glass.

Websites:

Reuse Glass (http://www.reuse-glass.co.uk/)

Rockware Glass (http://www.rockware.co.uk/index.html)

Berryman (http://www.berryman-uk.co.uk/)

Shanks

One of Europe's largest independent waste management companies, Shanks started life in the late 1800s as a construction company based primarily in the West of Scotland.

Waste management activities gradually increased and, in 1986, the then-named Shanks & McEwan acquired London Brick Landfill and an enormous landfill capacity in the northern Home Counties. This, together with successful Stock Market flotation in 1988, produced the foundation for organic and acquisitive growth, including the purchase of the former Rechem Environmental Services in the early 1990s.

The sale of the group's remaining construction interest, to concentrate solely on waste management, followed a re-organisation of the management team in late 1993 and 1994. Since then the group has grown significantly, both by organic growth and by acquisition. Shanks has increased the range of its waste management services and, in 1998, took its first steps into Europe with the acquisition of a significant group of waste management interests in Belgium.

Two years later, in March 2000, Shanks arrived in the Netherlands via the purchase of the eight principal businesses of Waste Management Nederland BV.

In June 2004, the sale of Shanks Group's UK landfill and landfill gas power assets to Terra Firma – owners of Waste Recycling Group – was formally completed, leaving Shanks positioned to further invest in its modern European operations and to concentrate on a suite of modern waste and resource management activities in the UK.

The range of products includes waste - both stable and hazardous - from laboratories, heavy manufacturing, factories and homes. The company is much more diversified in the management of waste than either ReuseR or NOW.

Based on interim accounts to September 2004, the following ratios can be calculated:

Gross profit margin	18%	ReuseR and NOW are doing much better
Net profit margin	3%	ReuseR and NOW are doing much better
Gearing (D/E)	0.87	ReuseR and NOW have much lower gearing, so raising debt to finance acquisitions may be perfectly reasonable
Debtor days	82	So ReuseR's and NOW's figures are fairly typical after all

Its current P/E ratio is 36!

Its website can be found at http://www.shanks.co.uk/

2 Précis the case

2.1 Background – the marketplace

The case this time involves two different companies operating in the recycling industry, mainly within the EU.

Recycling is a growing industry in its early stages.

Governments are keen to encourage recycling because:

- it reduces consumption of the world's resources
- it avoids over-use of landfill refuse sites, which in turn reduces pollution.

Businesses seek to recycle for the following reasons:

- company image
- green investment may command a share premium
- increasing legislation
- can give cost savings.

2.2 Reuse Refuse (ReuseR)

Introduction

- A quoted company in Northern Europe.
- Collects and recycles a wide range of products.
- Biggest product is glass (most profitable) which it supplies to 12 customers across 8 European countries. Also recycles wood, paper, metal and tyres.
- Sources waste from domestic collections and other sources.
- Expansion to date by acquisition of smaller companies.
- Majority of shares owned by directors and employees (53%).

Key senior management team

- Kurt Finehart - Chairman and Chief Executive (48)
- Jean Paul Gamell - Finance Director
- Clement Weiss - Business Development Director
- Allain Chambers - Operations Director (53)
- Ellouise Matin - HR Director

Cost control and logistics

Increased volumes/turnover has not resulted in increased margins.

Main reasons given are:

1 Extra spending on IT

2 Extra spending on recruitment and training costs

3 Higher transportation costs

4 Some products are not worth recycling

5 BUT collection costs are lower

Share holdings, share price and EPS

The main shareholdings were as follows:

Kurt Finehart	22.8%
Rest of the Board	12.3%
Institutional and other investors	46.4%
Employee shares	10.4%

In 2004 the price ranged from €1.91 to €2.61.

The company's P/E ratio is 10 (industry average 9) with EPS of €0.24. The five-year plan has a target EPS of €0.39 in 2009.

Middle East operations

ReuseR opened a recycling plant in October 2004 in a stable country in the Middle East with a very high record of recycling.

- Losses forecast for the first two years.
- To date, ReuseR has only signed two contracts.

Potential acquisitions

The guidelines for acquisition are:

- gross margin over 50%
- sales between €10m and €30m
- stand-alone company
- not hostile.

The plan is to acquire 8 companies in the next 18 months.

Initial finance is to come from a loan for €40m.

ReuseR Board meeting (February 2005)

The board agreed in principle to acquire three privately owned companies identified.

1 RED

Based in a new EU country and therefore has new market opportunities

Profitable but needs considerable capital expenditure

Has cash flow problems so may welcome an approach

2 KLL

Consolidates business in Northern Europe

Will create synergies but is a division of a larger company

3 MER

Based in Middle East

Growing market and expertise make this interesting

Finance secured (€40m) at 2.15% above base, repayable 2013.

2.3 No waste recycling (NOW)

No Waste Recycling Services Ltd (NOW) is a limited company that recycles paper, wooden pallets and glass.

- Recycled paper and wooden pallets account for 50% of its business.
- Recycled glass accounts for 20%

It sources waste from companies that it has built up long-term relationships with. Some are local government. Sells recycled waste to several European companies.

NOW is highly regarded, a leader in waste management and provides its customers with a high level of customer service.

Key senior management (NOW)

- Imran Patel - Chairman (46)
- Ernst Heist - Chief Executive (48)
- Peri Patel - Operations Director ((43)
- Val Rines - Sales and Marketing (37)
- Rik Mal - Finance Director (52)

NOW shareholdings

The main shareholdings are as follows:

Imran Patel	37.7%
Ernst Heist	23.5%
Peri Patel	16.0%

Growth since 1996

Business has grown rapidly since 1996 and has expanded into six European countries.

The business has been a strong cash generator and has used this cash for the expansion and to reinvest in the following:

1 Small recycling plants near to cities, providing flexibility and lower transportation costs.

2 New IT systems to provide customers with better, more immediate information.

3 'Recycle for cash' containers in shopping centres. These cost €3m, increased volumes by more than 180% and reduced costs as the waste became pre-sorted. However, they did displace some waste that would have been collected for free via other means.

During 2003/2004 NOW consolidated its operations. It is concentrating on core products:

- paper pulp
- wood
- glass.

Secure collection and pulping of waste paper

Further innovations included:

1 Supplying pulped paper to newspaper printers rather than waste itself. This saved transportation costs and gave higher revenue per tonne. The result was an extra 12% on gross margin.

2 Purpose-built vehicles to collect and pulp confidential waste. This resulted in eight large contracts by the end of 2004 for this type of business. Operational problems are being encountered as a result of high staff turnover. Customers have been let down and are disappointed but no business has been lost yet!

January 2005 saw two major new contracts:

1 Local government department worth €1.5m per year for six years. Hopefully this will lead to further wins.

2 A major IT company wants confidential pulping done for a trial period of two years. It could potentially be worth €5m per year if successful.

Board meeting to discuss strategy

Imran now considers that the time is right for further expansion following a small acquisition in December 2004.

A dividend of €0.245 was announced - total dividend €0.245 × 10.6m = €2.6m.

Five years ago each business was a separate SBU. This was changed to deliver better business solutions. It has outsourced many non-core parts of the business including treasury and IT development. It has a centralised finance function and IT operations.

SBUs are no longer geographical but product based i.e. paper, wood, glass, etc.

Pricing

Historically NOW set prices based on customers' ability to pay. In the last two years, however, there has been a decline in the prices NOW can command for recycled products.

One suggestion is to sell lower quantities to a few large customers, increasing sales by 15%. Val Rines does not think they should put customer loyalty at risk by going for short-term margin gains.

2.4 Appendix 1: European news extract

This is a European news article relating to ReuseR securing a bank loan of €40 million. The news was received positively, with share price going up 5.8% to €2.68.

2.5 Appendices 2 and 3: Financial statements for ReuseR and NOW

Both firms show solid balance sheets with low gearing.

Both income statements show good growth in revenue and profit. ReuseR has seen falling margins, however.

2.6 Appendix 4: Data on ReuseR's proposed acquisitions

Guidelines for acquisition:

- Gross margin over 50% - all qualify.
- Sales between €10 and €30m - all qualify.
- Stand-alone company - all qualify except KLL, an operating division of a private company.
- Not hostile - no real information other than RED would probably be happy to sell due to current financial position.

Other key information

	RED	**KLL**	**MER**
Location	Eastern EU	Northern Europe	Middle East
Products recycled	Glass, tyres, industrial waste	Domestic recycled waste only	Glass, chemicals, paper and other industrial waste
Other	Cash flow problems	Competitor	Same country as existing operations

3 ANALYSIS: BUSINESS STRATEGY PERSPECTIVE

3.1 Consolidate your understanding of the strategic positions of ReuseR and NOW using SWOT analyses

ReuseR

Strengths	*Weaknesses*
• Financials - good B/S, profitable, growing, good cash flow • Quoted, making raising finance easier • Seems to be in favour with the city, as shown by a higher than average P/E ratio • Experienced board (most been in place 5 – 10 years), which has remained stable. No conflict evident • Visionary chairman in Kurt • Kurt's government connections and reputation • Innovation • Share schemes should motivate employees • Strong head office finance team • Organisational structure gives a strong regional focus • Allain's expertise in transportation • Good rates of pay for staff • Looking to the future, wanting to grow the business and not just sit back and reap rewards	• Falling margins due to high transportation and staff training costs • Possible over-emphasis on new acquisitions at the expense of managing post-acquisition phase efficiently • Problems recruiting and keeping staff • Need more flexibility to reduce work loads - safety issues involved • Poor communication between head office and local offices • Operating structure may make it difficult to be client-centred • Lack of marketing expertise in senior management • Lack of division between chairman and CEO - poor governance • Possible conflicts of interest with Kurt being a NED for customer firms • Jean Paul is overworked and does not have time to resolve operational problems • May be recycling products that are not viable
Opportunities	*Threats*
• High growth market • Extending the range of products recycled e.g. chemical waste • Expansion into other EU countries • Expansion into Middle Eastern countries • Further acquisitions	• Over-dependence on 12 customers • New entrants • Existing firms seeking to expand • Larger clients decide to do their own recycling • May become exposed to significant foreign exchange risk in Middle East

The key issues facing the firm are:

- managing its acquisitions plans
- falling margins
- deciding which countries and products it should be involved in.

NOW

Strengths	*Weaknesses*
• Financials - good growth, profitability, improving margins, strong balance sheet • Customer-focused IT • Competitive advantage as a differentiator based on high quality customer care • Strong relationships with customers • Innovative e.g. recycle for cash • Has moved into higher margin businesses such as producing paper pulp rather than selling waste paper • Family ownership should result in less conflicts of interest • Good mix of age and experience at board level. Board has knowledge of the industry and strong links with each other. Either family as in the case of the Patels or personal as with Rik Mal or through investment in equity, they all have shares • Imran is a shrewd businessman and has experience of logistics • Ernst has a good reputation and strong links with the government of his home country • Peri has marketing expertise • Val has experience of working for local government departments • Rik has demonstrated good financial control • Operationally they have small recycling plants close to the city which keeps transport costs down and margins high	• Unquoted, restricting future financing options • Staff turnover • Complaints from some customers when schedules for dealing with confidential papers have not been met • Increasing centralisation may result in a loss of local flexibility and entrepreneurship • Has the current management got the experience to run a much larger company if the proposed expansion takes place? • Should they be paying dividends when they are looking for significant expansion?

Opportunities	*Threats*
• Being approved after the trial period for the large IT company has finished • High growth market • Extending the range of products recycled • Expansion into other EU countries • Further acquisitions	• New entrants • Existing firms seeking to expand • Larger clients decide to do their own recycling

The key issues facing the firm are:

- being successful in the trial for the large IT firm
- resolving the problems with recycling confidential papers
- retaining their strong customer focus while expanding.

3.2 Assess the recycling industry using Porter's five forces model

Competitive rivalry

Due to the market being in its early stages, the extent of rivalry varies considerably. The high growth in the market also allows firms to expand without having to steal market share. Overall, therefore, rivalry is not a major threat.

Threat of entry

Barriers to entry are expertise, capital requirements for specialist equipment and long-term contracts. Apart form long-term contracts, firms can get round these barriers fairly easily, so the threat of new entrants should be considered high.

Threat of substitutes

Low, given most (such as landfill) are becoming politically unacceptable and increasingly illegal.

Power of suppliers

Low.

Power of customers

Often dealing with large firms and local authorities who have the option of recycling their own rubbish. These customers can be considered to have high power.

In summary the key issues are:

- the need to reduce customer power
- the need to create barriers to protect existing operations from new entrants.

Both of these can be addressed by creating more switching costs to tie customers in.

3.3 Many firms, including ReuseR and NOW have grown via acquisitions. Assess the argument of acquisition v organic growth in the recycling market

Arguments for acquisition	*Potential problems*
• Speed - this does appear to be important as the market opens up in different companies • Synergy - there are economies of scale to be gained	• May be cheaper to grow organically but the premium paid on acquisition may be justified in gaining access to contacts and expertise in new areas • Cultural clashes • Selling off unwanted aspects • Post-acquisition management

Overall the need for quick entry appears to be the dominating factor.

3.4 Assess the three proposed acquisitions in Appendix 4

1 RED

Arguments for acquired RED

- The acquisition satisfies the criteria set by the Board (paragraph 25 of original document):

Gross margins ≥ 50%	YES 51%
Sales between €10 - €30 million pa	YES 12 million
Stand-alone	YES
Not hostile	Not stated explicitly but the company has been struggling with a cash shortage and has been unable to secure further loans, so existing owners would view an approach from ReuseR as a lifeline

- Geographical location - Eastern European EU - still have the advantages of being in the EU but an opportunity to break into new countries.

- Products recycled - glass (economies of scale), tyres (already do this to some degree) and industrial waste (?) - not much new.
- Investigations have shown operations to be efficient, so why the low NPM? This could indicate scope for cost-cutting synergies.

Arguments against acquiring RED

- Structure of deal – RED will be valued at approximately €9 million (P/E ratio of 9, profits of €1 million) less a discount for being unquoted. This needs to be paid in cash.
- Other synergy – large cash injection, part for operational needs but company also needs significant investment in new equipment, plant and vehicles.
- Why was RED unable to raise further loans? Lack of good assets to offer as security? Poor prospects?

2 KLL

Arguments for acquiring KILL

- The acquisition satisfies two of the criteria set by the Board (paragraph 25 of original document):

Gross margins ≥ 50%	YES 56%
Sales between €10 - €30 million pa	YES 18 million

- Geographical location – Northern European EU in a country where ReuseR already operates – aim is to gain a larger customer base to take advantage of new recycling facilities to gain operating synergies.
- Products recycled – domestic waste only?
- One less competitor.

Arguments against acquring KILL

- The acquisition fails to satisfy one of the criteria set by the Board and another is debatable:

Stand-alone	NO - an operating division of a larger company
Not hostile	The company has been successful in winning contracts by undercutting ReuseR, so why would they want to sell? There is a danger that ReuseR will have to pay a high premium for the existing owners to sell

- Structure of deal - KLL will be valued at approximately €18 million (P/E ratio of 9, profits of €2 million) less a discount for being unquoted. This needs to be paid in cash or shares. The cash would need to be generated in some way. As for equity, ReuseR is worth approximately 217m, so equity would not dilute existing holdings much.

- Potential problems integrating over 200 new staff.

3 MER

Arguments for acquiring MER

- The acquisition satisfies the criteria set by the Board (paragraph 25 of original document):

Gross margins ≥ 50%	YES 65%
Sales between €10 - €30 million p.a.	YES 28 million
Stand-alone	YES
Not hostile	Not stated explicitly but the Board considers that MER would benefit from ReuseR's experience and expertise

- Geographical location – Middle East in the same country in which ReuseR opened a recycling plant in 2004. The resulting economies of scale could turn around the forecast loss for this company. Region also forecast to one of high growth.
- Products recycled – glass (already have expertise), chemicals (new?) paper and other industrial waste (?).
- Investigations have shown operations to be efficient, so why the low NPM? This could indicate scope for cost-cutting synergies.

Arguments against acquiring MER

- Structure of deal – KLL will be valued at approximately €68 million (P/E ratio of 9, profits of €7.6 million) less a discount for being unquoted. This is much bigger than the other targets and, either way, we would have to look at the financing package more carefully.
- Geographical location – Middle East – outside the EU so potentially different legislation, currency risks.
- Potential problems integrating nearly 300 new staff.

3.5 Both ReuseR and NOW have considered rationalising the range of products recycled

Assess this strategy.

Arguments for	*Arguments against*
• There is evidence that specialists can be successful • Detailed legislation may be specific to certain waste products • Different equipment is needed to recycle, for example, glass and paper • Expertise gained in one sector may not transfer to others • One can focus on higher growth segments of the market e.g. paper	• ReuseR has won a number of long-term waste collection and recycling contracts (many with local government departments for the recycling of domestic waste) on the basis that over 80% of all materials collected will be recycled. Rationalisation may result in such contracts being lost • High level of joint costs - may have to be collected anyway so need to examine incremental costs of recycling only • Reduced risk exposure to changes in legislation

3.6 If given more information, what techniques could you use to assess which products should be recycled?

The problem is one of deciding on a portfolio. Consequently portfolio analysis tools such as the BCG matrix and even the Shell GE McKinsey Directional Policy Matrix (DPM) could be used.

Details on margins would be useful but care must be taken to separate out joint costs. Ideally one would look at the incremental cash flows of recycling compared with disposal. The firm will probably continue to collect the waste anyway - the issue is how much of it gets sorted and recycled.

The issue of customers wanting us to offer a comprehensive service is more difficult to incorporate - in effect we have joint products. Here one would have to consider the effect on the whole portfolio of removing particular products from recycling and examining the different possible scenarios.

3.7 Assess the strategic significance of IT to ReuseR and NOW using McFarlan's strategic grid

ReuseR

ReuseR has already implemented a €12 million IT project using satellite navigation technology that enables the company to track and monitor its large fleet of specialised vehicles. This has been stated to be a success.

The Board has also approved a project that will cost €1.5 million to eliminate delays due to incorrect or missing paperwork, and it will also speed up deliveries of recycled waste to ReuseR's customers.

The use of IT to improve logistics in this way does contribute to ReuseR's competitive advantage at present. In the future, however, it is likely that competitors will have similar IT in place, so this advantage will be lost.

This would suggest that, unless ReuseR finds new uses for IT, then it is in the factory quadrant of McFarlane's strategic grid.

NOW

NOW's use of IT has been more customer-focused – 'The company has also embraced the use of IT in the business, which enables its customers from whom it collects waste to monitor volumes collected as well as collection dates and times. Its IT systems also enable customers who purchase recycled materials to place their orders and get immediate confirmation of delivery dates and volumes.'

This is more forward-looking than ReuseR as the IT systems can create switching costs thus maintaining customer loyalty. This advantage could again be copied, but there is perhaps more scope here for the future use to be strategic.

3.8 Outline the key HR issues facing each firm

ReuseR

- High staff turnover despite paying high wages.
- High training costs.
- Integrating all the new staff from acquisitions.
- Managing and reducing high workloads for some staff.
- Maintaining staff safety.

NOW

- High staff turnover in the area of recycling confidential papers.

3.9 What are the main issues to discuss if a link up between ReuseR and NOW is proposed?

Get the question right!

- Clarify the nature of the link up - merger, acquisition or joint venture?
- If acquisition, then is it ReuseR buys NOW or NOW buys ReuseR?
- Who are you advising in the case – ReuseR or NOW? Predator or target?
- Are you an internal or external consultant?

Strategic arguments

- One less competitor.
- Quick entry for each into new markets - both product and country.
- Enables both firms to get closer to achieving critical mass in an industry with few really large players.
- Synergy - see below.

ReuseR's tests of an acquisition if ReuseR is buying NOW
(Note: This could be important even if advising NOW.)

Gross margins ≥ 50%	NO - 40% GPM quoted as normal, though pulp initiative has margins of 52%
Sales between €10 - €30 million pa	NO - revenue €55.8 million in 2004. NOW is bigger than the suggested targets
Stand-alone	YES
Not hostile	YES - the directors control the company, so if they are not happy it will not happen anyway. There is little scope for appealing to the shareholders in defiance of the directors

Product portfolio issues

- Both do glass, wood and paper - opportunities for economies of scale.
- Will there be scope for pulp to be sold to ReuseR's existing customers for recycled paper?
- NOW has been quicker to rationalise its portfolio - how will it feel about ReuseR's other products, such as tyres?
- ReuseR gets better gross margins (>50%) than NOW on

many products (40%) so maybe some scope for better cost control.

- Need further detailed information on precisely which countries each operates in.

Structure of the management team

- NOW has marketing expertise, ReuseR more logistics and HR.
- Who will be CEO and Chairman?
- Conflicts over posts.
- May lose key people.

Ownership

- Imran and Peri may not wish to relinquish control of NOW.
- If a merger, then valuation becomes critical to facilitate sharing out the new business.

HR

- Both have problems keeping staff – neither seems to have solved this.

IT

- Complementary focus – ReuseR's new system is better at logistics, NOW's is better at servicing customers.

Organisational structure

- ReuseR is more country oriented, NOW more product - this will cause a clash. Will NOW be forced to go back to a regional emphasis or will ReuseR embrace a product approach or should they both move towards a matrix structure including region, product and possibly, customer?

Transfer of skills

- NOW's customer focus could help ReuseR manage larger customers

Valuation issues

- ReuseR's P/E ratio is higher than industry average (10 > 9). Which would be used for valuation of NOW? Possible bootstrapping implications.
- Synergy estimates.
- Revised growth estimates.

Financing

- Depends on nature of link up – ReuseR buys NOW, NOW buys ReuseR, merger?
- ReuseR is worth €217 million, NOW approximately €110 million.
- Could ReuseR raise sufficient finance to buy NOW? The current plan is to buy a further 8 companies over 18 months. If it had average sales of €20 million, a net margin

of 10% and a P/E of 9, then it would be worth on average €18 million. Buying NOW is thus equivalent to buying six of these companies in one go. This is much riskier but, if the directors believe that they could finance the original plan, then they should be able to finance buying NOW.

- Could NOW raise sufficient finance to buy ReuseR? The deal would have to very highly geared or NOW would have to convince institutional investors to accept large amounts of equity. This would seriously dilute the existing shareholders' (especially Imran and Peri) shares. Overall looks difficult.

Other concerns

- Post-acquisition management – NOW has demonstrated more skill at this than ReuseR.
- Stock exchange regulations – especially if NOW wants to buy ReuseR.
- How will NOW directors feel about ReuseR's investment outside the EU?

4 ANALYSIS: FINANCIAL STRATEGY PERSPECTIVE

4.1 Analyse the financial statements of ReuseR and NOW using ratio analysis

ReuseR

Ratio	2004	2003	Comments
Growth in turnover	16.4%	-	Good growth in turnover
ROCE	29.2/(149.4+20.0) = 17.2%	28.1/(134.7+20.0) = 18.2%	ROCE has fallen - reasons highlighted below
GPM	Insufficient detail given.		
NPM	29.2/214.2 = 13.6%	28.1/184.0 = 15.3%	Significant fall in margins. Reasons are discussed in paragraphs 15 to 20
Asset t/o	214.2/(149.4+20.0)= 1.26	184.0/(134.7+20.0)= 1.19	Improving, possibly indicating that recent investments are showing better returns.
Current ratio	73.7/36.2 = 2.0	63.1/31.7 = 2.0	Safe but conservative
Quick ratio	(46.5+6.4)/36.2 = 1.5	(39.1+4.1)/31.7 = 1.4	Safe
Debtor days	46.5/214.2 × 365 = 79 days	39.1/184.0 × 365= 78 days	Seems high - what is industry norm? Are powerful customers using their influence to pay late?
Stock days	Insufficient detail		
Creditor days	Insufficient detail		
Gearing using D/E and market values	20/217 = 0.09		Extremely low whichever way you calculate it
Gearing using D/E and book values	20/149.4 = 0.13	20/134.7 = 0.15	
Interest cover	29.2/1.4 = 20.9	28.1/1.4 = 20.1	Very comfortable
Dividend cover		20.8/7.0 = 3.0	Comfortable

Overall the financial statements show a solid performance with good growth in sales and profit. The main problem is the fall in margins, which in turn has reduced ROCE. The other main observation is the low gearing.

NOW

Ratio	2004	2003	Comments
Growth in turnover	15.5%	-	Good growth in turnover
ROCE	16.6/(53.7+11.9+2.5) = 24.4%	13.2/(43.5+2.5+11.9) = 22.8%	ROCE has risen
GPM	Insufficient detail given		
NPM	16.6/55.8 = 29.7%	13.2/48.3 = 27.3%	Improving margins
Asset t/o	55.8/(53.7+11.9+2.5) = 0.82	48.3/(43.5+2.5+11.9) = 0.83	Worsened slightly, possibly due to new investment taking time to generate returns
Current ratio	21.1/9.3 = 2.3	19.6/6.5 = 3.0	Safe, but has got worse due to loan of 2.5m becoming current. If we exclude the loan from 2005 calculations, then we would have a current ratio of 3.1
Quick ratio	(12.9+2.3)/9.3 = 1.9	(12.1+0.4)/6.5 = 1.9	Safe
Debtor days	12.9/55.8 × 365 = 84 days	12.1/48.3 × 365= 91 days	Seems high but has improved
Stock days	Insufficient detail		
Creditor days	Insufficient detail		
Gearing D/E	11.9/53.7 = 0.22	(11.9+2.5)/43.5 = 0.33	Low and falling
Interest cover	16.6/1.4 = 11.9	13.2/1.4 = 9.4	Comfortable and improving
Dividend cover		9.6/2.6 = 3.7	Comfortable

Overall the financial statements show a strong performance with increasing sales, profits and margins.

4.2 As far as the information permits prepare a cash flow statement for both companies for 2004 and comment

ReuseR

	Working	€m
Operating profit		29.2
Increase in inventories	(20.8 - 19.9)	(0.9)
Increase in trade receivables	(46.5 - 39.1)	(7.4)
Increase in trade payables and accruals	(22.5 + 7.6 – 19.6 – 6.2)	4.3
		25.2
Tax paid	(5.9 + 6.1 – 6.1)	(5.9)
Interest paid		(1.4)
Dividends paid		(7.0)
		10.9
Increase in non-current assets (NBV)	(131.9 – 123.3)	(8.6)
Increase in cash and short-term investments	(6.4 – 4.1)	2.3

Comments:

- Not much excitement really; fairly conservative and safe.
- Increase in non-current assets could represent both tangible fixed assets and goodwill on acquisitions. It is also a net figure – once depreciation has been taken into account the level of additions will be higher.
- Not much spare cash to finance acquisitions in excess of current level, indicating a need for further financing.
- While the increase in trade receivables is significant, there is little evidence of the overtrading often associated with growing companies.

NOW

	Working	€m
Operating profit		16.6
Decrease in inventories	(5.9 – 7.1)	1.2
Increase in trade receivables	(12.9 – 12.1)	(0.8)
Decrease in trade payables and accruals	(3.3 + 0.6 – 3.2 – 1.1)	(0.4)
		16.6
Tax paid	04 paid	(2.2)
Interest paid		(1.4)
Dividends paid		(2.6)
		10.4
Proceeds of share issue		0.5
Increase in non-current assets (NBV)	(53.8 – 44.8)	(9.0)
Increase in cash and short-term investments	(2.3 – 0.4)	1.9

Comments:

- Not much excitement really; fairly conservative and safe.
- Increase in non-current assets could represent both tangible fixed assets and goodwill on acquisitions. It is also a net figure – once depreciation has been taken into account the level of additions will be higher.

4.3 Analsye the financing to date for each company and future financing opportunities

ReuseR

The existing financing structure of ReuseR

Very low gearing

- This reduces the gearing risk of the firm, which is particularly useful in a high-risk industry.
- However, the firm is failing to take advantage of cheaper debt finance.

Quoted

- Should make raising finance easier.

The announcement to raise a loan of €40 million

The loan will treble the gearing level. Normally this would be considered highly significant but in this case the gearing level is still very low.

As outlined in the commentary on Appendix 4, the rough values of the three approved acquisitions are:

RED	€9 million
KLL	€18 million
MER	€68 million

The loan of €40 million will not be sufficient for these alone, unless shares are agreed to be part of the consideration. The Board plans to acquire 8 companies over the next 18 months, leaving a question mark over how this will be financed.

The possibilities of raising further finance in the future

Debt

Further debt should be readily available due to the following:

- low gearing levels
- the company is profitable and growing
- the company is quoted.

But:

- Security - banks may be less willing to accept specialist recycling plants and lorries as security. The balance sheet shows non-current assets of €131 million but we do not have a detailed breakdown to see how much could relate to better security such as land and buildings. Given the sums involved, however, it is likely that adequate security exists.
- The falling ROCE, mainly due to a drop in margins, may worry lenders, as might the poor governance issue of Kurt being both Chairman and CEO.

Equity

Many of the above issues apply here. ReuseR should be able to raise the sums it needs via rights issues and public issues if necessary. Given the spread of shareholdings, there are unlikely to be any control dilution problems if new shares are issued.

Other

There has been no mention of government grants - one would have expected this to be a promising source of funding for new developments.

NOW

The existing financing structure of NOW

Very low gearing

- This reduces the gearing risk of the firm, which is particularly useful in a high-risk industry.
- However, the firm is failing to take advantage of cheaper debt finance.

Unquoted

- This will reduce the options available for equity finance - see below.
- The firm has been successful in accessing government grants - see Paragraph 41.

The possibilities of raising further finance in the future

Debt

Further debt should be readily available due to the following:

- low gearing levels
- the company is profitable and growing.

But:

- the company is unquoted.

Security – as with ReuseR, banks may be less willing to accept specialist recycling plants and lorries as security. The balance sheet for NOW shows non-current assets of €53.8 million but we do not have a detailed breakdown to see how much could relate to better security such as land and buildings.

Equity

The key issue here is that the firm is unquoted.

- The viability of a rights issue will depend on the owners' willingness and ability to inject more cash. On paper all of the main shareholders are millionaires but they may struggle to inject the sums required to finance further acquisitions. Val in particular has already invested €0.9 million secured on her home.
- Alternatives could include venture capital and flotation. In both cases there may be concerns over dilution of control - particularly from the Patel brothers.
- Note that the value of the firm (see below) would indicate that it is large enough to consider a full listing.

Other

Given past success, NOW should be able to access further government funding.

4.4 Calculate the WACC of ReuseR

K_d

Don't have a valuation for the loan notes, so assume they are valued at par and will be redeemed at par. Thus:

$K_d = 7\% \times (1 - 0.22) = 5.46\%$

K_e

The analysis of the five-year plan suggested a future growth figure of 10% pa (see analysis of Paragraph 22). Take this as an estimate of expected growth in dividends.

Take current market value as net profit × P/E ratio = €21.7m × 10 = €217 million.

Most recent dividend was €7 million

$K_e = \{D_0 \times (1 + g) / MV\} + g = \{7 \times 1.10 / 217\} + 0.10 = 13.5\%$

WACC

Weighting according to market values

$K = (217 \times 13.5 + 7 \times 5.46)/(217 + 7) = 13.2\%$

Given the low gearing level, it is likely that increasing gearing could reduce the WACC.

This figure could be used for investment appraisal.

4.5 Assess the market value of NOW using earnings, assets and dividend approaches.

1 *Earnings approach*

P/E ratio = 9 for quoted companies in the sector.

Earnings were €12.3 million in 2004.

MV = 9 × 12.3 = €110.7 million

However, given the lower marketability of unquoted shares, this figure should be discounted by between 10% and 25%.

A rough valuation would thus be in the range of €85 million to €100 million.

If one is considering a possible takeover, then synergies would need to be factored into the calculation.

2 *Net assets approach*

Book value of equity = €53.7 million

Less useful as goodwill usually understated!

3 *Dividend valuation model (DVM) approach*

To use the DVM we need to know a K_e and dividend growth. We can borrow the K_e from ReuseR (13.5%) but getting a suitable growth rate is more problematic.

Proposed dividend for 2004 is €0.245 per share, or 10.62 million × 0.245 = €2.6 million in total.

This is the same as for 2003 implying no growth in dividends.

Using these figures MV = dividend / K_e = 2.6 / 0.135 = €19.26 million.

This is far too low. The problem is the lack of growth in the dividends. In the long run one would expect dividends to grow in line with earnings.

From 2003 to 2004 profits grew from 9.6 to 12.3 million euros; growth of 28%. This is greater than the Ke! The DVM formula with growth is:

$MV = D_0 (1 + g) / (K_e - g)$

Putting this growth into the dividend valuation model gives a negative answer!

The DVM could be useful if a more representative growth figure could be obtained.

5 ANALYSIS: RISK AND CONTROL PERSPECTIVE

5.1 Assess the risks facing ReuseR and NOW under the following headings and summarise

Risk area	ReuseR	NOW
Business risks	• Growth by acquisition is generally more risky than organic growth • Risk of larger clients deciding to do their own recycling	
	• Risk of losing a major client will have a serious impact on the business as only have 12 • Risk of acquisitions not being successfully integrated into the rest of the business • Risk of losing international clients because the geographical structure is not client focused enough • The Middle East country concerned could be unstable politically (e.g. Lebanon) or a possible target for US action (e.g. Syria)	• Risk of losing customers due to problems with recycling confidential papers • Risk of not being approved at the end of the trial period with the large contract for an IT firm
Financial risks	• Low levels of debt so low gearing risk and low risk exposure to interest rate movements	
	• Low credit risk, though average debtor days is 79	• Low credit risk, though average debtor days is 84
	• Low exposure to currency risk except for any operations in the UK and in the Middle Eastern country mentioned. Even then, risk exposure will be low as most recycled waste stays within the country it was collected from giving costs and revenues in the same currency • Further expansion could be financed by local currency loans to hedge risk	• Low exposure to currency risk except for any operations in the UK
Political and legal risks	• Large upside potential due to increasing legislation forcing firms and individuals to recycle more	
	• Unlikely to face litigation except for safety issues	
Technology risk	• Risk of new methods being developed that will make recycling easier / cheaper	
Economic risk	• When firms and individuals have a choice whether to recycle, then demand may be influenced by trade cycles. Where demand is driven by legislation, then the risk is lower.	

Risk area	ReuseR	NOW
Environmental risk	· Upside potential as people are becoming increasingly concerned about the environment	
Reputation risks	· Low risk exposure as the marketplace is not brand driven	

Overall the key risks are business risks. For ReuseR the key downside risks relate to the possibility of losing clients and the management of acquisitions. For NOW key downside risks relate to losing clients. For both, the main upside potential relates to further changes in legislation opening up new markets.

5.2 Suggest some KPIs that could be used to monitor operations, using the balanced scorecard as a framework

Financial perspective
• ROCE and RI - overall and by SBU • Margins - overall and by product / customer - particularly important for ReuseR • Different costs as a percentage of sales e.g. transportation cost / sales • Sales growth • Cash flow targets • Market share
Customer perspective
• Percentage scheduled targets met – particularly for NOW's confidential paper recycling • Percentage repeat business • Number of complaints • Targets for new customers won
Internal business perspective
• Percentage waste recycled rather than dumped • Percentage utilisation of fixed assets - vehicles, recycling plants • Transportation cost per mile • Cost per tonne of waste collected - ESP for NOW's recycle for cash scheme • Staff turnover • Percentage of job offers accepted by suitable candidates • Number of safety breaches

Innovation and learning perspective
• Number of new product ideas launched • Targets for employee productivity • Percentage total revenue coming from new products

chapter

17

REUSER: MAY 2005 – UNSEEN MATERIAL

Contents

1 Exam question / requirement

You are Franc de Loore, the Business Development Director at Shard.

You have been requested to write a report to the Board of Shard, following the recent Board meeting, concerning how Shard could secure the sources of recycled materials in the longer term.

Your report should cover the issues discussed at the Board meeting, as minuted in Appendix 5 of the unseen material.

2 Rest of unseen material

Shard

Background

In recent years many large international manufacturing companies have been building up their own recycling divisions. Shard is a major European company, listed on a European stock exchange. Shard has two main business areas, manufacturing glass and newspaper publishing and printing, which are both profitable. The company manufactures glass for a significant proportion of the new cars manufactured in Europe and it also manufactures over six billion glass jars and bottles annually.

Shard also owns eight European newspaper titles, which it acquired in a move to diversify over nine years ago. All titles are operating profitably, but margins are becoming tighter.

Shard operates three divisions, which are glass, newspapers and recycled materials. The glass division is the largest and, in the year ended February 2005, generated over 82% of Shard's operating profit. The newspaper division generated almost 16% and the balance of Shard's operating profit was generated by sales of recycled products.

Shard has achieved significant growth in turnover, profitability and EPS in the last 10 years through internal growth, geographic growth and external growth through acquisitions. The company has a stated aim of achieving productivity gains of over 4% per year and of continually improving its EPS.

The company's share price has fluctuated due to global economic factors, but is currently near its high for the last 12 months at €13.95 per share.

Shard is also at present negotiating for a major new contract, which could result in an increase in glass production from its current level of 81% of capacity, up to 89%. However, there are several other manufacturers bidding for the contract and Shard may, or may not, be successful in being awarded it. The outcome will not be known until the end of 2005.

Shard and recycling

Shard plans to achieve cost savings by continually upgrading its industrial efficiency and also by acquiring some of its key raw material suppliers, thereby controlling supply and price of these crucial inputs into its glass manufacturing and newspaper printing process. Furthermore, like many industries, the glass and newspaper industries are under increasing pressure to meet recycling targets. Shard currently uses recycled glass for about 38% of its raw materials in the glass division and around 16% of its total paper supply for newspaper printing is recycled paper.

In a benchmarking exercise, Shard's Finance Director identified that some competitors use higher levels of recycled materials. Shard's Finance Director has reported that he considers that Shard should aim to significantly increase the levels of recycled materials used by the glass and newspapers divisions within the next three years. He considers that Shard should have targets of 60% for recycled glass and 75% for recycled paper.

Shard currently operates a small number of recycling plants in several countries that supply glass and paper to the main businesses, but these have failed to grow significantly over recent years. Shard has believed for a long time in the importance of recycling glass and the cost benefits of obtaining recycled glass for its raw materials. The higher the proportion of recycled glass, the better the gross margin is on that batch of glass output, due to lower raw material costs and also lower energy costs in production. The glass industry globally is under pressure to reduce costs to remain competitive. In addition, the European glass industry is being put under pressure to increase the level of recycled glass by the EU authorities. Furthermore, the newspaper industry is also trying to reduce costs without affecting quality.

Shard has been obtaining higher levels of recycled glass and paper over the last five years by establishing links with over 20 recycling companies, of which two are ReuseR and NOW. ReuseR has supplied and worked closely with Shard for many years. ReuseR's Chairman and Chief Executive, Kurt Finehart, is also a non-executive director of Shard, having been invited to join its Board three years ago.

Proposed expansion of Shard's recycling division

The Shard Board of Directors has long been considering expanding its recycling division and feels that the time is right to embrace the challenges of corporate social responsibility. Not only does it feel that it is right for society, it also makes good commercial sense as each Euro saved on raw materials improves Shard's profitability. Its own recycling division currently acquires waste materials, including glass and paper as well as other materials from a range of sources, mainly from contracts to collect waste from other manufacturing companies. Shard's recycling division sells unwanted recycled materials to other companies, but retains all recycled glass and paper for Shard's two businesses.

The Shard Board met on 23 May 2005 and Franc de Loore, Shard's Business Development Director, was requested to investigate the possible acquisition of a recycling company. It was considered that this would enable Shard to have access to a much higher level of recycled materials much more quickly than it could if it continued to build up its own recycling division, which has not grown as expected. The Business Development Director had already eliminated a number of recycling companies from the shortlist of possible companies to acquire, as they handle a wider range of recycled goods than Shard is interested in. The two alternative recycling companies that Shard is considering acquiring are ReuseR or NOW.

The Shard Board is not united in its decision to progress the acquisition of a recycling company and the comments made by Directors at the Shard Board meeting on 23 May 2005 are shown in an extract from the minutes of the meeting in **Appendix 5**.

Kurt Finehart (a non-executive director of Shard) was present at the Board meeting on 23 May 2005, and he also had access to the Shard Board papers concerning the potential acquisition of ReuseR, where he is Chairman and Chief Executive. His reaction to the possible acquisition of ReuseR is also shown in **Appendix 5**.

At the meeting, Franc de Loore was requested to prepare a report for the next Shard Board meeting in June, concerning whether either company were suitable for acquisition.

Shard's key financial data

Summary key financial data for Shard is shown below:

	Year ended February 2005	Year ended February 2006
Shard group revenue € Million	2,040	1,940
Operating and administrative costs € Million	1,692	1,595
	———	———
Operating profit € Million	348	345
Interest and other finance charges € Million	(68)	(72)
Taxation (30%) € Million	(84)	(82)
	———	———
Profit for the period € Million	196	191
	———	———
No of shares fully paid up	214 million	214 million
Earnings per share (EPS)	€ 0.92	€ 0.89
Dividends per share (DPS)	€ 0.37	€ 0.35
P/E ratio	15	15
Market capitalisation (at end February each year) € Million	2,941	2,870
Net debt € Million	802	895
Capital expenditure during year € Million	87	82
Share price - range in year	€ 13.24 - 14.01	€ 12.68 - 13.45

Due to Shard's current long-term debt repayment schedule and continued expansion, the company has decided that it is not able to acquire either recycling company for cash.

Shard's post-tax cost of capital is 9%. Shard's share price at 20 May 2005 is €13.95 per share.

Shard does not yet have access to detailed management accounts from either ReuseR or NOW, which would give a breakdown of profitability by sector. The only accounting data that Shard currently has access to is the statutory accounts for both companies (of which extracts are included in Appendices 2 and 3 to the pre-seen material). From the statutory accounts, Shard also has details of operating cash flows generated, which are shown below.

Forecast effect on Shard's cash flows if a recycling company is acquired

It is forecast that Shard could achieve operating efficiencies and cost savings through the use of higher levels of recycled glass and recycled paper, assuming that the majority of production of recycled glass and paper that is currently sold by ReuseR or NOW is supplied to Shard and contracts with existing customers are not renewed.

The after-tax effect on the Shard group's cash flows is forecast to be as follows:

After-tax effect on Shard's group cash flows	**If ReuseR is acquired** € million	**If NOW is acquired** € million
Glass manufacture:		
Savings to Shard due to price differential between recycled glass and 'new' raw materials	3.6	0.8
Energy savings(through the use of greater amounts of recycled glass)	3.5	0.7
Increased transportation cost to Shard factories	(1.6)	(0.3)
Newspaper printing:		
Savings to Shard due to price differential between recycledpaper pulp and new paper	4.0	2.8

It is forecast that, if Shard chose to acquire ReuseR, it would sell some areas of the ReuseR business and the effect would be a one-off net benefit to Shard of €5 million (post-tax). This benefit to Shard is not included in the cash flow figures in the table above. The management of Shard does not forecast any substantial changes if NOW were to be acquired.

The two companies being considered for acquisition have generated the following post-tax operating cash flows in the year ended during 2004:

	ReuseR € million	**NOW** € million
Post-tax operating cash flows for year ended during 2004(as extracted from latest statutory accounts)	33.6	17.8

Franc de Loore has forecast that, if ReuseR were acquired, its post-tax operating cash flows could grow by around 10% per year. He has also forecast that if NOW was acquired post-tax operating cash flows could grow by around 20% per year.

Shard's acquisition policy states that it evaluates potential acquisitions over a six-year period.

Investigations on ReuseR and NOW

Franc de Loore has investigated ReuseR and NOW as part of his research prior to the possible acquisition of either of these two companies. He has been able to obtain the following information about the companies:

ReuseR

ReuseR's audit

ReuseR's audit identified a number of problems:

- criticisms of how a recent acquisition had been accounted for, including an overstatement of the valuation of stocks and other assets
- a number of minor frauds had occurred during 2004, one involving substantial cash movements, which had already been identified by ReuseR management and the employee involved has left the company
- weaknesses in the ReuseR's finance team, particularly in certain countries.

Safety issues at ReuseR recycling plants

During April 2005 there were two separate accidents at different ReuseR recycling plants and in one of these accidents there were two deaths. One worker had got trapped in a machine. A fellow worker tried to help and both were fatally injured. Safety instructions had not been followed.

The Health and Safety (H & S) authorities had investigated the latest accident and their preliminary report found that there was widespread ignorance of safety issues and that, at some ReuseR plants they had visited, there were inadequate safety instructions and a shortage of safety equipment (including safety goggles and safety hats). The report gave ReuseR management 28 days before a further inspection during June 2005. There is a possibility of the H & S authorities imposing fines or the possibility of one, or more, of the recycling plants being closed down until safety measures have been improved.

ReuseR share price

ReuseR's share price has fluctuated between €1.91 and €2.61 during 2004. Following news of the accidents at ReuseR recycling plants in April 2005 and subsequently the H & S report, ReuseR's share price had slipped to around €2.20 by early May 2005. On Friday 20 May 2005, ReuseR's share price had been boosted to €2.31 as it had just announced the successful acquisition of RED in an Eastern European country.

NOW

1 *NOW's staff problems*

Franc de Loore has identified that NOW is experiencing staff recruitment and staff retention problems. The terms and conditions of employment in NOW are poor in relation to industry practice. Although NOW employees receive regular training, they work long hours and many NOW employees are less skilled than those in other recycling companies. Many NOW employees feel under pressure from working long hours and they have a demanding waste collection schedule to achieve. Many of NOW's staff feel that they cannot meet the demands of their jobs.

2 *NOW's problems with its secure waste paper collection and pulping service*

NOW operates a fleet of specialised waste paper recycling vehicles that deal solely with pulping confidential waste paper materials on customers' premises. Franc de Loore has investigated NOW and has identified that it is experiencing problems with its secure collection and pulping service. The information has come from reliable sources.

In early May 2005, NOW had one of its contracts terminated by one of its largest customers, LW, which has also filed a legal charge against the company. LW has claimed that NOW did not securely dispose of all of its confidential waste paper, which should have been collected and pulped on LW's premises. LW has discovered that large quantities of commercially sensitive papers were instead disposed of in a standard waste disposal site. LW's management is very concerned at this major lapse of NOW's secure collection and pulping service of LW's confidential papers. NOW is investigating how this lapse in its confidential waste paper disposal service has occurred, when the papers should have been pulped at LW's premises. NOW is tightening procedures, and trying to rebuild confidence in its waste paper pulping service before other customers learn of this problem.

Franc de Loore has been advised that the lapse with LW's confidential waste paper is not the first time such an incident has occurred. He is also reliably informed that the NOW Board is aware of the problems with its collection and recycling service for confidential waste paper. He has also been made aware that Val Rines (NOW's Sales and Marketing Director) is very annoyed that she had not been informed of all of the previous problems. Val Rines is understood to have been in favour of temporarily suspending the confidential waste disposal service, but the NOW Board disagreed.

3 *Valuation of NOW*

NOW is not a listed company. The Shard Board has an acquisition policy of valuing non-listed companies using a multiple of six times the level of its latest post-tax earnings.

Appendix 5

Extract from the minutes of Shard Board meeting held on Monday 23 May 2005	
Item 5 from agenda: Securing long-term supplies of recycled materials	**Responsibility**
5.1 There was a detailed discussion about how Shard could secure long-term supplies of recycled materials.	-
5.2 The Director of Glass and the Procurement Director both consider that Shard should enter into long-term contracts with its key suppliers, not acquire them. The latter has been very outspoken in his criticism of the proposed strategy to strengthen the recycling division of Shard.	-
5.3 Shard's Chairman and Finance Director of Shard are in favour of Shard's proposed enlargement of its own recycling division. Both directors consider that this would lead to significant cost savings in raw materials and energy costs.	-
Shard's Chairman and Finance Director are both in favour of acquiring a recycling company to enlarge Shard's own recycling division. The Board agreed that a strategic analysis of the benefits and problems of acquiring a recycling company is required.	
The Chairman also wants the Board to consider recommendations of which, if either, of the two alternative companies (ReuseR or NOW) should be acquired.	
5.4 The Finance Director stated that there is a need to ensure that the acquisition valuations recognise the need to improve Shard's shareholder value.	-
The Finance Director also reminded the Board that the success of any acquisition is usually determined by the acquiring company's ability to plan and implement a successful post acquisition strategy.	
5.5 Kurt Finehart, a non-executive director of Shard (who is also the Chairman and Chief Executive of ReuseR) stated that he personally was not in favour of Shard acquiring ReuseR. He proposed that Shard acquired NOW.	-
5.6 The Business Development Director has been requested to prepare a report for the next Shard Board meeting.	**de Loore**

END OF UNSEEN MATERIAL

chapter

18

REUSER: MAY 2005 – SAMPLE SOLUTION

Contents

1 Introduction

What follows is a possible answer for the ReuseR May 2005 exam. As always, it is one possible solution and alternative interpretations may be valid.

2 Sample script

REPORT (CONFIDENTIAL)

To: The Board of Directors, Shard

From: Franc de Loore, Business Development Director

Date: Today

Shard: Current issues and future strategies

Contents

Appendices

1 Introduction

Shard is a major listed European company with two main business areas, manufacturing glass and newspaper publishing and printing. The company has achieved significant growth in turnover, profitability and EPS in the last ten years through internal growth, geographic growth and external growth through acquisitions.

In each of its main markets Shard is under pressure to reduce costs without compromising quality and to increase the proportion of recycled materials used. These two pressures are consistent as recycled materials often involve lower costs.

The key challenge facing Shard is thus to determine how best to secure the sources of recycled materials in the longer term. This could be through better contracts with suppliers or vertical integration. If vertical integration is the preferred option, then this could be achieved through organic growth or acquisition.

2 Terms of reference

This report has been prepared at the request of the Board of Directors of Shard, to examine and advise on the future strategies for Shard, looking in particular at how the company could secure the sources of recycled materials in the longer term.

3 Prioritisation of key issues

A detailed SWOT analysis of Shard is shown in Appendix 1. Out of these the key issues facing Shard are as follows.

3.1 Top priority: Whether Shard should be vertically integrated with respect to recycled materials

The first decision to be made is whether Shard should be in the business of recycling materials. For example, why cannot the firm exercise its buyer power to obtain cheap, quality supplies from outside suppliers of recycled materials, as advocated by the Director of Glass and the Procurement Director? This decision must be made first before considering how to pursue further backwards integration.

This issue is discussed in more detail in section 4 of this report.

3.2 Second priority: Whether backwards integration is best achieved via organic growth or acquisition

Should the decision be made to integrate backwards further, the next key question is how. Should Shard focus on developing its existing recycling division or pursue a policy of acquisition?

This issue is discussed in more detail in section 5 of this report.

3.3 Third priority: Evaluation of ReuseR as a potential acquisition target

Should a policy of acquisition be adopted, the next logical step is to find suitable targets. To some degree these two issues are related - acquisition may only be acceptable should a suitable target be found but, for the purposes of this report, they are separated. Two targets have been identified - ReuseR and NOW - and both are discussed to assess their strategic fit with Shard.

The evaluation of ReuseR as a possible target is discussed in more detail in section 6 of this report.

3.4 Fourth priority: Evaluation of NOW as a potential acquisition target

The evaluation of NOW as a possible target is discussed in more detail in section 7 of this report.

3.5 Fifth priority: Post-acquisition strategies

The post-acquisition management phase is critical to the overall success of any acquisition. Should Shard proceed with either ReuseR or NOW, key steps will need to be taken to ensure a successful integration of the businesses concerned.

This issue is discussed in more detail in section 8 of this report.

4 Whether Shard should be vertically integrated with respect to recycled materials

The main decision Shard needs to make is which business it wants to be in.

The arguments for Shard using more recycled materials are compelling:

- EU legislation
- the large cost savings that result
- the benefits towards Shard's green image.

However, there are different ways of increasing supply; rather than increasing in-house supply, Shard could look at developing its relationships with external suppliers.

The main arguments concerning backwards vertical integration, as applied to Shard, are as follows:

- *Economies of combined operations* - Shard should benefit from not contributing towards suppliers' profit margins.
- *Reduction in supplier power* - this is a weak argument for the acquisition as Shard exercises considerable buyer power over suppliers. This could save costs without the need for organic growth or an acquisition.
- *Better scheduling* - it is not clear whether there have been problems with deliveries to Shard from external suppliers but, if there have been, then vertical integration would solve this. Again this might be possible simply by Shard exercising more customer power over existing suppliers.
- *Better internal control* - there may be scope for Shard to change how ReuseR and NOW prepare their glass and paper to make it more suitable for Shard's purposes. Yet again this might be possible simply by Shard exercising more customer power.
- *Flexibility* - a powerful argument against the move is that Shard would lose the flexibility to switch suppliers as market conditions change.
- *Stability of supply* - this is unlikely to be a problem for Shard as the industry is made up of many firms eager to supply recycled glass and paper.
- *Control of supply* - Shard could stop ReuseR and/or NOW selling glass and paper to any of its competitors. However, the structure of the industry with many small suppliers would mean that competitors could easily find alternative sources of supply.
- *Increased operating gearing* - a glass manufacturer / printer like Shard is likely to have high fixed costs anyway, so acquiring suppliers' fixed costs rather than simply paying a variable cost for recycled glass and paper seems unwise.
- *Growth opportunities* - the recycling industry may offer Shard more opportunities for growth than glass manufacturing and printing.

Overall the strategic argument for vertical integration does not look convincing. Shard may be able to achieve all of its objectives by exercising more customer power rather than buying a supplier or increasing its existing recycling business. This is the strategy of firms such as Rockware Glass in the UK.

5 Whether backwards integration is best achieved via organic growth or acquisition

The main arguments concerning acquisition and organic growth as applied to Shard, are as follows:

- Speed - acquisition is generally quicker than organic growth. Given that the Finance Director wants to increase the percentage of recycled glass from the current 38% to 60% and paper from 16% to 75% in three years, it may be that organic growth will be too slow to hit these targets.
- *Cost* – the purchase price of any acquired company will usually include an element for goodwill. Organic growth is generally cheaper as only assets need to be bought, not goodwill. The question is thus whether Shard needs the goodwill of the target companies. Given the poor performance of Shard's existing recycling division, there is an argument that Shard would benefit from the expertise and contacts that existing external suppliers possess. However, it would be cheaper to recruit people with suitable expertise rather than to buy a supplier.
- *Product range* – Shard requires glass and paper products only, so there is little point in acquiring a supplier who recycles other products as well, such as tyres.
- *Reputation of the target company* – both ReuseR and NOW have serious ethical problems that could affect Shard's reputation if not dealt with quickly. These are discussed in more detail in section 9 below.
- *Control* – growth is easier to control if organic.
- *Clash of cultures* – any acquired business may have a different culture to Shard's resulting in integration problems and possible clashes. Organic growth allows a smoother growth process.

On balance organic growth is preferred to acquisition primarily owing to the cost issues involved.

6 Evaluation of ReuseR as a potential acquisition target

The arguments for and against buying ReuseR are as follows.

Arguments in favour of buying ReuseR

- Incorporating possible synergy into a discounted cash flow analysis values ReuseR at €277.8 million (see Appendix 3 for detailed calculations). Given ReuseR's current market capitalisation of €207.9 million, this would still allow a bid premium of 20% to be offered and leave Shard with a potential gain of €28 million.
- ReuseR has strong positive cash flow.
- Net savings of €9.5 million a year could be gained.
- Directors already know Kurt Finehart.

- ReuseR appears to have strong management with good contacts with government.

Arguments against buying ReuseR

- ResueR has seen its margins declining due to high transportation and staff training costs.
- Recent health and safety and financial control problems will need to be addressed - these issues are discussed in more detail in section 9 below.
- ReuseR may be recycling products that are not viable.
- ReuseR has problems recruiting and keeping staff.
- The management of ReuseR has struggled managing the post-acquisition phase after buying companies.
- ReuseR has contracts in the Middle East - does Shard wish to have an interest in this area?

Viewed in isolation the arguments for buying ReuseR outweigh those against, so the acquisition is recommended. However, when comparing ReuseR and NOW, NOW appears the better target (see section 7).

7 Evaluation of NOW as a potential acquisition target

The arguments for and against buying NOW are as follows.

Arguments in favour of buying NOW

- Incorporating possible synergy into a discounted cash flow analysis values NOW at €185.9 million (see Appendix 4 for detailed calculations). Even if NOW's current shareholders attempt to value the business using the industry average P/E ratio of 9, giving a value of €110.7 million, this would still allow a substantial bid premium to be offered and leave Shard with a large potential gain.
- NOW shows stronger financials than Reuser - higher historic growth in net profit (29.7% rather than 4.3%), higher forecast growth (20% rather than 10%), higher net margins (29.7% rather than 13.6%) and higher ROCE (24.4% rather than 17.2%).
- NOW has implemented customer-focused IT systems.
- NOW has built up strong relationships with its customers
- NOW has demonstrated its ability to be innovative e.g. the recycle for cash scheme.
- NOW has moved into higher margin businesses such as producing paper pulp rather than selling waste paper.
- NOW has recently won two new large contracts for paper
- A smaller target than ReuseR, so will be easier to integrate.

Arguments against buying NOW

- With NOW being unquoted and with 77.2% of the shares owned by three people, the bid process for NOW should be cheaper and simpler. However, should the existing owners refuse to sell, there is little Shard can then do. With ReuseR being quoted, there is scope to start buying shares and then appealing to the wider shareholder group to secure over 50% of the shares.
- There may be problems retaining key directors as they are currently shareholders who will benefit from the sale and may choose to retire or leave.
- NOW has had some major problems with its secure collection and disposal service - this issue is discussed in more detail in section 9 below.
- Valuation is more difficult with an unquoted company, increasing the possibility of paying too much for the company.
- NOW has a problem recruiting and retaining staff, reflecting poor working conditions.

Out of the two targets identified, NOW appears the better prospect due to the greater potential gains and better underlying financial performance.

8 Post-acquisition strategies

The success of post-acquisition management depends on five key areas.

There must be scope for adding value to the target

It is vital that the current ethical problems identified are addressed in the acquired company as an urgent priority:.

There must be a common core of unity between the two businesses

A key reason for acquiring either company is the potential synergy. Particularly if the synergy is factored into the offer price, it is vital that action is taken to turn forecast gains into actual gains.

To do this some of NOW's (or ReuseR's) supplies will have to be diverted to Shard. This will involve identifying whether spare capacity exists, which existing contracts can be cancelled and implementing the switch. Most of the synergies identified should follow directly once the proportion of recycled materials used by Shard is increased.

A key aspect for Shard will be the extent to which the acquired business and Shard's existing recycling division are integrated or kept separate.

Management must understand the business being acquired

The issues involved in recycling are different from manufacturing glass and paper. It is vital that the Board of Shard meets with the management of the target company to fully understand the critical success factors involved.

The buyer needs to put in a quality management team quickly

Where there are skills gaps with the target firm, Shard will have to appoint new managers or allocate responsibility for the matters involved. For example, ReuseR has a lack of marketing expertise in its senior management, so Shard would have to ensure that this area is transferred to Shard's marketing director

The buyer must be able to hold onto the best management of both companies

It is essential that Shard does not lose the expertise and experience inherent in the Boards of ReuseR or NOW. Most directors in the target companies hold shares so are less likely to be convinced to stay by financial incentives. Key staff should offered senior roles in Shard.

9 Ethical considerations

The main ethical issues facing Shard are as follows.

Corporate responsibility

There is a possible ethical conflict between maximising profit for shareholders and protecting the environment. For Shard this conflict is not a major problem as the use of recycled materials is both good for the environment and is usually cheaper. Ongoing legislation is putting pressure on firms to use more recycled materials so Shard could take a lead here and recycle more than the legislation requires.

Possible conflict of interests for Kurt Finehart

Kurt Finehart is a non-executive director of Shard and is also the CEO and Chairman of ReuseR and holds 22.8% of the shares in ReuseR. There is a clear conflict of interest here as Kurt has to represent the interests of both Shard and ReuseR shareholders. While one would expect him to act with full integrity when advising the Boards of Shard and ReuseR, it is recommended that he is not asked to contribute to Shard's discussion of the potential acquisition of ReuseR or NOW to avoid such a conflict.

ReuseR

The audit report has highlighted control problems within the accounting function of ReuseR, as highlighted by recent minor frauds. If ReuseR is acquired, then steps must be taken to ensure that the accountant involved acts with greater competence and the principles of corporate governance are adopted.

There have also been breaches of health and safety within ReuseR and some plants have been threatened with closure. A culture of safety needs to be put in place as soon as possible.

NOW

NOW is facing litigation from a customer over a failure to dispose of confidential material securely. This appears to be a systematic problem rather than a one-off and is due to poor staff training and motivation. The management of NOW has failed to address these issues and has failed to suspend the service until it is rectified.

Shard will need to act quickly to reassure customers if it acquires NOW.

10 Recommendations

Before considering potential acquisitions in more detail, the Board needs to examine the arguments for continued outsourcing in more detail. It is recommended that Shard enters into long-term supply contracts with key suppliers to ensure supply and limit price increases. The exercise of buyer power over external suppliers will enable Shard to achieve the same objectives as switching to more in-house supply.

Should further backwards integration be preferred, then it is recommended that Shard continues to develop its in-house recycling division rather than buying an existing supplier. The extra costs of acquisition do not cover the benefits. To facilitate further growth it is recommended that a new head be appointed.

However, should acquisition be seen as the best route forwards by the Board then either target would be an acceptable acquisition. When choosing between the two, it is recommended that NOW is a more suitable target than ReuseR. This is because of the greater potential gains to shareholder value and the stronger underlying financial position of the firm.

It is recommended that the Board of NOW be approached in the immediate future to commence negotiations.

Should either company be bought, however, there are significant ethical issues that will need to be urgently addressed. The other key post-acquisition issue will be the retention of key staff.

11 Conclusion

Shard needs to increase the percentage of recycled materials used within its glass and paper businesses to reduce costs and to continue to exceed environmental legislation. The main challenge facing Shard is thus how best to secure extra supplies of recycled materials. This report has recommended that outsourcing be investigated further before increasing the degree of vertical integration within the firm and that organic growth is preferred to acquisition.

Once these decisions have been made Shard should have a clear platform for future growth.

Appendix 1: Position analysis of Shard using SWOT framework

Strengths	***Weaknesses***
· Large, well-established business · Share price at a high, reflecting market confidence in the business · Has achieved significant growth in turnover, profitability and EPS over the last ten years · Strong management team · Listed, making raising finance easier · High capacity utilisation in glass manufacturing · Use of benchmarking to improve performance	· Some competitors are using higher levels of recycled materials than Shard · Shard's own recycling division has not grown as expected, partly due to a weak management team · The Board is not united regarding future strategies · Plans to repay debt restrict the methods of consideration to share for share exchanges if acquiring new businesses. This may not be acceptable to vendor shareholders
Opportunities	***Threats***
· Increase the % of recycled materials used to reduce costs and enhance Shard's reputation for social responsibility · Acquisition of ReuseR or NOW · Manufacturer flat glass · Increase capacity utilisation · Exercise buyer power to reduce the cost of recycled materials from suppliers	· Intense competitive rivalry · Global pressure to reduce costs · Increasing legislation regarding the use of recycled materials - especially within the EU · Rivals may buy ReuseR and/or Now and restrict Shard's access to cheap recycled materials.

Appendix 2: Key ratios

Ratio	Shard	ReuseR	NOW
Revenue growth	5.2%	16.4%	15.5%
Growth in net profit	2.6%	4.3%	28.1%
Growth in EPS	2.6%	4.3%	26.1%
Net margin	9.6%	13.6%	29.7%
ROCE	N/A	17.2%	24.4%

Note: The most recent available figures have been used for each company:

- Shard - y/e Feb 2005
- ReuseR - y/e Nov 2004
- NOW - y/e Dec 2004

Appendix 3: Valuation of ReuseR

1 Market capitalisation

The current share price of ReuseR is €2.31, though the highest price in 2004 was €2.61.

Clearly ResueR shareholders will not accept a price of less than €2.31 and would probably want a reasonable premium above this to be convinced to sell. The €2.61 would give a premium of 13%, though for greater chance of acceptance a premium of 20% would be preferred.

This would value the shares at 120% × 2.31 = €2.77.

ReuseR has 90,000 million shares in issue, giving total market values as follows:

	€million
Current market value	207.9
Market value with share price of €2.61	234.9
Market value with premium of 20%	249.3

2 Discounted cash flow analysis

Incorporating potential synergies, the value of ReuseR can be estimated as follows:

	2005 *Year 1*	**2006** *Year 2*	**2007** *Year 3*	**2008** *Year 4*	**2009** *Year 5*	**2010** *Year 6*
Operating cash flows (W)	48.5	53.4	58.7	64.6	71.1	78.1
One-off benefit of selling some areas of ReuseR	5					
Net cash flow	53.5	53.4	58.7	64.6	71.1	78.1
Discount factor @9%	0.917	0.842	0.772	0.708	0.650	0.596
Present value	49.1	45.0	45.3	45.7	46.2	46.5
NPV	**277.8**					

This would suggest that the maximum Shard should pay for ReuseR is €277.8 million. A price higher than this would erode shareholder value, not enhance it.

Furthermore, even with a 20% premium over market price, there is still scope for Shard to gain by over €28 million.

Working

	€million
2004 operating cash flows	33.6
Estimated cash flows for RED (using net profit)	1.0
Savings on glass prices	3.6
Savings on energy	3.5
Extra transportation costs	(1.6)
Savings on paper and pulp prices	4.0
Net cash flow	**44.1**

To get the figures for 2005 onwards, this has been increased by 10% each year.

Note: An alternative approach would have been to exclude the synergy from the growth.

Appendix 4: Valuation of NOW

1 Valuation based on net assets

The book value of NOW's equity at 31 December 2004 was €53.7 million.

2 Valuation using P/E ratios

Shard's policy is to value unquoted businesses like NOW using a P/E ratio of 6.

NOW's earnings were €12.3 million in 2004.

Thus the market value is given by:

MV = 6 × 12.3 = €73.8 million

However, the P/E ratio for quoted companies in the sector is 9, giving a market value of:

MV = 9 × 12.3 = €110.7 million

However, given the lower marketability of unquoted shares this figure should be discounted by 25%, say, giving a rough valuation of €85 million.

Given the high growth anticipated within now, a high bid premium would have to be added to the above figures to encourage acceptance.

3 Discounted cash flow analysis

Incorporating potential synergies, the value of NOW can be estimated as follows:

	2005 *Year 1*	**2006** *Year 2*	**2007** *Year 3*	**2008** *Year 4*	**2009** *Year 5*	**2010** *Year 6*
Operating cash flows (W)	26.2	31.4	37.7	45.3	54.3	65.2
Discount factor @9%	0.917	0.842	0.772	0.708	0.650	0.596
Present value	24.0	26.4	29.1	32.1	35.3	38.9
NPV	**185.9**					

This would suggest that the maximum Shard should pay for NOW is €185.9 million. A price higher than this would erode shareholder value, not enhance it.

The difference between this evaluation and an earnings-based one allows great scope for negotiation leaving Shard significant gains to shareholder value. For example, an opening bid of €100 million, say, would indicate to the Board of NOW that Shard is serious. This could be negotiated up to €130 million, say, and still leave a potential gain of €56 million.

Working

	€million
2004 operating cash flows	17.8
Savings on glass prices	0.8
Savings on energy	0.7
Extra transportation costs	(0.3)
Savings on paper and pulp prices	2.8
Net cash flow	**21.8**

To get the figures for 2005 onwards, this has been increased by 20% each year.

Note: An alternative approach would have been to exclude the synergy from the growth.

3 Commentary

Beware of the twist!

Most students expected to be writing to the Board of either ReuseR or NOW. Instead a new business, Shard, was introduced. It is vital that you answer the question here and don't rely too heavily on your expectations for the pre-seen material – a SWOT of ReuseR, for example, is not very useful whereas a SWOT of Shard is essential.

Requirement

There is no guarantee that the question requirement will be the same every time. In this case the requirement is more structured and thus it should have been easier to structure your report accordingly. Rather than prioritising random issues from the SWOT, the key here is to present the different issues regarding vertical integration, organic growth verses acquisition, ReuseR v NOW, valuation and post-acquisition management in the most logical order.

Marking grid

The grid for this case has 10 marks for technical skills rather than the usual 5. This reflects the higher level of calculations required.

Likewise diversity is given 10 marks, not 5, indicating that the examiners expected you to bring in more real-world examples, for instance.

Sample answer

The main strengths of the sample script are as follows:

- Good structure.
- Well argued.
- Very good overall flow of argument and logic.
- Clear prioritisation of key issues.
- It addresses all of the major issues facing the firm and gives clear recommendations for each.
- The report feels finished in the sense that most managers would have been happy to send it to a client.
- Good writing style with no waffle.
- Detailed calculations clearly explained with a range of options incorporated.

The main weaknesses are as follows:

- More reference to real-world companies would have gained further diversity marks.
- 'Other issues' have not been addressed anywhere, throwing away some easy marks.
- More could have been said on alternative courses of action and why they were dismissed.